HIDING IN HOLLAND

A RESISTANCE MEMOIR

SHULAMIT REINHARZ

ap

ISBN 9789493322691 (ebook)

ISBN 9789493322707 (paperback)

ISBN 9789493322714 (hardcover)

Publisher: Amsterdam Publishers, The Netherlands

info@amsterdampublishers.com

Hiding in Holland is part of the series Holocaust Survivor True Stories

Copyright © Shulamit Reinharz 2024

Cover image: Max Rothschild (author's father) milking a cow in the Netherlands, circa 1940

All Rights Reserved. No part of this publication may be reproduced or transmitted in any form or by any means, electronic or mechanical, including photocopy, recording or any other information storage and retrieval system, without prior permission in writing from the publisher.

CONTENTS

Introduction   v

1. Resisting as a Child in Germany   1
2. Resisting and Hiding in Holland   60
3. Coming out of Hiding   230
4. Postscript   298

Acknowledgments   321
Amsterdam Publishers Holocaust Library   325

INTRODUCTION
MULTIPLE BEGINNINGS

In the winter of 1974, my husband, Jehuda, and I visited my parents in their suburban New Jersey home where I had grown up. When we all sat down for a meal, I was in for a surprise that changed my life. It all started when the heating system growled and shut down. Not knowing what to do, my father sent Jehuda, an historian, to the cellar to "fix it." I came along to assist.

After rummaging around, Jehuda decided to kick a large, old machine. To deliver the blow, we cleared away some disintegrating boxes nearby. Strangely, a motor somewhere in the basement suddenly sprang to life. With this bizarre success behind us, we opened one of the cartons to see what was inside. Lo and behold, it contained a large collection of notebooks in Dad's handwriting along with documents in German.

Curious about this crumbling mess, we brought one of the notebooks upstairs. "What's this?" we asked my father. "*Oh, that's nothing. In fact, I don't really know what it is. You can throw it away.*"[1] We didn't comply. Instead, with Dad's permission, we took the contents of about ten cartons to our home in Ann Arbor, where I put each item in a page protector and organized the whole set of materials into 3-ring binders clearly labelled by date. Unfortunately, I was too busy to read any of it. But 45 years later, I had the material translated professionally from German, Dutch, Hebrew, and French into English.

A Survivor

Among other identities, Dad was a Holocaust survivor. He preferred the phrase "lived through the Holocaust" or "lived through the Hitler years." But there is no question that he was a survivor – born in Germany, nearly killed in the Netherlands and finally a refugee in the US. Dad managed to escape death repeatedly, sometimes by his clever actions or the help of kind people, and other times by sheer luck or what he called "miracles."

In 1976, when Dad was 55, I gave birth to his first grandchild, Yael Dalia. Perhaps the overwhelming phenomenon of welcoming the first member of our family's next generation propelled him to write about his wartime experiences. Using an old manual typewriter, my then newly retired father engaged in a common activity among aging survivors – he wrote his memoirs.

Three and a half decades had elapsed since his liberation from Nazi rule in the Netherlands on May 5, 1945, and yet he wrote without reference to published books or even the materials he had collected. It was as if everything he had undergone was etched permanently in his brain. Added to his astonishing feat of memory is the inexplicable fact that my father somehow retained personal papers, report cards, invoices, and certificates of all sorts from the years before he came to America, even though he mentioned that most of his papers were burned either deliberately by those trying to protect him or by chance during bombings in the Netherlands.

It also turned out that the boxes in the basement were merely the tip of the iceberg, a fraction of the remarkable treasure trove scattered throughout the house. Dad didn't know what he had kept or where he had put it. But I knew. The papers, just like Dad, himself, had survived by hiding – under beds, in books and the backs of drawers, from the attic to the basement.

The account my father wrote approximately 40 years after being freed is a first-hand retelling of what happened to him before and during (but not after) the Holocaust. To learn what happened *after* liberation, I used the letters that he sent and received from the early moments of freedom until his departure for the US in 1947. Dad's letters concern such major events as the German invasion of the Netherlands, as well as small details of life, such as piano pieces he heard. And yet, in the opening paragraph of his memoir, he claimed that regardless of all the facts he included, his memoir was not objective.

It is impossible for me to be objective in my writing. How can any living man, how can a person with a heart, be "objective" about the Hitler era, about that absurd, bizarre sequence of events which in the last analysis can never be explained fully, but only described?

The Next-to-Last Move

Another decade passed. My parents sold their house and moved into a nearby senior residence. My sister, Tova, in New Jersey, chose the facility; my brother, Jonathan, on Long Island, organized our parents' finances; and I, having moved to Massachusetts, drove south to New Jersey and watched the movers take away the heavy items. I then scoured closets, bookshelves, and cabinets for anything my parents might want to take with them. In the process, I found hundreds of papers. Things that had nothing to do with one another were stapled together. Unmailed contributions to obscure charities were tucked in envelopes provided by other charities. Once again, I took everything home, this time to Boston. And just as before, my parents said, "*We are not really interested in this old stuff.*" I, on the other hand, was exhilarated – I had found a treasure trove hidden right before my eyes – a veritable *Genizah*![2]

By then I had earned a Ph.D. in sociology and developed a successful career leading to tenure and an academic chair at Brandeis University. As we entered the second millennium, I started thinking about my retirement from Brandeis, scheduled for early summer 2017. Soon after I left the university, I decided to look at what I had collected from my parents' house throughout the years. Perhaps I could write a book that would integrate Dad's notebooks, correspondence, and documents with my comments and interpretations. To accomplish this, I read extensively about all the topics he discussed. Examining his memoir closely, I realized that for Dad, hiding in the Netherlands was the major element in the whole saga of his survival and had become a symbol of his life's journey. Thus, the title of this book.

Roots

Jehuda and I married in fall 1967, exactly 50 years before I began writing *Hiding in Holland*. Nearly every summer for the first few years of our life together, we travelled throughout Eastern and Western Europe on five dollars per day or less, always starting with buying a car at Schiphol Airport in Amsterdam and usually ending by selling the car in Athens. I didn't realize at the time – Alex Haley's book, *Roots*, would not appear until 1976 – that we were taking "root trips," not just "road trips." Our first adventure happened to include a several days' drive-through of Germany, a country "in the way" as we headed slowly and circuitously from the Netherlands toward Greece.

Having been born into a German-Jewish family, my being in Germany even for a short while was painful. I was rude and snappy to everyone I encountered. All around me I saw the wealth that German people, and their nation, were enjoying. How much of it was stolen from Jews? How much had American taxpayers given to Germans through the Marshall Plan? Where was justice?

The mere sound of the German language gave me the uncanny sensation that all these people were Jews because back in the States, my parents and grandparents spoke German all the time. Thus, I had acquired a passive knowledge of the language, i.e., understanding well, speaking with lots of errors, and writing not at all. My mother explicitly forbade me to learn or speak the language of the people who killed her parents, so I never actually studied German. Growing up, the only people I heard speak German were members of my extended family or other German Jews. But none of the people I encountered in Germany were Jews, I had to remind myself repeatedly. It was difficult to stop asking myself what the people my parents' age or older had done during the Holocaust and what they had taught or hidden from their children.

I had other associations: a person I saw with Down Syndrome reminded me of my father's uncle Paul with the same condition, whom the Nazis felt no qualms about using for target practice. When trains sped down German railroad tracks, I "saw" the train that brought my mother's mother to her death. I saw children in playgrounds and flashed to the one and a half million Jewish and other children who had been murdered. Why should German non-Jewish children be playing happily while German Jewish children were being gassed and burned? Later, my friend, historian Joanna Michlic, told me that the percentage of Jewish *children* murdered was much greater than that of Jewish *adults*: "Only six to eleven percent of Europe's prewar Jewish population of children numbering between 1.1 and 1.5 million survived, as compared with 33 percent of the adults."[3]

A few years passed. Jehuda and I were invited by the German government to an all-expenses paid, guided tour of Germany using an itinerary of our own creation. We chose the concentration camp near the town of Dachau, where Dad's Father had been incarcerated.[4] We visited Munich where Dad had gone to high school and where we saw the memorials to "The White Rose," a rare anti-Nazi protest group of German university students. We drove to the Wannsee Museum outside Berlin where the Nazi leadership met to adopt the "Final Solution" as official government policy. We traveled to Leipzig and saw the apartment in which Jehuda's grandparents had raised a large family. We visited Essen where Jehuda's father grew up and saw how the synagogue in that city had been repurposed as a museum. Jews had become museum pieces, just as Hitler wanted when he conceived of a "Museum of the Extinct Race" (i.e. Jews) that he would locate in Prague.

After Germany, we traveled to the Gurs Concentration Camp in southern France, where my maternal grandfather starved to death and from whose confines my mother's mother was shipped by train, first to Drancy outside Paris and then to Auschwitz. Each visit

Jehuda and I took was like placing a pebble on our relatives' missing tombstones, as is the custom when visiting the grave of a Jewish person.[5]

Reconciliation

During every subsequent trip to Europe, I became more pensive and peaceful. One fall I traveled alone to Gunzenhausen, the Bavarian town where my father was born and lived until age 14. In advance, I emailed the German Consul in Boston, asking him for the name of the current head of the Jewish community there. He wrote back saying that there is no Jewish community in Gunzenhausen. The town had been *Judenrein* [cleared of Jews] since 1939. Today the term might be "ethnically cleansed."

Although I felt embarrassed by my naive question to the consul, I did travel to Gunzenhausen and to my surprise, opened another chapter in my life. Not only did I gather information about Dad's birthplace, but I came to enjoy warm relations with numerous people who live in the town today. During the Covid pandemic, we established a bi-weekly discussion group on Zoom consisting of eight descendants of Jews who had lived in Gunzenhausen and eight people who live in the town today. Recently we created a Zoom-based lecture series about "memory activists" and "memory culture" in Germany. In summer 2023, along with 30 Jewish descendants of former inhabitants of Gunzenhausen from all over the world, we gathered to participate in memory activities in the town, including the planting of trees as a symbol of life.

The Netherlands

In January 1939 at age 18, Dad fled from Germany to the Netherlands. Little did he know that the Netherlands would become the Western European country with the highest percentage of murdered Jews, approximately 85 percent. The comparable Belgian number is 44 percent; the French 25 percent; the Danish, 10 percent and Portugal, which was neutral and not invaded by

Germany, none! Eighty-five percent represents a near complete genocide of Dutch Jewry. Why was the Netherlands such a failure in protecting its native Dutch Jews and German Jewish refugees? That was my prevailing question.

I traveled to the Netherlands numerous times to find some answers. I devoted the first few visits to spending time with the Dutch people who saved my parents' lives. A few years later, I spent eight weeks in Utrecht to get a feel for the country. I also wrote eight op-eds for the Boston-based *Jewish Advocate*. During that summer, I had many typical Dutch experiences, including going to an Ajax soccer game where I heard antisemitic chants shouted from the stands.[6] Another common experience in the Netherlands was to have one's bicycle stolen. Mine disappeared at the Utrecht train station one day and someone offered to steal a bike for me to replace it! I sadly acknowledged that even today, the Netherlands was not just tulips and windmills.

I visited tourist sites in Amsterdam, focusing especially on museums, memorials, and the Jewish Quarter. I visited people in The Hague connected to the International Court. I had wonderful conversations and recorded interviews with Dutch historians, survivors, archivists, fellow Jews, and a former mayor of Amsterdam. Jehuda came to the Netherlands and drove me around the country for one week so I could visit all the places my father had written about.

In Utrecht, I attended a lecture by Dutch military historian, Christ Klep, who asked: "How did the Dutch react to being occupied by Germany from 1940-1945?" "In three ways," he answered. "By active resistance (a minority); by collaboration (perhaps a majority); and by accommodation (a clear majority of the population)." He added that there was a thin line between accommodation and collaboration. He concluded his lecture with the sentence, "During the German Occupation, the Dutch *government* did nothing to save its Jews."

When I was growing up, the stories my parents told me about Dutch people deviated from Klep's conclusions. My parents' stories were about individuals who had saved them (not about the government that didn't). Thus, I had generalized erroneously, thinking that the Dutch were good to the Jews. Only when I began my research did I realize that my parents were atypical – they were two of the very few Jews in the Netherlands who lived to see the end of "the Hitler period."

Using the dates 1933-1945 as the span of the Holocaust, Dad lived half that time in Germany and half in the Netherlands. While in Germany he saved his life – without knowing it – by joining a Zionist youth group. He saved his life in the Netherlands when he decided to hide rather than obey the Nazi order to report for the fictitious "Harvest Help" program. When he arrived in the Netherlands in January 1939, Dad knew only one Jewish family there, relatives of his mother. By the time he decided to hide three and a half years later, he had developed a large set of non-Jewish and Jewish friends who would protect him even if the government did not.

The Holocaust: More than Auschwitz

The Holocaust has become equated wrongly in the public mind and even in the minds of survivors – if it is remembered at all and not denied – almost exclusively with concentration and extermination camps, particularly Auschwitz, which has become a symbol of the Holocaust and a tourist destination. People are familiar with the horrific images of Jews about to die or already dead, of living skeletons staring out from wooden bunks, of ghost-like people. Perhaps some non-Jews derive sadistic pleasure from seeing pictures of suffering Jews. The focus of study is not on survival. The Auschwitz iconography of Jewish death is so powerful that many survivors who were not imprisoned there don't consider themselves Holocaust survivors at all.

My father's experience presents an alternate image – a living person crouching silently in a basement or attic waiting for the war to end. It is a picture of life, albeit a difficult one, not of death. One of the motivations behind my writing this book is to urge us to remember and learn about the 3.5 million who survived, just as we remember the six million who were murdered.

Telling Stories

My father's ability to describe the first 24 years of his life (from 1921 to 1945) was strengthened by his telling his three children stories about his experiences while we were growing up (I was born in 1946, my sister in 1949 and our brother in 1954). A few of these stories concerned situations about which Dad felt intense guilt. He may also have told us so many stories because he had a lot of pent-up anger – anger at the BBC; at "arm-chair theorists;" at the Nazis, of course; at the Allies; at the Dutch government-in-exile; at the Church; at the Zionist leadership; at the US government for taking in so few Jews; at the obsequious Red Cross; at Hannah Arendt; at know-it-alls who pontificate about the Holocaust; at those who benefit financially from memorializing the Holocaust; and more. He experienced "survivor rage" rather than survivor guilt. And his rage was muted by humor.

Throughout his life, Dad studied the Old Testament (Torah) and other Jewish sacred texts such as the Talmud. He knew that his anger violated Leviticus (19:18): "Don't take vengeance and don't bear a grudge... but love your neighbor as yourself." Nevertheless, he did harbor grudges against Jews and non-Jews alike. He told us about these people in jokes. He mocked people who didn't know what they were talking about when they talked about the Holocaust.

And what do we see today? Word-makers, wise-guys of all sorts. I should have liked to see some of these people, just for a moment or two, living through those times; I should like to have observed all those loud-mouths, to see how they would behave during a "normal" Nazi round-up, or let's say, half an hour in Buchenwald...

Hiding

The German Nazis who ruled the Netherlands between 1940 and 1945 were committed to killing every single Jew who lived there. Sadly, most Jews chose not to hide, nor could they get visas to emigrate, and thus had almost no chance of surviving. These men, women and children were gathered systematically on Dutch soil through a process of sudden raids (called *razzias*) and government decrees. And then without their understanding what was happening, their killers shoved them into trains which carried them to their deaths. The German occupiers and the Dutch natives did this labor together.

Of the 140,000 or so Dutch Jews, 20,000-25,000 hid.[7] [Another 300,000 non-Jews hid as well.] In the Netherlands those Jews who went into hiding were far more likely to survive than Jews who did not hide. To take one example from the Dutch town of Almelo where my father lived for several years, a Yad Vashem document states:[8] "The greater part of the Jewish inhabitants of Almelo did not return from the camps; from the 265 deported, only six returned. By contrast, 160 of Almelo's Jews were hidden during the war and survived."

In the Netherlands as a whole, about half the Jews in hiding were caught and then killed. Other than the Jews in hiding who survived, there were about 5,500 Jews who returned from liberated concentration and extermination camps. By hiding, my father outlived Nazi rule in the Netherlands. Dad survived because his rescuers did a good job of helping him. Hiding was his choice and saved his life. And, in some ways, it became a theme in his life ever after. When he emerged into broad daylight at the end of the war, Dad brought the trauma of hiding with him. It shaped his consciousness and to some extent, it shaped our family.

The Future Holocaust

Fast forward 40 years to the mid-1990s. World War II had been officially "over" for half a century. Jehuda, our two daughters, and I had just moved into a large, old house in Newton, Massachusetts. During my parents' first visit, Dad asked me for a tour. So I showed him around and even led him down to the basement. At the bottom of the basement stairs, he stopped and declared, *"This would be a perfect place to hide!"* Clearly, he had his eye out for good *places* in which to hide. In a very practical and not morbid way, my father assumed that Jews would also need good *people* to hide them in the future – he needed trustworthy people and safe places. Having internalized this idea, I, too, found myself evaluating non-Jews in terms of whether I could rely on them to hide me when (not *if*) the need arose.

My father believed that a Holocaust was and will be a recurrent phenomenon against Jews. And so he wanted us to be prepared. The Police Department of Brookline, Massachusetts, where I now live, has done the same. They train synagogue members how to hide from active shooters. Like many people, I frequently wonder if American democracy is strong enough to ward off fascism. In Philip Roth's 2004 novel, *The Plot Against America*, it took only one election to change the course of US history. In contemporary America, this potential is strikingly real. Although Israel is militarily strong, it, too, cannot guarantee Jewish people's safety. There, too, it makes sense to train people to hide if necessary. My father believed strongly that the war against the Jews would continue for a long time to come and sadly, I believe he has been proven right.

Unfortunately, mass killings are typical for our age. We stand at a crossroads again except that this time, in the 1980s, annihilation will come to all of us, to all mankind, and being a Jew will no longer mean to be singled out for murder. This time is worse because there is no way out; there is no different route we can choose. This time we cannot go into hiding. When the button is pushed by somebody who thinks this is his duty, it will mean the end for all that breathes, and even if one of us should escape the first atomic or hydrogen or cobalt explosion, the poisonous clouds that ring around the globe are sure to reach us.

America's dropping of nuclear bombs over Japan on August 6 and 9, 1945, the Cuban missile crisis that unfolded during twelve agonizing days during October 1962, and the proliferation and testing of nuclear arms during the Cold War persuaded my father that nuclear war could not be averted. In the 1980s, anti-nuclear protests and activism were spreading across the US. At least 50 novels about the post-apocalyptic world were published. On June 12, 1982, one million people demonstrated in New York City against nuclear weapons and for an end to the Cold War arms race, the largest anti-nuclear protest ever organized and largest political demonstration in American history. My father was not an activist. He didn't march; instead, he worried, wrote, planned, and told us stories about his life.

A Deeply Jewish Document

To tell the truth, when I began writing these memoirs, I did not intend to put the Hitler years in the center. And yet, I cannot get away from them. Everything in my life, it now is apparent, was influenced by that trauma. It has been said that we shouldn't be captives of bad memories, but the fact is that those years left their imprint on everything that followed.

Today a great deal is being denied about that period. We know why, of course. Not only denied, but argued about, debated in the sense that maybe this or that Nazi misdeed wasn't that terrible, after all. And above all...that repetition we hear ad nauseam, both in the courts and outside, in speech and in print, that those poor Germans were forced, absolutely against their will, to do all those bad things to the Jews, things which... never really happened anyway.[9]

It is for my children that I want to write the story of my life; for them, and for my grandchildren, and whoever comes after them, if they are at all interested, and...if our world still exists at that time. Not that my own life is of such importance that any time and paper should be expended on it.

But I have lived through some experiences that are typical for our age, and for a part of the history of my Jewish people. The memory of those experiences ought to be kept alive for the sake of continuity, for the sake of our own self-respect, for the sake also of those who would rather forget, who do not like to hear of certain things any longer.

My own purpose in writing is broader. I hope to convey something about the disappearance of nearly the entire Jewish community of the Netherlands, the importance of Zionist organizations, the necessity of not cooperating with the oppressor, the significance of hiding as a form of resistance, and the fact that alongside the six million Jews who were murdered during the Holocaust, three and a half million Jews survived. My father declined to give an oral testimony. I think he believed a memoir that he could design would be more accurate than a format not under his control.

In telling stories, Dad was carrying out a Jewish obligation or *mitzvah* that instructs parents to teach their children how to live. He knew it was incumbent upon him to teach, not just tell, his children about his life so that they could learn from it. As a result, and in contrast to most survivors/parents, Dad talked about his experiences constantly. This was not a sign of neurosis, in my view, but rather the fulfillment of an obligation. The Holocaust was too important not to share with one's family.

I am writing for my children about a few of the important moments in my life... Some of those moments described in these pages will probably remain with me to the very end. Perhaps I can also confess the mistakes I made. But I feel that life can be lived, when seen in proportion, yes, it can be lived, even if it seems hopeless at times.

Dad's awareness of the Jewish people's survival – not only its catastrophes – gives his writings an uplifting undertone at times. When he was 12 years old, Dad promised his dying mother that he would "survive" without truly knowing what that meant. About ten years later, the concept was clear. At that time, he made a promise to himself that if he survived, "leading a Jewish life" would become a principle to which he would adhere. When I started reading Holocaust survivors' memoirs, I was surprised that, typically, Jewishness is hardly mentioned. Anne Frank mentioned it only once or twice in her diary. I also noticed that survivors who wrote memoirs were likely to be assimilated, in contrast to observant (i.e., religious) Jews. My hunch (later confirmed) was that assimilated Jews were more likely to survive (and thus be able to write memoirs) than religious Jews, because assimilated Jews were more likely to mix with Gentiles who might help them.

While growing up in Gunzenhausen, my father, Max Michael Rothschild, was a Jewish boy in an observant, traditional Jewish community of family members, relatives, and friends. He went to synagogue regularly; he ate only kosher foods; the family celebrated all the Jewish holidays. But when he moved to bustling Munich as an early teenager, he chose to join – from many closely related options – a Zionist youth organization that was *indifferent to religion*. He could have chosen a group that was both Zionist and religious as his sister Hannah did. Instead, he chose the group that shed most Jewish religious activities, while retaining a few: Friday night welcoming of the Sabbath, Bible study, learning the Hebrew language and examining Hebrew literature.

Dad's teenage response to Nazism was to embrace secular Jewish Socialism, also called Labor Zionism. Some Jews responded in the opposite direction, by moving away from assimilation and embracing Judaism for the first time. In general, Nazism destabilized Jews' approach to their religion. When Dad later came to the US in 1947, he adopted Conservative Judaism (not Orthodox Judaism) and was ordained as a rabbi in that movement, a perfect choice for him.

My father's voluminous writing combines stories, descriptions of everyday life and unusual events, confessions of guilt, evaluations of people's behavior, and philosophical ponderings. This range of topics differentiates his memoir from a straightforward chronological account. I have newspaper articles he published, travel journals, book reviews and countless letters. Letters are especially valuable because in general, they are written shortly after the events they describe, giving their contents added credibility. While in hiding for almost three years, Dad wrote a diary that focused on a longed-for better world as defined by socialism's key concepts – the brotherhood of man and the classless society. After the war he wrote hundreds of sermons. Although Dad was cooped-up "during the war" and unsure that he would survive, he also dreamt of a beautiful future "after the war" when he could do meaningful work. This dream sustained him. When the war ended, he continued writing, this time for his job and to earn a Ph.D. The stories and endless jokes he told were as telling as his writing. I was privileged to hear this "oral memoir" all the time.

The Post-Hiding Phase of the Holocaust

On May 5, 1945, soldiers from Canada and other Allied countries liberated the northern part of the Netherlands where a tiny remnant of Dutch Jews and German Jewish refugees were still hiding. In a few concluding sentences of his memoir, Dad described the Dutch reaction to Germany's surrender. I continue the story showing what life was like for my parents during the 18 months immediately after they came out of hiding. During this period, the Dutch government was completely insensitive to what the Jews had undergone during the Holocaust. It amazes me that Jews were contrasted with the "real war victims," i.e., non-Jewish Dutch people.[10]

What was it like for my father to leave hiding places and try to live as a normal human being once again? The answer lies in the correspondence between Dad and his parents. After the war, even before they were married, my father and mother wrote constantly from the Netherlands to Dad's parents who had escaped to the US. My parents also wrote to a few relatives who had arrived safely in Palestine. His letters concern my parents' problems: medical problems, wedding problems, housing problems, visa problems, the search for missing people and more. Although they no longer needed to hide, life clearly was difficult. Later, after arriving in the US, Dad wrote brief job-seeking resumés summarizing his accomplishments to date. Some of the information in these resumés revealed yet additional information about Dad's war-time experiences that I had not known. He also wrote essays required by teachers of the courses he took at Boston University.

Although Dad frequently disparaged himself by saying that his writings were worthless, I think that overall, he believed there was merit in what he wrote. His writings convey his voice and interpretation of events, his apologies, gratitude, and regrets. His two hands as a survivor wrote countless pages in various forms; my two hands as a sociologist and daughter tried to integrate everything I found. In my imagination this partnership is analogous to the times when the two of us played piano duets for four-hands. His part was the melody; mine, the accompaniment. And so it is with this book.

---

1. I use italics for material my father wrote or said, and regular font for my voice. The italicized material is either a direct quote or summarizes his writing on a topic.
2. A collection of deteriorated prayer books, documents, and other papers that a Jewish community preserves.
3. Joanna B. Michlic, "A Young Person's War: The Disrupted Lives of Children and Youth," in: Simone Gigliotti and Hilary Earl (eds.) *A Companion to the Holocaust* (New York: John Wiley & Sons, 2020), pp. 296-310, p. 296.
4. As a sign of respect, Max used a capital "F" when writing about his Father. I do the same.
5. My mother's father had a tombstone in the Gurs concentration camp; my mother's mother had no grave or tombstone because her remains evaporated into ash or were destroyed in Auschwitz.
6. See Claire Moses, "Dutch Police Arrest 154 Soccer Fans Singing Antisemitic Songs and Chants before a Match," *The New York Times,* May 8, 2023, p. A4.
7. In October 1995, the Government Printing Office of the Netherlands brought out "In Memoriam," The Hague, ISBN 90 12 09178 5, which states that of approximately Dutch 130,000 Jews at the time of the invasion, the Germans (with Dutch cooperation) killed 100,000. Other estimates are in the same range, although the number 140,000 is most frequently used.
8. Yad Vashem, founded in 1953 and located in Jerusalem, is Israel's national memorial to the victims of the Holocaust.
9. Erich Goldhagen has shown that this is not true; there was room for Nazis to refuse to carry out atrocities. See his *Hitler's Willing Executioners: Ordinary Germans and the Holocaust* (New York: Vintage, 1996).
10. See Bela Ruth Samuel Tenenholtz, *Land of Many Bridges: My Father's Story* (Oegstgeest: Amsterdam Publishers, 2022), p. 200.

1

RESISTING AS A CHILD IN GERMANY

In summer 2023, as a guest of the Gunzenhausen town government, I traveled from Boston to Gunzenhausen, the town in which my father was born and where he lived until his bar mitzvah at age 13. Jews had lived there since 1343. My purpose was to meet with people who live there today. Joined by about 25 relatives and friends from the US, Israel and Germany, the program for our several-day visit included an evening talk by Peter Schnell, the Assistant Mayor of Gunzenhausen, reminding the large audience of townspeople what had happened there as the Nazis came to power. The packed lecture hall was completely silent as the crowd listened to Schnell's words. The Jewish descendants of the Jewish former residents of Gunzenhausen were profoundly moved to hear an account of the Holocaust-era in Gunzenhausen, as written and read out loud by a current resident and town leader. Schnell felt responsible for the deeds of the older generation and used the pronoun "we." "We harmed Jews; we harmed your families." Here follows (a lightly edited version of) what he told us that night:

> Nazism didn't fall out of the sky. Our town was a Nazi stronghold from the start and the Christian residents of Gunzenhausen were cruel to their Jewish neighbors. In 1922, we damaged the

gravestones in the Jewish cemetery. In 1923, we smashed the synagogue windows. In 1932, in the Reichstag election, the NSDAP received 64.9 percent of the votes in Gunzenhausen. The Mayor of Gunzenhausen, Dr. Heinrich Münch, joined the Nazi party in 1932, making the Nazis presentable.

Following Hitler's appointment as Reich Chancellor on January 30, 1933, Gunzenhausen was the first city to rename its market square the Adolf-Hitler-Platz. Three months later, a Hitler monument was built in the nearby Burgstall forest, the first of its kind in Germany. In the last free Reichstag election in 1933, the Nazis received 67.1 percent of the vote in Gunzenhausen, 23 percentage points more than the national average in Germany. In March 1933, Jews were physically attacked on the streets and the windows of many Jewish shops were smashed.

When the National Socialists seized power, 181 Jews were living in our town. State and municipal restrictions on Jewish activity increased noticeably. In the fall of 1933, the last advertisement for a Jewish business appeared in the local newspaper, the *Altmühlbote*. Unrestrained antisemitic agitation met with lively approval from the residents of Gunzenhausen, culminating in the pogrom of March 25, 1934, one of the first in the Third Reich, and always referred to as "Bloody Palm Sunday." Up to 1,500 fanatics, out of a population of around 5,000, participated. The rage began when a group of SA men led by Obersturmführer Kurt Bär entered Simon Strauss's Jewish inn to extract a non-Jewish guest who showed solidarity with Strauss.

This event was so significant that *The New York Times*, thousands of miles away, described it in a short column.

Kurt Bär and 24 other men were charged in court with rioting against the local Jews and damaging their property. Kurt Bär received a prison sentence of only one and a half years. When the innkeeper couldn't find him, Bär and his accomplices forcibly dragged the innkeeper's son, Julius Strauss, out of the inn. Young Strauss was brutally beaten until he fell to the ground unconscious. His parents rushed to his aid and were threatened with a gun. 35 Jewish residents, including six women and Max's father, the town physician, some in their nightgowns, were dragged out of their homes and thrown into the local prison. Two Jewish citizens, Max Rosenau and Jakob Rosenfelder, died from the violence that night.

Another 20 defendants were sentenced to between four and twelve months in prison. A few days later, the sentences were reduced: Bär received ten months, 18 other defendants between three and seven months in prison; the rest were acquitted. Additional riots later occurred in Gunzenhausen.

On July 15, 1934, Kurt Bär, who was freed prematurely, broke into the Strauss family's apartment. Bär attacked Simon Strauss and his son Julius, who had testified against him and his comrades in court. Bär fired shots at them with his pistol. Simon Strauss succumbed to his injuries on the spot; his son was taken to the hospital, seriously injured. The profound impression that the riot left on the members of the Gunzenhausen Jewish community led to the first wave of emigration. Nearly 50 Jews left the city, hoping to survive the Nazi madness in the supposed anonymity of larger cities.

By fall 1938, only 55 Jews lived in Gunzenhausen. On the night of November 9, the antisemitic attacks organized and directed by the Nazi regime all over Germany (*Reichspogromnacht*) hit the Jewish citizens of Gunzenhausen with full force. A week after the Reichspogromnacht, Gunzenhausen celebrated the end of the Jewish community in a conspicuous way: the two domes of the synagogue were torn down in the presence of a packed crowd of spectators. The following day, the local newspaper hailed the "end of Jewish rule." Josef Seeberger and Martha and Albert Klein, the last Jewish residents, left our town on January 25, 1939, rendering Gunzenhausen *Judenrein* (rid of Jews). No Jewish community was ever re-established here.

One hundred and seven Gunzenhausen Jews subsequently were murdered in such concentration camps as Dachau and Theresienstadt, in the gas chambers of Auschwitz and Sobibor, or in deportation locations such as Kaunas in Lithuania. It took some time before citizens in Gunzenhausen started to come to terms with the local history of National Socialism. I, Peter Schnell, was born in 1951. When I went to school, I never heard a word about that terrible time. This silence lasted until the 1980s when we began to examine our history, culminating in the groundbreaking work of teachers Emmi Hetzner and Franz Müller in the 2000s. With the help of the city archivist Werner Mühlhäußer, ninth grade students researched the history of Jewish families and their houses in Gunzenhausen.

In 1934, soon after my Bar Mitzvah, I moved by myself 180 kilometers due south from my small hometown in the rural Bavarian region of Germany, to the cosmopolitan city of Munich. My new address was my grandmother's apartment. Jews had lived in Gunzenhausen as a small minority for centuries, sometimes severely persecuted and sometimes less so. After departing as a young teen, I never lived in Gunzenhausen again. I visited only once, immediately after the war, to kill a Nazi.

Much had already happened to me before I moved to Munich. When I was barely one year old, my mother, Thekla, or Mammiah as we all called her, gave birth to a second son, my brother Manfred, whose short life ended about a year later in a tragic accident. Mammiah went on to deliver two girls, my sister Hannah in 1924 and Eva in 1929. Sadly, at the same time, Mammiah's latent heart ailment took a downward turn, and four years later, in 1933, she died in our house. Fortunately, I still had my loving Father whom I adored. Throughout our lives, I leaned on my dependable Father and likewise, I tried to help him in whatever way I could.

In our last heart-to-heart talk, Mammiah asked me to promise I would survive, a request I thought was strange. But perhaps she intuited how bad the situation was already becoming for us Jews. As it turned out, Mammiah's final request was propitious and guided me when I had to make life-or-death decisions, which was quite frequently. After Mammiah's burial, her tombstone in Gunzenhausen was vandalized repeatedly, and in 1946, when I visited the town's Jewish cemetery, no evidence of her tombstone remained. (And so it is to this day).

Notwithstanding the deaths of my brother and mother, it would be incorrect to say that my early years were bleak. Already as an infant, I was introduced to the beauty of Gunzenhausen's synagogue life, where I absorbed the melodies and images that contributed to my becoming a Jew. When I reached three years of age, Father arranged a private local tutor for me, Mr. Rehfeld. As he was my first teacher in Hebrew and Jewish subjects, I owe a great deal to him. In fact, I might even have loved Mr. Rehfeld and his wife, although "love" is a big concept for a boy so young. I think I was the only child in town to have the opportunity to study Jewish subjects for at least two years before kindergarten.

As it turned out, Mr. Rehfeld became one of the great influences in my life. Years later, when I was languishing in the Buchenwald Concentration Camp, I had a bittersweet daydream of seeing him in the camp, as if he had come to help me. That was not the only time I "saw" Mr. Rehfeld. I also "brought him" into my hiding places in the Netherlands. There we "engaged in conversations" about Jewish studies and Hebrew poetry. But later, I also suffered from guilt because as a youngster I didn't always treat Mr. Rehfeld with the respect he deserved.

In 1924-5, when Adolf Hitler was preparing Mein Kampf for publication, and I was three and then four years old, I started attending the Jewish elementary school (grades 1-4) in Gunzenhausen. It turned out that I was a good student and even skipped a grade, allowing me to enter the Realschule (grades 5-10) one year early. Unlike my first school, the Realschule was not managed by the Jewish community, and antisemitic ideas seeped freely into my school education.

This education left a deep impression on me. So much so that years later when I hid in the Netherlands, I devoted time to contemplating if and how the German educational system could be transformed to prevent German students from becoming fascists once again.[1] I concluded that German teachers had used their authority to create a generation of Nazi criminals. In the Gunzenhausen Realschule, teachers differentiated between the Jewish and Gentile students and were hostile to the Jews.[2] An example is the requirement that all the pupils memorize a particular booklet about German history. Among other falsehoods, the booklet asserted that Jewish men did not fight for Germany during World War I. I knew this was a lie. In fact, my Uncle Max (Father's brother and only sibling) enlisted voluntarily and died on a French battlefield fighting for Germany. I was named after him. Naively, I treated the booklet assignment simply as a memorization challenge and paid no attention to the meaning of the words. Father, whose formal name was Dr. Karl Kalonymus Rothschild, also served in the German military during World War I. He became a compassionate physician on the front, after which he became a highly regarded doctor in Gunzenhausen, treating Jews and gentiles, "rich" and poor.

Teachers also humiliated Jewish students by compelling them to march regularly through town in those inane Nazi productions – not with their own classes but as a separate unit to be laughed at and spat upon.

Much of my personality and many of my interests had been formed by the time I moved to Munich in 1934, dubbed "the Capital City of the Nazi Movement." For example, I was already studying the piano seriously. It is difficult to describe how much classical music meant to me, and how proud I was when my teacher called me "an exceptionally proficient pianist for my age." Later, when I had to hide for three years, these memories became something I turned to, to maintain my sanity.

As a child, I developed a vivid imagination and thought I saw God in the synagogue decorations. Or sometimes it was Jesus, as suggested by the Gentile maids who lived in our household. Just like my friends, I participated actively but sometimes impatiently in the religious services and holiday celebrations of the synagogue, the center of Jewish life in Gunzenhausen. Because the Jewish community was so small, we had only an itinerant rabbi [something Dad became years later in America]. The lectures or sermons of distinguished Jewish visitors who came to Gunzenhausen also appealed to me. Even as a child, I was allowed to attend these talks and quietly listen to the intellectual salons in my parents' home.

I don't wish to brag but within Gunzenhausen's Jewish world, I was always defined as the best, the favorite, the smartest, etc., in other words, "an exceptional child." But being exceptional did not mean that I was always well-behaved or obedient. I would call myself a rascal, a boy who *frequently got into trouble and was regularly spanked by Father. Perhaps my largely tolerated disobedience as a youngster helped me defy – or resist – Nazi officials and edicts in Germany and later in the Netherlands.*

I was not unique in this regard – my friends were rascals, too. Together we got into endless trouble by sneaking into Father's medical instrument cabinet and experimenting with the mysterious tools. Sometimes we explored forbidden parts of the synagogue. I shamelessly wrote "nasty poems" about my schoolteachers and even ran away from home on my bicycle, not to be heard from until several days had passed.

Early Resistance: The Jewish Sports Arena

When I was 12 in 1933, Giora Josephtshal (1912-1962), a 21-year-old German Jew, visited our town to try to shake us out of our lethargy and denial of reality. Gunzenhausen Jews did not understand – or did not want to understand – our precarious position in Germany. The Jewish adults rationalized their humiliation and tried to maintain life as usual. Josephsthal came to town to offer an alternative – the embrace of Palestine as the Jewish homeland and the concept of Zionism as a feasible, practical solution to our hardships. I was so inspired by Josephsthal's talk that on the spot, I decided to mobilize the Jewish boys in Gunzenhausen to form a Zionist group that would do what Josephsthal urged – study Hebrew (the language of Jewish Palestine) and Zionism in preparation for living in Palestine/Israel.

Our Jewish boys' group built a "sports facility" with our own hands, a place where we could train and compete with one another. We got spades, shovels, rakes, and other tools, and went to work on a track, a soccer field, and a jumping pit. We got more ambitious every day. It was as though a fever had taken hold of us. We worked for hours after school, and we were totally self-organized and self-disciplined. It was a wonderful new spirit. We were extremely proud that our initiative did not involve parents or any community leaders.

At long last, the dignitaries of our congregation got wind of what we were doing. Then the president and his associates, having duly inspected our work, gave their official approval. For a few months after our "sports arena" was completed, we had a great time at track, handball, and lots of other sports. I was intent on having fun and was put off by the older people's passivity. It is important to understand this episode of creating a Zionist youth group as an early act of resistance because, to me, it represented departing from the role of weakling and victim. It was a positive, non-violent form of resistance. We club members did not endanger ourselves. That was to come a few years later in high school.

Berlin authorities asked the pro-Nazi town mayor, Johan Appler, to slow down "the public persecution going on in Gunzenhausen because Berlin wanted to control the development of pogroms rather than leave it to local hoodlums." Soon a vicious Nazi was elected mayor of Gunzenhausen, a position he kept until the war's end.

One additional change in my life before my move to Munich was the arrival of Henny (or Henriette) Tuch, who became my stepmother when she married Father. I respected and admired Henny and was always grateful for the way she treated her new husband and his three children. After she and Father married, I called Henny "Mutter" (mother) for the rest of her life.

Despite having been jailed with the other Jewish men in Gunzenhausen for no reason other than being a Jew, Father did not attempt to take our family out of Germany. He simply could not tear himself away from the town where his beloved [first] wife was buried. The one practical measure Father took was to send me to Munich and enroll me in its Luitpold Oberrealschule, a well-regarded high school. Neither Father nor I realized that Munich was an awful choice for someone trying to escape Gunzenhausen's antisemitism.

After school I immersed myself in piano lessons, in a Zionist youth group, in Munich's synagogue choir, in religious studies at the Hebrew Language Institute, and, most important, in a relationship with the first serious girlfriend I ever had, Ilse Strauss, whom I married a decade later. High school, itself, was not my top priority.

At the same time, my family in Gunzenhausen was growing restless. Things were getting worse, and gradually Father decided to leave, "sell" the house, give up his [medical] practice, and settle, like me, in Munich. In retrospect, I wrote, "This was the one great mistake Father made during that period. He should have had the foresight and courage to give up

Germany altogether and to emigrate. At that time, it was still possible to do so."

Zionism

Among the most important positive aspects of my new life in Munich was the opportunity to become part of an actual Zionist youth group. From the many options with different ideologies, I chose Habonim [Hebrew: "the builders"].[3] Through this involvement, I not only met my girlfriend, Ilse, but I changed the plan my family had for me to obtain a visa for the United States as soon as possible. In retrospect, it is amazing that the visa arrived just as I was graduating high school, and even more amazing that I ignored it! Instead, I wanted Zionism, and I wanted Ilse.

My earliest curiosity about Zionism was aroused by a very large portrait Father had sketched, depicting Theodor Herzl (1860-1904), leaning famously on a railing over the Rhine River in Basel, Switzerland during the First World Zionist Congress in 1897. The sketch hung prominently over the desk where Father talked with his patients.[4]

Neither Father nor I saw Judaism and Zionism as opposed. Perhaps we might even hasten the arrival of the Messiah by our own actions, we thought. The young people I met through Habonim became my new family – my new brothers and sisters, just as the leaders or counsellors were additional "parents." I appreciated Habonim for focusing on the future of German Jewish youth, rather than mourning our past or dwelling on our dismal present. We had our regular meetings several times a week, a combination of social get-together and discussion, not only of Zionist topics, but also of sex, love, etc. We lived our real lives in our youth group. We were so closely connected with our friends, so involved with the discussions of our Zionist ideals, that we became oblivious to the realities of Hitler. Soon after joining, I became a discussion leader for younger members.

Life in our youth organization overshadowed everything. The family took second place. In those early years of the Nazi regime, Zionist youth groups played a role in our lives that can hardly be overestimated... Zionism, positive Jewishness, the proud association with other Jewish youngsters, and just being together as young Jews gave us enormous moral support during those difficult times. It was then that I started using the word "us" rather than "me," and "we" rather than "I." Our youth group gave meaning to our lives when Nazism questioned our very value. Our Zionist youth group gave us self-respect and hope; it gave us something to strive for; it gave us many hours of happiness and joy, singing and dancing, going on hikes and camping together, when outside, everything was gray and ugly, oppressive, and dangerous. A different world was created in which we could live a normal youngster's life, more than just subsist from day to day, as was the case with many of our parents.

In short, Zionism offered me an alternate reality. Instead of being hated, as I was by the larger German society, I was now part of a group of young people who adored one another. Instead of being the "Unglück" or "misfortune," as Hitler labeled Jews, I began to dedicate myself to the task of building a Jewish society in Palestine.

But Zionism also entailed a grave danger. This important point, which nagged at me for years, stemmed from the fact that developing a Zionist identity meant delaying getting out of Germany. Habonim's message was not "go now!" but rather "go after you are trained in agriculture!" No one realized that the longer we stayed, the greater the danger to our very lives. Because the leaders did not perceive the situation as an emergency, they focused on training us in Zionist ideology and in becoming skilled farmers who could build the new country. The four years I spent as a member of Habonim in Munich indoctrinated me to not apply to college and to not immigrate to the United States. To violate these taboos was to become a "moral outcast." My girlfriend would most likely have dropped me.

The Habonim Youth Group as Resistance

I can only be grateful for the moral support we were given by our Zionist youth movement. To be able to study, to listen to a lecture by a famous Jewish personality, was sheer bliss. Today I would go so far as to say that "this was real, positive, courageous and highly valuable resistance to Nazism." This point is worth emphasizing, given that some postwar critics of Jewish actions during the Third Reich lambasted Jews for not resisting, for going like sheep to the slaughter. That accusation does not consider what Jews experienced as resistance. In my case, I began resisting Nazism through my Zionist activities in Gunzenhausen and I continued resisting in Munich as a member of Habonim.

High School and a Major Act of Resistance

To my surprise, things were very orderly in March 1934 when I entered Luitpold High School. In fact, most of the professors were still quite friendly. We even had a Jewish professor, Mr. Schaalman, a man who taught math and was active in the organization of German-Jewish war veterans, with its emphasis on loyalty to the Fatherland and opposition to Zionism.[5] I did well in school and my report cards reflect my performance. Teachers praised me for my "sense of duty," a term whose meaning is not apparent. By contrast with the orderliness of the school, however, the outside world was chaotic and preparing for war.

To graduate from a German high school, students had to pass the "Abitur," the climax of the pre-university curriculum. Like everyone else, I took the Abitur two months before graduating, even though, as a Jew, I had little chance of being admitted to a university, no matter how good my grades were. My certificate for having passed my Abitur meant nothing. It was not a ticket to higher education and a career. And it was not a shield against antisemitism. During my junior year of high school, it had become illegal for Jews to obtain doctoral degrees in German institutions. Nevertheless, we thought the Abitur was important, and for the school administration, everything preceding this event was geared towards it.

My Abitur took place in March 1938 at the exact time when Germany invaded, or rather was "welcomed" by Austria during the Anschluss. Despite the creeping and ever-increasing discrimination against the few remaining Jewish students in my school, the fact that Father had been on active duty at the front in WWI helped me somewhat. It certainly made it possible for me to be enrolled at all. But the restrictions, and later the daily humiliations... Could I help it, I often asked myself, that I was the best in my class?

The weeklong Abitur exams were major events, dreaded by all who took their studies seriously. "Aryan" (i.e., non-Jewish) boys were luckier than Jews, however. As active members in the younger ranks of the SA or SS, Aryan boys were called up for immediate duty in the Anschluss operation, freeing them from further exams in the Abitur, securing for them 'A's' all around. The French language was an especially dreaded subject. But this problem disappeared overnight for students who would soon be soldiers. What excellent planning on the part of the German High Command to invade Austria on a Tuesday morning during Abitur week, precisely when French exams were scheduled!

The [English] exam was given by a miserable Nazi professor, a smug, unprincipled individual who presided with his eternal smirk over six or seven Abitur classes. The professor grinned triumphantly at me, the only Jew in the room, as he explained the exam rules repeatedly. We were handed sealed questions and had to translate from English into German. The text – an excerpt from the English edition of Hitler's Mein Kampf! All ideology aside, one should have been able to conceive of a more representative example of "English" literature. In that segment of Mein Kampf, Hitler claims that no Jews fought at the front during his tour of duty during World War I. And so the drivel went on.

This insult made me want to stand up to the Nazis... some unseen force drove me...When I reached the point in Mein Kampf where Hitler's diatribe against the Jews began, I halted. By stopping there, I knew that I would get a D at best, thus ruining not only my English grade but also my general average and the class average. I finished the exam, first among the several hundred students, and walked through the rows of scribbling and pencil-chewing boys to hand my paper to the astounded professor. He couldn't see how anybody could finish so quickly.

A few hours later, I saw my English professor, Dr. Lorentz, a devout Catholic who also taught French, Latin, and Spanish, and who knew some Hebrew. He was one of the few men in our school who was decent... We talked about the exam. Naturally, he wanted his students to succeed. In the corridor where everybody could see us, I told him about my Uncle Max who had volunteered to serve at the front for the German army in 1918 and was killed. "How could I forget all human decency and put on paper the garbage that was in Hitler's book?" I asked Dr. Lorentz. "I understand you fully," said Professor L., "but I'm sorry that my best student had to fail the final exam."

This event loomed very large at the time...I feared I had jeopardized the good will of an imagined immigration official at the American consulate who saw that my English skills were very poor...But I did what I did, rather than insult my honor as a Jew. I didn't feel like a hero, and I didn't strive to be one. I just could not help myself... When I returned home, the family was proud of me. But my English grade was ruined. And I was officially excused from the final graduation exercises.

When Dad graduated high school on March 23, 1938, he picked up his diploma with the following run-on sentence summarizing his performance: "Max Rothschild, son of the practicing physician Mr. Dr. Karl Rothschild, born on February 20, 1921 in Gunzenhausen, of the Jewish religion, who was from May 2, 1934, a student of the Luitpold High School in Munich, passed the Abitur this March, and, is declared capable of entering college. Behavior: very commendable, Diligence: very commendable... He is a decent, respectable, and dutiful student. His essay for the German exam contained good ideas in a flawless composition. He participated in Latin classes and in the aeronautics association with diligence and good results." A good report card in every respect.

The document concluded with the signatures of the representative of the Ministry of Education and the school principal, in this case, the same person. Between these identical signatures was a stamp of the "Presidency of the Luitpold High School, Munich" containing a swastika. *For all the lovely evaluations of my behavior and achievements, the only two items of significance on this diploma were "Religion: Jewish" and the swastika.* They defined his place in German society and became the rationale for his landing in the Buchenwald Concentration Camp eight months later.

Outside the high school's walls, the Nazi government in Berlin issued a steady stream of edicts to forge the Third Reich. It is therefore no surprise that on the streets of Munich, the government's wild rhetoric sparked violence against Jewish people and property. As early as March 1933, Nazi thugs had burned books by Jews. The violence is now well known. But ironically, despite its intentions, one of the new directives helped Jews and can be said to have saved Dad's life.

On July 13, 1936, while I was still in high school, the Reich Educational Ministry authorized the establishment of "retraining schools" for Jews in preparation for their emigration. On September 13, 1937, Heinrich Himmler [head of the Gestapo][6] *decreed that Jews may be released from "protective custody in concentration camps" if they can provide evidence of their imminent emigration. Clearly, Hitler wanted the Jews to leave! He even gave us a way to do it.*

Despite the venom around me, I remember my teenage years as positive. Strange as it may sound – the time before the storm broke, I had a good life divided between music making at home, the Zionist youth movement, and my growing affection for my girlfriend. It was as though the Nazis didn't exist.

But, of course, they did exist. In September 1938, the Nazis took over the Sudetenland based on the deceitful Munich Pact. The first Nazi war already had started and the second had not yet commenced. The first was the Nazis' war against European Jews that was in effect for five years before Hitler annexed a single country. For some reason these events didn't register as a "war against the Jews." How could Dad not have noticed that Father was no longer permitted to practice medicine? Jews could hardly do anything they used to do or wanted to do.

The "war against the Jews" might have been normalized, invisible or foggy to Dad as a high school student, but it rested on easily understood racist decrees beginning with the Nuremberg Laws declared on September 15, 1935. Two months later, the German government passed a law defining who was a Jew and barring him/her from being a citizen of the Reich, leaving the person with no right to vote on political matters or hold public office.

Approximately a year later, in a secret memo of August 1936, Hitler announced collective Jewish accountability for crimes committed by individual Jews. Half a year after that, on December 16, 1937, the Nazis voided all German passports issued to Jews and ordered a restricted reissuing of passports that now had to be stamped with the letter J [for *Jude,* or Jew]. As of that date, all German Jews became stateless and vulnerable. On April 12, 1938, state prosecutors could open court proceedings to establish a person's Jewish or non-Jewish ancestry.

Music: An Island of Peace

Even with increasing tension in high school and in German society at large, I made time for music. Music touched my soul in a way that transcended the sound of the notes. It was vital for my very existence. Had it not been for the Holocaust, I might have aimed at becoming a professional pianist, a dream I had to relinquish as I focused on the larger goal of saving my life. It is the fortunate piano teacher who discovers that among all the youngsters who give the piano a try, one or two are serious. I was one of them.

Long emotional passages Dad wrote about Gunzenhausen, Munich, and later, the Netherlands, are devoted to memories of his piano teachers, his nostalgia of sweet evenings of music-making with the family, and the opportunity later to practice one full day while in hiding. When Ilse and Max married after the war, they bought a piano before any other furniture. In the 1930s, music strengthened our family's cohesion in a world disintegrating beyond recognition.

Henny, an excellent soprano, allowed me to accompany her regularly. Thus, between a Beethoven violin sonata or a Mozart trio, and a handful of Schubert or Schumann songs, we spent many a happy evening with our friends and family in the Thierschstrasse apartment in Munich. I think back with nostalgia to those evenings of Hausmusik [German: house music] when everything outside was gray and ugly, especially when, as Jews, we were not allowed to attend concerts any longer.

Within the walls of our apartment, there was an island of peace...The sweet magic of our concertizing made us forget the grim reality of ever-increasing terror. Our music...transported us "into a better world," as the well-known Schubert song has it. Perhaps the answer to the question about how I could describe my Munich years as a "good life" is that, despite what was going on around me, I focused on activities and relationships I cared about. And I saw in this, vital resistance against the Nazis. Not a resistance of guns, but of dignity. Music sustained my spirits beyond the pleasure of playing the piano. Later, it helped me endure the vicissitudes of hiding when I remembered the notes and melodies.

An undated entry in Dad's German-language "War Diaries: September 1942-October 1944" describes his feelings about music while he hid:

Last night in this attic room, the insufferably slow composition of a Beethoven piano sonata cut through my very being. This music is like lime tree balm on my wounded soul... Beethoven's composition entails so many life lessons for me... As long as we live, we have hope. I must keep this in mind. Life is always worth living... Yes, even the sadness of loneliness can be useful when we understand it properly as part of life.

When I listened to or made music, Nazism didn't exist. Music took its place. And so when I came back to Munich in British uniform in the spring of 1946, one of my chief objectives was to visit my superb piano teachers, Miss Schroeder and Julia Menz. Sadly, because both had passed away, I couldn't tell them how the music they taught me had saved my soul.

Choosing Hachsharah

Typically, a high school graduate must choose a next step. In 1938, as a 17-year-old Jewish boy in Nazi Germany, Dad saw three options. He could try to emigrate to Palestine immediately, either clandestinely or by obtaining an almost impossible-to-acquire British Certificate that would allow him to enter Palestine legally. Second, he could try to emigrate to the United States. And finally, he could stay in Germany and become more deeply involved with Zionist and other resistance activities. The third option entailed moving to a Zionist farm in Germany, called a *Hachsharah* (Hebrew: "preparation"), where he would be trained to become a farmer in Palestine. That was the choice he made.

As soon as I moved to Munich and joined Habonim in 1934, I began to "strive towards Hachsharah," which is the language we used. I would go to a training farm that would transform me into a farmer and then a pioneer in Palestine. In 1937, the German national office of Habonim located in Berlin tried to make this plan possible by establishing a Hachsharah farm in Ellguth, a town in northeast Germany in a region called Upper Silesia, close to the Polish border, an area that repeatedly changed hands: from Germany to Poland and back again.

The farm itself stretched over 600 acres and belonged to the Jewish Fräenkel-Pinkus family of textile manufacturers. Auguste Fräenkel-Pinkus' (1838–1919) factory in Neustadt, Germany (now Prudnik, Poland) was one of the largest producers of fine linens in the world. This successful and generous businessman allowed The Synagogue Community Association of Upper Silesia to set up the *Habonim Hachsharah* on his farm. The year-round camp/farm offered trainees total immersion: 24/7 Zionism, agriculture, Judaism, Palestine, Hebrew, friends and even love.

Little did I know that the Hachsharah farm education would also save my life. I refer to the Nazi order of July 13, 1936, authorizing the establishment of "retraining schools" for Jews in preparation for their emigration, foreshadowing Nazi efforts to compel Jews to emigrate.

Leonard Gross, author of *The Last Jews in Berlin*, had this to say about the decree: "In the 1930s, before the mass exterminations began...the Nazis had their favorite Jews: the Zionists. Although their motives could not have been more different, the Nazis – Adolf Eichmann among them – and the Zionists were united in their desire to see the Jews leave Germany for Palestine."[7]

Choosing *Hachsharah* put Dad in a minority position among German Jewish youth. Many Jews his age wanted to emigrate immediately, particularly to the United States, but also to Palestine even if they were not yet trained in farming. After July 1, 1920, Great Britain had the Mandate for the Palestinian area in the Middle East and had decided to grant immigration certificates only to 10,000 Jews per year to balance Jewish desire for immigration with Arab opposition. From 1933 until 1939, 10,000 German Jews per year emigrated to Palestine – a paltry percentage of the much larger number of Jews whom the British blocked for lacking a certificate to enter.

If they had a visa to another country, Jews began leaving

Germany as soon as Hitler took power. As early as 1933, 37,000 Jews out of a total population of 523,000 German Jews saw the writing on the wall and left.[8]

As is well known, many more Jews tried to get out of Germany than were allowed to enter other countries. This was true during the entire Hitler period and mirrored all the governments of the world who chose not to accept Jews. All these governments were complicit indirectly or directly in contributing to Jewish deaths during the Holocaust. Closing the gates to Jewish would-be-immigrants enabled Hitler to commit genocide. For this reason and others, we can consider the Holocaust as a world war against the Jews. In some cases, Jews were pursued by killers and in other cases, Jews were forbidden to reach a place of safety.

If Father had somehow forced me to forsake agricultural training and go to America, that would have been a decisive conflict for me. I probably would have joined the US Armed Forces as a volunteer, following the example of so many other young refugees from Germany... [Or] I would have been drafted and either would have been killed at one of the fronts or would have come back to marry some respectable Jewish girl, started a family and a career.

The way Dad put this made the American alternative seem a poor second choice to marrying Ilse Strauss, his girlfriend.

Had I gone to the US, I would have been spared the horrors that befell me in Buchenwald and the Netherlands. But none of this outweighed being in love: if I had gone to the US, I would never have gotten Ilse, the most wonderful girl, as my wife... Father relented and let me join the Hachsharah. He knew that Habonim ideology was not the chief magnet drawing me to the farm in Ellguth, a place so far from Munich that it took almost two full days to get there by train!

When I arrived in Ellguth, I found close to 100 boys and girls my age plus two married couples who functioned as educators and inspirational leaders. These were Giora and Senta Josephsthal, and Edgar and Elly Freund, four of the most outstanding figures in the Zionist movement of those times. These couples hired local non-Jewish farmers to instruct us in farming. The leaders themselves worked with us off and on, but their talents were required behind a desk or telephone. That is what saved us.

After the war, Senta published a book describing her work with her husband on the Habonim farm. She wrote that their goal had been to "guide the youngsters in learning to be farmers. Half the day was spent working and half in studying. The study program aimed to develop the youngster's ability to think for her/himself, increase her/his thirst for knowledge and provide tools for independent study." Senta was impressed with the youth: "They had all the qualities needed to constitute a fine nucleus for a [*kibbutz* in Palestine]," she wrote.

Hachsharah trained us, but it did much more. The fact that we German Jewish middle-class youth were supposed to become working-class farmers gave us the strength for enormous moral resistance, something everybody needed. This was the foundation of our Jewish resistance to Nazism, real resistance, positive, morale-building resistance, which those who open their mouths from almost half a century's distance will never understand. In fact, I often wondered how other young people who did not grow up in a Zionist youth movement, who did not experience this intense life as we did in Ellguth, how they had the strength to cope with the ever-growing Nazi oppression.

One subtle aspect of Habonim was to distance ourselves from our parents' control by molding us into strong groups with weakened attachment to our families. We were taught that we belonged to one great family, i.e., the family of fellow halutzim [Hebrew: pioneers]. *This new belief generated the courage to resist actively and continuously.*"[9] *Parents could be loved, but they represented "Old Jews," literally and figuratively. The Labor Zionist ideology held that "Old Jews" did not know how to cope with Nazism, whereas "New Jews," i.e. the youngsters, did. "New Jews" fought back. Simply by being in Habonim, New Jews were resisting the Nazis. I lived, learned, discussed, and taught these ideas day and night in Ellguth.*

Love in the Time of Hachsharah

I have already mentioned that my enthusiasm for Zionism stemmed from an additional attraction – Ilse, my girlfriend, "my first erotic involvement." Like anyone who has ever been "madly in love," I sought ways to spend time with this dark-haired, rosy-cheeked Jewish girl with the conventional German name – Ilse. In Ludwigshafen, her home city, she had to deal with antisemitic hostilities in her classrooms and among her disloyal girlfriends. It became so bad that she dropped out of school in tenth grade. It was then that her parents sent her to Munich to live with relatives. Soon her family followed.

By chance, Ilse joined my Habonim group. Later, when she left Munich for the Ellguth training camp, I caught up with her soon after I graduated high school. And so a new life began for me. Within a few weeks, my things were packed, and I started the long trip from Munich via Dresden and Breslau to Upper Silesia, a route that only a few years later would become the final one for tens of thousands of my fellow German Jews being transported to concentration camps in Poland.

Ilse wrote, "In Habonim I found my life's philosophy, i.e., a return to Judaism from my assimilationist past and a dedication to building up *Eretz Yisrael*..." Ilse knew very little about Judaism, so she quickly adopted Zionist ideology as her way *into* Judaism. By contrast, for my father, Zionism represented a distancing *from* Judaism, which he knew very well. For both, *Habonim* was a youth movement of ideals. Ilse loved her parents (her lawyer father and her homemaker mother) and her two sisters. But beyond that, she believed she belonged to the family of fellow *halutzim*, and for her, this attitude generated the willpower and courage to resist the Nazis.

My love for Ilse and the ideology of Habonim contributed to my decision to turn down the US visa when it arrived. But shame was also at play. Going to America meant being a traitor to the Zionist cause. The personalities of our leaders exerted a magnetic force...and you simply had to follow them for fear of being a moral outcast. The thing to do was to go on Hachsharah, change your life from a student to a farmer and then wait patiently to receive a British Certificate for emigration to Palestine. You would go when your time had come, together with your group from Habonim, and then you would build a new outpost together in Palestine.

The Inverted Pyramid

To understand the fervor with which some middle-class Jewish youths committed themselves to becoming working-class farmers requires understanding two things. First, farming in *Eretz Yisrael* was valorized. It meant being in touch with the Holy Land physically, the theme of many *Habonim* songs. Only by working the land could one truly "possess" it. The Holy Land would become the ground on which the Jewish future would be built.

The second idea was *Habonim*'s insistence that the Jewish demographic structure needed to change. "A new society in a new land!" According to this ideology, the old structure consisted of a tiny base of blue-collar workers supporting a huge top layer of "unproductive" philosophers, Talmud scholars, and academics. Young Jews who, under normal circumstances, would have headed straight to universities after high school needed to become part of a new society of dignified, useful manual laborers. Instead of being *Luftmenschen* with their heads in the clouds, they would become farmers with their feet on the ground and their hands in the soil.

All Jews, *Habonim* contended, needed to move to *Eretz Yisrael* and become "New Jews," he-men who were physically strong and not necessarily learned. By contrast, the image of the New Jewish Woman was poorly defined and certainly not new: cooking, laundry, and childcare, with a few exceptions.

For us in Ellguth, the "Palestine or nothing" attitude ruled our lives. We dreamt of becoming farmers, or, in some cases, mechanics. In retrospect, we did not see the similarity between the images of Aryan men and women and the images of the New Jews. Zionism asserted that the Jews' upside-down occupational structure had to be changed. Hence the various plans for re-training, called "Umschichtung" in German. The motivation to prepare oneself for life in Eretz Yisrael stemmed from a longing for freedom and a land of our own, guided by the theory of the "occupational pyramid" of the Jews. Even from the distance of decades, this theory continues to plague me, leading me to write about it repeatedly and extensively. I also witnessed this theory later in the Netherlands, where the leaders of the Vereeniging [Dutch name of the

Jewish Zionist refugee organization] had absolutely no interest whatsoever in any intellectual pursuits on the part of their charges, of which I was one. If you could milk a cow, could talk and smell like a farmer, and you were healthy, you were normal. More than normal – admirable.

My views changed over time, and years later, I criticized the presumption of anyone telling me what to do with my life. To save myself from physical extermination, I would be willing to do almost anything. But to agree with Hitler's attacks on the Jewish people and make a Weltanschauung [worldview] out of this, that is entirely different. I am proud to be a member of the "People of the Book." I am proud that so many Jews have won Nobel Prizes. I am proud that we are so "disproportionately" represented in the professions, in art, in science and in commerce. But then, when we pulled sugar beets out of the mud, we loved that, too, because we were told that this was our generation's life goal. But I wasn't sure. While there were moments of contentment in milking the cows and spreading manure, I was never able to see in this my personal destiny.

The previous paragraph represents a major confession. It illustrates that I did not fully internalize my Zionist youth group ideology. True, I turned down the opportunity to go to America – that was "virtuous," but that was also motivated by love. Not seeing a farmer's life as my personal destiny was blasphemy. The only exception to repudiating intellectual education was our intense study of Hebrew – this we did with zeal.

A Visit Home

In September 1938, I received permission from someone in authority to leave my Hachsharah paradise in Ellguth and spend the High Holidays with my parents and sisters in Munich. In addition to missing my relatives, I missed Judaism. While socialist Zionism at the camp had its own rituals, songs, symbols, language, godlike figures and more, the Jewish religion itself was not a central part of Hachsharah life. At Ellguth, Zionism replaced Judaism. But when I arrived in Munich, I participated happily in synagogue services and sang in the choir, just as always.

The trip home after five months in Ellguth opened my eyes in many ways. The family was glad to see me, but I looked different to them, and I saw them in a different light. Our parents' friends were not the same any longer either. They huddled together, discussing emigration possibilities all day long, spreading rumors of every kind. And then, shortly after the holidays, my world fell apart. Just before I was scheduled to return to Ellguth, an overnight razzia and the deportation of Polish Jews began in our neighborhood. On October 28, 1938, German police arrested 17,000 (!) Jews of "Polish nationality living in Germany."

These so-called "Polish Jews" were long-time German citizens; many had even been born in Germany, but now they were stripped of their citizenship without having committed any crime. For the sole reason that they were "Polish Jews in some way," they were evicted by truck and "returned" to Poland, 1,122 kilometers from Munich.

When they arrived at the German/Polish border, the Polish authorities turned these people back to Germany, because "they had no use for any 'extra Jews, Polish citizens or not.'" My relatives, the Kalters, and many whose homes and possessions had been stolen, were then housed in prisons. Or they stayed for several months in "hastily constructed, closely guarded camps in "No-Man's Land" near the border, until the Poles let them in.

I did not barricade myself inside my grandmother's apartment while this round-up was underway. Rather, I ran to the Central Train Station in Munich where I met Ilse's two cousins, the Gerns. Together we stood in a truck that had been put at our disposal by the owner of one of Munich's Jewish department stores, and we distributed woolen blankets and other necessities to the deportees. For the first time in my life, I saw Nazi brutalities, mild, of course, in comparison with what happened later. A police inspector...kicked little children who were looking for their parents. Ilse's cousins and I worked through the night. We did not imagine it would happen to us, just to those poor Polish Jews.

I even thought that the evictions fell into the realm of normal possibilities: here was a group of foreigners some of them probably without the necessary documents permitting them to reside in Germany [not true; they were Jews recently deprived of their German citizenship] *and the German authorities removed them from German soil... This scene was "normal" only because I could still find a way to rationalize it and even blame the victims. If I had allowed myself to realize it was not normal, I would have had to identify with the Ostjuden (German: Jews from Eastern Europe) and recognize the extreme danger I, myself, was in. True, I cared about the Polish Jewish deportees as fellow human beings, but I also felt separate from them, grateful to be spared their fate. After all, I was German, not Polish. Little did I know that soon this distinction would count for nothing. The only important identifier was "Jew."*

The expulsion of 17,000 Polish Jews had enormous, unforeseen consequences. To punish the Germans, Herschel Grynszpan, a young "Polish" Jew and son of deported Jews, assassinated a German diplomat in Paris.[10] Ernst vom Rath's death provided the Germans with an excuse to unleash an extraordinary attack on German Jews and their property 12 days later when the infamous, government-sponsored *Kristallnacht* took place all over Germany.

Abandonment on the Farm

At the end of my Rosh Hashanah vacation, I left the delights and horrors of Munich for Ellguth once again, traveling via Dresden, where I met Ilse who, like me, had been home for the holidays. And then, I had a shocking experience I never forgot. We discovered upon our arrival at the Hachsharah camp that our leaders had disappeared: they had gone on Aliyah, an ideological way of saying they had "left for Palestine."

In other words, the leaders of the Zionist training camp had abandoned the youth when they personally had the opportunity to leave. Apparently, the same phenomenon occurred at other *Hachsharot* as well. Senta Josephstal's biographical essay about her husband, Giora, contains a few sentences about the "abandonment." She wrote: "In September 1938, an unexpected opportunity arose to emigrate to Palestine. Without checking with Berlin, the district commissioner issued a passport to Giora...We took immediate advantage of this piece of luck and crossed the border into Czechoslovakia."[11] Senta did not speculate about what their departure meant to the youth they were leaving behind... Nor does she mention whether she or her husband had made provisions for them or even left a note.

And so we youngsters were left to our own devices. Rumors of new Nazi terror started to penetrate our little world. But we did not care too much. Our Zionist ideas were more important than the events outside. We could manage even without leaders! At the end of October 1938, as Ilse and I returned to the Ellguth Hachsharah, we still did not feel particularly endangered. Just forgotten. It took until Kristallnacht a few days later, on November 9, 1938, along with the subsequent incarceration of Jewish men and boys in concentration camps, to rouse the Zionist leadership to recognize how dangerous the situation had become in Germany.

I have used the term, Kristallnacht, even though I am angry at myself for doing so. The German label – Reichspogromnacht *– is more fitting because it names the persecutors. To me, Kristallnacht represents one of the typical misunderstandings and half-understandings that characterize the post-World War II approach to the Nazi catastrophe. As though all that happened during that fateful night in November 1938 was the smashing of some knickknacks German Jews kept in their homes. "That is not what happened," I want to shout. "That many Jews were killed, that tens of thousands were dragged off to concentration camps, that most, if not all, of our synagogues went up in flames (where is that American respect for 'houses of God'?), that Torah scrolls were defiled and burned, in short – that our communities and our world were destroyed... All of this is passed over. It has no place in the conscience of the Western world, a conscience that feels much more comfortable when it can speak of bric-a-brac [i.e., crystal]." And then, I argued against what I had just written: "I have to acknowledge that history and historians show greater understanding when past events are given names."*

Ilse preferred "November 9th" and until she died in 2013, she commemorated the date annually by lighting a memorial candle. I grew up commemorating November 9 with her as the day her parents lost their possessions and were shipped west to Concentration Camp Gurs in France – the beginning of the end.

The Ellguth leaders' abandonment provoked a painful ethical debate, or better put, an imagined trial in which I judged the Zionist movement. The "accused" were charged with not protecting the youngsters. We should have been taught that we faced an emergency demanding extraordinary measures. Then many of us would have saved our lives – not by waiting for a British Certificate to go to Palestine as agricultural pioneers, but by availing ourselves of every possible means to leave Germany under any circumstance.

Romanticized ideologies did their part in closing our eyes to these realities. The Zionist leaders did not recognize or even discuss the emergency, did not prepare us to escape, but when they had the opportunity to leave, they took it and abandoned us. Although I was adamant in labeling the leaders' actions as abandonment, I now recognize that there is a possibility they fled because they feared arrest. Although Ilse and I stayed in touch with Senta and Giora over the ensuing years, we never got a full explanation from them of the circumstances of their sudden departure.

Was Pioneering Zionism Dangerous for Jewish Survival?

Thus, an unwelcome dent appeared in my Zionist euphoria. Were the Habonim leaders irresponsible in setting up youth movements in Germany when they should have focused on getting us out? Why did the leaders keep us in Germany? What were they waiting for? After all, violent state antisemitism had already been in place for more than five years. Dozens of restrictions had already been enacted. The leadership must have known about the deportation of innocent Jews from Munich, an outrage I had seen with my own eyes!

But there were no signs that our leadership had any conception of the true problem of Jewish survival. In addition, I began to see my own family in Munich in a new light. They sought survival at any cost, discussing emigration to any country that had an open door. Our Zionist youth leaders showed no such attitude. If their thinking had been different, their moral coercion – I hesitate to use this harsh term – of going to Palestine would have given way to organized efforts at emigration to other countries, regardless of where, to secure our survival.

Instead, they preached chalutziut [Hebrew: pioneering] and nothing but chalutziut.

I do not want to overlook the positive side of what we were doing. For many of us, working with hoe and rake was the only occupational therapy that could help us cope with, or forget, our troubles as persecuted Jews. I also credit many of my experiences in Nazi Germany with enabling me to withstand the difficulties of hiding later. Being abandoned on the farm prepared me to make my own decisions, to rely on myself.

Ironically, because of the strength of Zionist ideology, some of the leaders on whom we relied were unable to perceive the fundamental danger facing the Jewish community. Our leaders acted as though nothing had changed since the publication in February 1896 of Theodor Herzl's Judenstaat, *the pamphlet that presented the idea of a possible and necessary Jewish state. Young Zionist Jews were cornered: they were "morally forbidden" to go to America, and "legally forbidden" to leave for Palestine until they received British Certificates. Instead of viewing America-bound youngsters as having found a way to save their lives, such emigrants were considered traitors.*

Had the leaders known what really was at stake, they might have devised a compromise – America on the way to Palestine. But it seems harsh to judge the leaders for not knowing what the entire world did not know, i.e. that the Nazis would soon endorse a plan to exterminate European Jewry.

Kristallnacht on the Farm

Despite the lack of adult leadership, the Hachsharah at Ellguth continued to function for a week or so after our return from Munich. We had our usual daily routine of work and study, and we believed things would go back to "normal." But then my utopian world collapsed entirely! One evening, we were studying Hebrew after our meal, when somebody came in to tell us that a day earlier, synagogues had been burnt, stores destroyed, and some Jews had been taken away.

We learned that Propaganda Minister Joseph Goebbels had "explained" that the assassination of the German diplomat in Paris was the product of a "World Jewry" conspiracy. Later, we learned that in response, Hitler ordered "spontaneous" public demonstrations and instructed the police not to intervene. The order not to protect Jewish life and property ignited nation-wide violence that reached into the major cities, small towns, and remotest spots in Germany. Some of us got a bit nervous when we heard this story, but we did not feel insecure. "Nothing could happen to us," I wrote.

Then the unexpected did happen. My friend, Jacobus [Hannemann], came rushing into the rooms where our diverse study groups were meeting. He was pale but he tried to tell us in a calm voice that we were to assemble in the dining hall at once. At that moment, we knew that the thing we had subconsciously feared during the last few weeks had come to our doorstep. We stumbled down to the ground floor. When all of us had gathered, the policeman addressed us roughly. He had orders to confiscate all our weapons and knives. We were stunned. What was this all about? There was even a "question and answer" period! Were pocketknives permitted? No. Kitchen knives? Only a few essential ones! "As long as I am here, nothing is going to happen," the officer said.

I can hear him now. But we still didn't understand. I think we didn't want to understand; we were conditioned not to understand. Somebody behind me whispered that he had thrown his pocketknife into the pond and would try to fish it out later. The whole scene was over in a few minutes. We calmed each other down – not really, I think – but each of us got up some courage by telling the next person that nothing serious was going to happen. We went back to our study groups as soon as the policeman had left. I think I even taught that night. Two of our members were on night duty in the chicken coops where it was nice and warm. What they could not have known is that by remaining in the coop, they had saved themselves from being taken to the Buchenwald concentration camp.

An hour or two later there was a great noise, people were running and screaming throughout our large building. Somebody yelled: "Everyone outside; everyone line up outside." We scrambled, and suddenly, several local thugs attacked us, armed with sticks and clubs and belts, hitting us wherever they could. One of our boys had blood running down his face. Somebody else was brought up from the basement with a bandaged head. So this was it, the real thing! Perhaps the policeman who had come earlier to make sure the camp members had no weapons had been setting up the conditions for the hooligans to attack us more easily. The violence I had known during the pogroms in Gunzenhausen was now everywhere in Germany. The police did not control the attackers; they collaborated with them! There was no escape and no person to turn to. Certainly, no leaders.

And next came the sinking realization that it was most likely a non-Jewish person training us on the farm who had betrayed us. This person was responsible for the farm's operations and for instructing the youth in agricultural skills. The violent vandals on the outside were colluding with the agricultural trainers on the inside! Our foreman and other non-Jewish workers, whom we knew, had joined the thugs! They helped beat up both boys and girls amid disgusting gestures and remarks. It was all so grotesque: a few hours earlier, we had been working together harvesting our sugar beets. They did not kill us or injure us seriously. Perhaps their superior had told them not to go too far.

The attackers seemed not to know what to do. They didn't understand the orders and so they made up everything on the spot. They could have hit harder. But most of them were busy stealing and grabbing whatever they could lay their hands on. They wallowed in the girls' bedrooms among underwear and boxes with sanitary napkins, which they handled with great delight. This combination of violence, theft, and a kind of salacious voyeurism became the overarching pattern of the Nazis' relations with us throughout that night and beyond.

Immediately after these frightening events, the Nazi establishment decided that since the Jews were to blame, they were legally and financially responsible for the damages incurred. Accordingly, a fine of one billion marks was levied on the German Jewish community for the slaying of vom Rath, and the six million marks paid by insurance companies for broken windows was to be given to the state coffers.[12]

The *Hachsharah* camp in Ellguth was not the only institution that Nazis violated in Upper Silesia. According to an article in the *Guardian*, patients in the home for consumptives (i.e. tuberculosis patients) were driven out during the night and the home demolished. The institution for Jewish infants was also destroyed.[13]

In Ellguth and later in Buchenwald, I was aware of the sexual underpinning of the Nazis' behavior. Even on this night of terror, I was struck by the raiders' obscenities and their fascination with the girls' intimate possessions. I must confess that at one point, we were concerned that they would abuse our girls, but nothing serious happened, except that those yokels handled the girls' breasts in a clumsy way, something I had to witness against my will.[14] All in all, scary as it was, this command performance led by the local SA in its usual "courageous" manner, seemed a half-hearted exercise, much milder by comparison than what awaited us.

Ilse also wrote about Kristallnacht on the farm. She did not mention the sexual humiliation, but focused instead on the violence. "Our life was brutally interrupted on November 9, 1938, when we were rounded up by locals and were beaten until we were lying on the ground. Seventy boys and girls, 17 or 18 years old, were put on a truck and shipped to the Polish border."[15]

Sociologist Lenore Weitzman's interview of Ilse decades later contains additional description and interpretation of that night: "We were sitting a whole night at the border. I was 18 at the time. The Polish border guards said they did not want us. Later, I realized that this refusal saved our lives, because if they would have taken us in, we would have been in Poland when the Germans invaded in September 1939, and that would have been the end of us. They took us to a city named Posen and we had to stand with our faces against the wall for a few hours.[16] We thought it was the end. But then they decided that they would take the boys to the camp in Buchenwald."

When the truck finally returned the girls to Ellguth, the thugs' leaders said that the girls could go home to their families. That was the end of Ilse's ordeal on Kristallnacht. For me, it was just the beginning.

The Trip to Hell

We boys were allowed a few minutes to go to our rooms and get some belongings to take "to where you will be sent." We saw how our attackers helped themselves to whatever they liked. It was all over in minutes. They then lined us up outside the main building for a headcount, repeatedly, and there was an occasional kick in the shins for us. The bad thing was that we had no leader, no spokesman. The thought of resistance, other than trying to protect your head against the blows – was totally out of the question. We were unarmed. We had no plan. We had to submit.

We stuck together, leaderless, facing the grins of our former neighbors and co-workers who surrounded us. Everybody nursed his bruises and tried to cope as best as we could. In one or two of our attackers there was a touch of humanity left: they did not assault the married bookkeeper or his family; they stayed away from his little children and even put a bandage on the head of his little boy who had been badly hurt in the turmoil. All in all, it was a strange mixture of stupid brutality and a vestige of humane behavior, as though those Nazi brutes, at that early stage in the game, were not sure how far they should go.

After a while – and by now it had become totally dark – we were loaded onto open trucks, which had arrived at our farm "spontaneously." Boys and girls were separated as we drove off. It was bitterly cold. Now and then the truck would stop to permit us to urinate over the side. We finally wound up in a small border town that somebody was able to identify as Kreutzburg. German border police came out of their barracks and led us to their office building, not knowing what to do with us. It now had become clear that the thugs who had originally attacked us wanted to push us into Poland. We sat on the stairs and the floor in those border police headquarters while the leaders of our attackers negotiated inside. If we, ourselves, had had any leaders, I am sure that somebody would at least have been heard. Instead, we were bombarded by screams between the Polish border police and the Nazis.

Apparently, our attackers demanded praise for their brave and patriotic action, but the policemen, who, as always, went strictly "by the book," did not know what to do: here were a hundred or so unwashed, hungry, half-sick and scared Jewish youth. Chasing us across the border would do no good: those Poles would chase us right back again, as had happened several times before during those weeks. At this stage, Jews were not yet shot on sight.

A few commands were snapped at us and then they beat us back into the trucks again. Meanwhile, it had become light outside. They began to drive us in a different direction [west!]. We came to a nice town, which somebody recognized as Oppeln. In the distance, we saw a synagogue burning. That was when we finally knew that this action did not concern us alone, but that it was part of something bigger. They drove us up to the town prison and stopped in the large courtyard. The girls were with us again. We had to face the prison wall and stand in absolute silence. At that time, we feared that they would shoot us. I could do nothing, not even pray, so I looked at the neck of the girl in front of me – I can still see it, every single hair.

After a while, one of those incomprehensible things took place: the wife of the prison warden came around with mugs of a hot brew and we were able to relax, to warm ourselves, even to go to a toilet in the prison building. We had not eaten for many hours. That hot liquid, whatever it was, brought us some relief. May that woman be remembered for good!

The girls were called out – surely a bad sign. Maybe the thugs wanted to shoot only us boys. Again, we were lined up against the wall. We tried to wave good-bye to our girls. But suddenly, we [boys] were packed into a waiting line of police vans or paddy wagons that had arrived outside the gate. It was the first time I sat in something like that. You are squeezed into a very narrow cell good for only one person and you face the grating, giving out onto an aisle of sorts.

The new destination was a train station where we boys had to get out once again. We were lined up against the tracks. A not unfriendly police officer negotiated with some minor Nazis about the number of contingents from various towns and villages where Jews had been rounded up during the night. All were to be assembled at this local collection point in Oppeln. Nothing was said about a concentration camp, but we knew at that time from overhearing discussions between the people who called themselves "in charge" that all Jews were to be sent somewhere far away by train. They even passed around mugs of hot coffee. We were treated like common criminals who had been rounded up in a mass action, and apparently "the book" said that you had to give them coffee. Then, one of the officers made the rounds and asked every single one of us whether we had any physical complaints.

Dad loved irony and taught me to appreciate it as well. And here was a wonderful example. The Jewish boys had been beaten, thrown into open trucks, driven to a border where they were rejected, made to stand facing a wall, thrown back into trucks, forced into paddy wagons and denied any information about where they were going. And yet the police officer asked each one of them if he had any complaints! It was almost funny.

But this was no farce. I told the officer about my stomachache – something that came over me automatically during the rest of the Hitler era in situations of high tension. "I will make a note of it," the officer said, "and the doctor will take care of you upon arrival at your destination. Just report to the doctor when you get there." This was said in all earnestness, and I believed it. Maybe the officer believed it as well. I sometimes said, jokingly, that I spent the entire war on the toilet with my stomach aches.

We huddled together in the train. All we knew was that we were going west. Going west meant that for the time being I was staying in Germany and not being forced to cross into Poland. After a while, we fell asleep, exhausted. I dreamt. We woke up with a jolt. Sleep had been only a fitful dozing through the long November night on the hard, wooden benches of our train compartment. The train was slowing down. I rubbed my eyes and immediately remembered the situation. B., next to me, started to cry. That was something I had never seen my friends do. The train stopped. Nazi Storm Troopers yelled excitedly on the platform – "raus, raus, ihr Saujuden" [German: out, out, you Jew pigs] *– the doors to our compartment were torn open and a handful of uniformed men climbed in, beating us, and yelling all the time, "Saujuden raus!"*

In Hitler's hierarchy of life forms, Jews were lower than insects. And yet, Jews were regularly called pigs. Perhaps this epithet was meant to be particularly derogatory since Jews who eat only kosher foods do not eat pig products. Pigs represented filth.

When the train halted, one of the Nazis took the wristwatch of my friend, Shushu, threw it on the floor and trampled on it, yelling "Judenuhr, Judenuhr" [German: Jew watch]. *It was all so absurd. Suddenly we found ourselves in the wide underground passage of the train station that connected the platforms.*

We were pressed against the wall in rows of ten or 15. There were hundreds of us. The Nazis beat the last and next to last men mercilessly to have all of us squeeze against those in front to create more room. The Nazis were anxious not to have this scene observed by outsiders – I still do not know what all this secrecy was for.

In *The Politics of Cruelty,* however, Kate Millett explains that after torture was nearly universally outlawed in the early 1800s, it became covert. After all, even those who engage in torture today try to keep it a secret. But it was unlikely that 10,000 Jews who were imprisoned in Buchenwald from all over the country on Kristallnacht could have been brought to this camp or others without people who lived nearby noticing. By the month's end, the number of men in the camp exceeded 18,000.

Why, of all the experiences of the Hitler era, and most of them much more horrible than this one, why do I hear to this very day the voice of one of the SS men, a strapping youngster, not much older than I was, yelling and hitting without interruption so that the rows of baffled Jewish men and boys would arrange themselves to his liking – "Geh doch ruber, in sanner glied, du Judensau" [German dialect: Get the hell over there into the other row, you Jew pig]. I still hear him. He wasn't the worst. You could duck his lashes, and his truncheon did not always hurt so badly. Perhaps I remember his voice because it was my introduction to the world of Buchenwald, a new dimension of life for me. Buchenwald was both a place and a concept. For me, aside from its horrible physical aspects, it was an intense education in survival and a precursor of future German horrors.

Buchenwald, Prisoner #27384

Located five miles north of Weimar, Buchenwald [German: beech forest] was one of five concentration camps established in Germany between 1936 and 1939. Large groups of prisoners were incarcerated there shortly after it was established and by mid-1937, a year and a half before *Kristallnacht,* Buchenwald had become one of the largest camps in Germany, eventually spawning 130 satellite camps and extensions. Following actions by the Nazi government, Buchenwald's prisoner population grew continuously. The first female prisoners were incarcerated in 1942.[17]

On Kristallnacht, Father and I were sent to two different KLs [German: Konzentrationslager, concentration camps]: I to Buchenwald and he to Dachau. Father's dates of incarceration were November 19 to December 19, 1938, more than five weeks. His prisoner number was 20098. It is reasonable to assume that he was grabbed [from his home?] in Munich and sent to Dachau, only ten miles away. Father talked very rarely about this experience, but on January 12, 1954, a little less than a decade after the war ended, he received a formal document from the Allied High Commission for Germany, stating that he, prisoner number 20098, had been incarcerated in order to place him in "Jewish protective custody."[18] *In October 1939 (almost a year after I had been released), it became a rule that nobody was to be released from protective custody for the duration of the war.* This term – Jewish protective custody – represented one of the most severe "legal" measures which the National Socialist State applied against anybody who had been declared an "Enemy of State and People." With the elimination of formal reviews of Gestapo procedures by the courts, Gestapo imposition of protective custody...cleared the way for any special treatment that the National Socialist leadership wanted to employ, i.e., the physical liquidation of any prisoner.[19]

Following *Kristallnacht*, "Thirty thousand Jews were dragging around in various concentration camps...for four to eight weeks. [The Nazis] hoped that the barbarous treatment of the Jews at the hands of the Nazis would increase the pressure on Jews to emigrate from Germany, leaving their property behind."[20] This strategy worked. The remaining Jews in Germany did everything in their power to leave. The "only" thing lacking was a country to which they could emigrate.

I want to continue describing my Kristallnacht experience: On the far side of that underground passage in the train station, over to the right from where we had come, we could glimpse a commotion. We were not allowed to look up – we had to keep our heads down – but we felt that something was going on out there. Only a few of us had an idea that a concentration camp called Buchenwald existed and was nearby.

I speak of "we" rather than "I," as if I could assume that everyone was thinking the same thing. Perhaps this sense of unity gave me some strength, the strength derived from not being alone. But, as with everyone else coping with such a situation, I preferred that if someone had to be beaten, it not be me. And so each of us edged deeper into the pack so as to avoid the random blows.[21]

Out there it was broad daylight. The rows of Jews pressed against the wall eased up a little, the pressure of bodies became less, and we saw that row after row to our right disappeared towards the opening. When our turn came, I was pushed and kicked and told to run fast. The SS formed a gauntlet,[22] hitting and yelling, "faster, faster." I stumbled with my nailed boots I had kept from my mountain climbing days, solid high boots that stood me in good stead. But the boot-nails slipped on the cobblestones. Another kick in the rear, and I was up in an open truck, head down, thrown in together with a few dozen fellow Jews.

Anyone who raised his head would get a smack from the rubber truncheon of the SS man guarding us. The Nazi guards forced the Jews to keep their heads down so that none of the people of Weimar should see our faces – at that time it still seemed to matter to them. I had the distinct feeling that they were a bit ashamed, or at least acting as though they knew they were doing something not right. The trip up to the camp from the train station was long and bumpy, but my discomfort came mostly from the heads-down position. The painful heads-down requirement prevented us from seeing where we were going.

But this position was important to Nazis for other reasons. Humans and many animal species recognize the heads-down posture as a sign of weakness, inferiority, deference, or surrender. By having to keep our heads down, we Jews could not look the Nazis in the eye to express defiance nor identify the individual Nazi and his actions. Moreover, the backs of our necks were exposed to dangerous beatings. Then everything slowed down. There were rows of barbed wire, many barracks, a gate with the inscription "Recht oder Unrecht, mein Vaterland" [German: My Fatherland, right or wrong]. "Down with that Jew head" – bump, and then, as the back of the truck was opened, we were chased out. Finally, we realized that we were prisoners in a concentration camp.

The Bok Story – The Inability to Act

Later, in 1942-3, when I began writing what I called "A Wartime Diary from a Place of Hiding," I did not start with the day I went into hiding. Instead, I began with an early Buchenwald experience, which in retrospect, had become painful all over again. I close my eyes and I can see my fellow Jews once more. They were standing with their faces against the stone wall, the prisoners shaking against the wall.

Suddenly, the "punishment commander" came over and randomly chose one person to be punished. The "commander" got the prisoner out of the line and forced him to get "the stand" himself. The prisoner then had to drop his pants. And then he was buckled onto a device – the "bok." The first blows of the heavy leather whip swished down hard onto his bare flesh; the poor man's feet moved in agitation, and he emitted such heartrending wails that we thought the earth would open and swallow everybody. The straps of the whip tore deep into his flesh, and that human soul cried louder and louder for God. Oh God.

Every five lashes, a new policeman took a turn because they wanted to strike the prisoner with all their might. How the man was able to get off the wooden stand, I do not know. But I still remember very clearly that all of us, including me, stood by with our bread in our arms and said nothing. Not one word. Being immobilized and unable to help my fellow prisoner plagued me forever. No one helped, not even me. Why couldn't I give the suffering brother a sign of comradeship and sympathy, and by doing so perhaps ease his pain?

I have tried to atone for what I define as my sin. I know that I closed my eyes for one second when I didn't think I could bear the sight any longer. And today, after so many years...these pictures of the past come up repeatedly. I have a feeling of shame. Who knows if this poor man is still alive. Will he ever forgive me for standing by and keeping quiet as he was being whipped? One shouldn't say "we couldn't do anything" in a situation such as the one I described. That's not a way to answer the lifelong puzzle posed by one's conscience.

My father's story about being unable to act while a fellow Jew was being tortured reminds me of Niek Schouten, a magnificent non-Jewish Dutchman who later, with his wife Aag, sheltered my parents. Niek told me the life-defining story about how he decided to act in the face of Nazi terror. When he witnessed Nazis marching Jews through Rotterdam to the train station, he struggled with the question, "What should I do?" Niek remembered the very spot where the question arose. At that moment, he came up with three options: do nothing; somehow kill one or more Nazis; or somehow save one or more Jews. He chose the last option. And ultimately, he did save several Jews. But Dad could not save the man on the "bok."

I was tormented by witnessing extreme torture and remaining immobilized. I believed that I had "abandoned the victim." In my torment, I defined "standing by mutely" not as fear-induced paralysis but as a choice not to act, a choice not to sacrifice myself. First, there was the horror of witnessing an innocent, helpless man being whipped viciously. And then there was my profound guilt for not having done anything in response. Both horrified me.

While in hiding a few years later, I wrote: It is difficult to fend off the constantly recurring feeling of shame. Today we can find many words to justify our inaction in 1938, but our guilt from that time cannot be put aside. I know that I would never have thought that way about those occurrences were it not for the fact that I am in such a difficult situation myself right now [i.e., hiding and starving]. I would not want other people to react the way I did toward my brother on the "bok." I did not want to be the silent onlooker. I wanted to be the boy who organized the sports center, the boy who refused to translate Mein Kampf *on his Abitur. I keep on thinking about this brother on the "bok." And by thinking about him, my conscience won't leave me alone. This was a moment that forms people, that turns us in a particular direction. From the experience I had, I learned the truth about myself.*

Photographed and Measured

On the day of our arrival, a few of us were photographed. We were unwashed and unshaven after the three-day trip to Buchenwald. Our heads had been shaved by old inmates with old razors, and everybody looked like a criminal. But some, including myself, looked more awful than others, what with my Jewish features, especially my long nose. I was a natural, so to speak, for eager photographers who appeared on behalf of German magazines. The photographers went down on their knees before us to take their shots, aiming their cameras upward so that our faces appeared distorted, more mug-shot-like, more inhuman. Precisely the stuff that would attract the readers of the Nazi magazines: a row of typical Jewish criminals. For my photograph, I posed next to an open barrel, the temporary outdoor toilet we used during the first days in camp.[23]

A few days later, there was an announcement: "Jew birds that had their pictures taken" must report immediately to a special officer. I was terribly afraid because to be singled out from the big crowd of fellow prisoners was the worst that could happen. It was a murky November day and they ordered me to an office where an SS doctor told me to take my dirty shoes off to prevent soiling his place. He was quite polite, if the term can be used, being interested solely in "racial studies." He measured my nose and my facial features, but he did not mistreat me.

As soon as I realized the absurdity of it all, part of my courage came back. He asked me how long my ancestors had lived in Germany and where they had originally come from. With an unwavering voice, I said: "Since the 16th century, and we were originally from Czechoslovakia." What difference did it make which idiotic story I invented? I sounded so convincing to that "scientist" who entered all my answers to the questions on the questionnaire.

Interrogation – Micro-Resistance

The next office was more unpleasant. It was the commander's main office near the entrance to the camp to which I was led by two guards, again with my shoes off. It was mid-November, and I shivered all over. The commander, I think his name was Koch – a Bavarian brute described exhaustively by Buchenwald survivors – was seated behind his desk, flanked by several of his cronies. He sat there, toying with his leather whip and pistol.

This commander, Carl-Otto Koch, was a mid-level SS officer born in 1897 and executed by firing squad in April 1945. He had become an adherent of Nazism two years *before* Hitler came to power. He was also a thief who stole valuables from murdered Jews. Koch commanded Buchenwald between August 1937 and September 1941, which includes the time Dad was imprisoned there. Apparently, when Koch was in charge, rules called for camp commanders to be punished for misdeeds. Thus, Koch was later punished and dismissed on allegations of corruption, fraud, embezzlement, drunkenness, sexual offenses, and murder. Two of his murder victims were hospital workers who had treated him for syphilis and whom he had killed to cover up his disease. SS officers themselves were Koch's chief critics and defied his order that they murder several officers. Hard to believe, but Koch was accused of bringing shame to the SS!

It was into the office of this man that I was now ushered. While I was being interrogated, a few guards pointed their guns at me, making it difficult to stand erect. My knees would literally give in every few minutes. First, I was shown some photos and told to identify the people; most of them were my old friends of our Hachsharah group, including my best friend, Shushu. Then came the personal questions – about my school, my plans, etc. I pulled the old trick that I had tried a year earlier in a forced school essay, namely about my wanting to fulfill the Führer's wish to see the Jews leave Germany, and that I had taken up agricultural training in a Zionist camp to make it possible for me and many others to help the Führer carry out his plan. All of what I said was true, except for the fact that I was not motivated by a desire to help Hitler.

Then they asked about Father, and all my protestations that he had been on active duty for the Fatherland during WWI, that he had been awarded the Iron Cross, and that I was named after his only brother who had died fighting for Germany – all of this led nowhere. What they were after was something else. They wanted to know whether Father examined non-Jewish women and girls in his medical office; whether I had watched him, and I quote verbatim, "pull their legs apart on his examination table." Furthermore, they wanted to know how many non-Jewish girls I had fucked – there was no inhibition whatsoever in their language. When this part of my interrogation was reached, the commander and at least one other SS crony touched their genitals and seemed to derive great pleasure from masturbating. It is as disgusting for me to put this on paper as it will be for you who are reading these lines. I have mentioned repeatedly the Nazis' sexual perversions. It seems to have been particularly arousing for them to visualize a male Jewish doctor giving a gynecological exam to a non-Jewish woman.

Nazi edicts outlawed Jewish/Aryan contact of the sort described above. Clearly "the forbidden" was enticing to the camp commander and his cronies. Nazi stereotypical beliefs about Jewish men included their hyper-sexuality, an idea that was taught in German public schools. In a study of German children's drawings of Jews, a "13-year-old German girl drew a Jewish man as a lecher, intent upon seducing a young German girl. The young victim ably defends herself and the Jewish man backs away."[24] This whole scenario was a Nazi fantasy displaced onto the Jew. As is well known, accusations of hyper-sexuality are commonly applied by those in power to such minority groups as black men, women, Romas, immigrants, gay men, and Jews. Nazi visual propaganda is replete with images of physically unattractive Jewish men who pose a sexual threat to the virginal, beautiful, innocent Aryan girl or woman.

The King David Story

The interrogation continued uninterrupted, but I had another trick up my sleeve. I have had one or two moments in my life when I felt an intervention from a mysterious power. I should like to think that it was divine help, although I certainly was not worthy of it. That point in the interrogation by the commander of Buchenwald was one such moment, and it has stayed with me because I could never explain it. Some voice told me to play the dumb idiot.

Suddenly, I remembered the Biblical King David when he was captured by the Philistines. The verse is as follows: "When David realized that he had been recognized, he panicked, fearing the worst from Achish, king of Gath. So right there, while they were looking at him, he pretended to go crazy, pounding his head on the city gate and foaming at the mouth, spit dripping from his beard. Achish took one look at him and said to his servants, 'Can't you see he's crazy? Why did you let him in here? Don't you think I have enough crazy people to put up with as it is, without adding another? Get him out of here!" [Samuel 21:12-15]

In response to the sexual questions, I acted as if I did not understand what Herr Oberkommandant [i.e., Koch] was talking about. "But surely," Koch said, "a young fellow with such good grades in the Oberrealschule, a fellow who had even skipped a grade must know what it means to fuck a girl." [How did Koch know I skipped a grade?] Next question: "Did I ever pull the panties off a Christian girl? Did I put my fingers in her cunt? But surely, you must at least have masturbated," he said, and the expression he used belongs to the German underworld, too dirty and too complicated to be repeated here.

To all this, I did not even shake my head in denial. My mouth was agape. My eyes started to bulge out. And I stared ahead, totally dumb, surely an acute case of dementia praecox. Sounding like the Biblical Achish, King of Gath, Koch yelled, "Let's get rid of that imbecile who doesn't even know what it means to masturbate" – using that impossible expression again. And I was thrown out of his office without further ado. It amazes me that the Oberkommandant did not recognize that I was simply acting the part of an imbecile. Whereas before I feared I would be executed or tortured or castrated, my shaking heart was now filled with a prayer of gratitude...to King David.

After witnessing torture, being photographed, and finally measured and interrogated, I was given my prisoner number – 27384.[25] In the camp at that time, numbers were not tattooed on prisoners' forearms. However, once I received this number, it was illegal for my captors to address me by my name – I was solely prisoner 27384. It may sound strange – but after a few days of getting into a certain camp routine, most of us found Buchenwald somehow...bearable. The main thing for us was to find our friends, our chaverim [Hebrew: friends] from Ellguth. Once we were together again as a group, everything was easier.

Generally speaking, we so-called protective arrestees were a great deal better off than the regular prisoners. Of course, the camp was bad, but it was not yet an extermination camp. Shortly after our arrival, a whole row of wooden coffins was carried near us by a detachment of "regulars." I still don't know if it was for the purposes of intimidating us, whether there were real corpses in those coffins, or whether it was a personal joke of one of the commanders. I had the feeling that it was nothing but a stupid bluff by some ingenious Scharführer (German: Squad Leader) *who was eager that another star for valor be added to his medals.*

I did not think of my fellow camp inmates as saints, but rather as prisoners who sometimes were very hard on each other in the struggle to survive. Hunger, thirst, and some infighting among us were probably just as much a cause of our suffering as the uncertainty of what would happen next. The filth was especially bad. You couldn't wash, and nobody had a change of clothes. I was terribly upset having to watch the evening line-up of "regular prisoners," separated from us by barbed wire in the wet November cold, preceded by the forced running and marching after a hard day's work, singing always that same banal song about the old, little mother waiting for her son to come home from the front.

There were also mysterious announcements that somebody was missing from a work detail – usually a suicide – only to be corrected afterwards to the extent that "the dead Jewish bird has been found." Several times we had to witness a beating, but I will spare you the details. We heard endless screams from the isolation bunkers during round-up time and prayers yelled from solitary cells during the mass count when everybody had to keep absolutely silent. The latrines, a row of rough wooden beams over giant pits filled to the top with feces and urine, were horrific. You would sit there with your bare buttocks on a piece of pine over that stinking pit; the "brave" young SS trainees pointed their guns right at you from behind the outer barbed wire fence – others have described these dismal scenes much better and in far greater detail. But I, the 17-year-old, was deeply impressed for the rest of my life.

There isn't a scene I have forgotten about Buchenwald. The camp lives on with all its colors and smells, with all its indignities and humiliations, with the various attempts at coping, with the occasional flickers of human nobility and self-respect that the Nazi swine could not destroy. Once there was an elderly professor sitting next to me over the latrine, trying to relieve himself. "I feel that I have atoned now for all my sins," he whispered to me. Once I overheard a few of the doctors among us arguing over the early symptoms of somebody's appendicitis. I remember that one of my friends from Ellguth had brought along a pocket edition *of... Kant, Immanuel Kant OF ALL THINGS, and spoke of the possibility of a merely "contemplative existence!" And there was my Uncle Richard from Dresden, in whose apartment Ilse and I had recently been such happy vacation guests. He would slip me a piece of bread occasionally. The fact that Uncle Richard slipped me, his nephew Max, who was much younger than he, an occasional piece of bread illustrates dramatically, how little food was available and how precious it was.*

Dad's story of sharing bread is an example of "stealth altruism," Arthur B. Shostak's useful concept to describe people helping each other when it is forbidden to do so.[26] According to Primo Levi, "Bread [was] our only money," and sharing it was both a sign of stealth altruism and a sign of affection.[27]

Once I helped carry food from the kitchen. It consisted of a steaming soup, not without taste, I must say, filled with pieces of heavy lard, and the whole mess was in metal garbage cans that had to be carried by two men, one at each handle. The loamy ground of Buchenwald was slippery from the heavy fall rains, and one of us fell, spilling the boiling hot stuff all over the mud. Within a moment, we were surrounded by dozens of fellow prisoners who tried to pick pieces of lard out of the slime. Others stood there, quietly admonishing their neighbors to show some dignity, to suppress their hunger, and not to behave like animals.

I quickly became used to eating such non-kosher foods as "heavy lard" because in Jewish law, saving life is the highest good and takes precedence over everything including the prohibition against eating unkosher food or desecrating the Sabbath. The greatest challenge for Buchenwald prisoners, a challenge greater than withstanding terror, the lack of food, the biting cold, the grueling labor, or the foul stench, was to retain one's humanity and dignity. That's what some prisoners tried to express to their friends who were picking through the slime.

The Sweater Dilemma

Prisoners struggled to reconcile what they needed to do to survive with how they should act in terms of their moral code. How do you behave morally in a lethal, criminal environment? One survivor, Aron Greenfield, answered the question this way: "I awoke one frigid morning to find that the man on whose stomach I had rested my head was dead. People asked me, 'What did you do?' What do you think I did, recite the Kaddish? [Jewish memorial prayer]. Of course not. I stole his shoes. By that time, you didn't believe there is a God. 'He's on vacation' is what we used to say."[28]

For me, the challenge of remaining a moral human being was symbolized by what I call "The Sweater Dilemma," a story that haunted me forever after Buchenwald. In our bunk, 5B, I wore an old but very heavy woolen sweater. At night I took it off and used it as a pillow. I slept on the very top layer of bare pine boards in our bunk. It was, after all, a great deal easier for us youngsters to climb up there than it was for the older men. The top bunk was also the best, in the sense that no one could urinate on us in the middle of the night. And more privacy was available than in the bunks below.

Head-to-head with me was an elderly Jewish gentleman... One night I felt a heavy tug under my head, and as I awoke, I realized that the older man was trying to pull my sweater from under my head to use for himself. I pulled the sweater back into a more secure position and turned onto my side facing away from the "thief." This incident bothered me a great deal, not because the old man had done what he had done but because I had no empathy for his misery.

In my youthful self-righteousness, I whispered to the old man: "Why didn't you ask me for my sweater? I would have lent it to you." The man looked sick. But I took my sweater back because during the day I needed it badly. The nights were relatively warm, especially up there on the top layer where all the body warmth and odor of those hundreds below us created an atmosphere of hot air and warm stench. I did not know the man's name. I do not know whether he survived, but I keep thinking of him, even after almost half a century! Let great armchair moralists and ethics specialists analyze the case and tell me how I should have handled it. I have no patience for "armchair moralists," people who never had to undergo actual, painful moral dilemmas with real-world consequences. The moral dilemma of the sweater pained me both because the man who tried to steal humiliated himself and even more because I was rudely ungenerous.

Writing in the 1980s, I was frustrated by people who were not

Holocaust survivors and yet claimed to have understood what was going on in Germany in the 1930s. They even had the gall to lecture survivors about what they should have done. From their high horses and armchair comfort in America, they pronounced verdicts on Jews who had to cope with the actual situation.

Familiar Faces

In the large mass of men imprisoned in Buchenwald, it was possible sometimes to recognize someone from one's hometown or even from one's family.

Not only did I find Uncle Richard, Henny's brother, but I also found Uncle Leopold, Henny's brother-in-law. Seeing Uncle Leopold, all grey and bent... was heart-wrenching. The poor man had been in Buchenwald for more than two years (!!) after having been falsely denounced for having made a derogatory remark about Hitler by a neighbor who owed him money. The family had spent a fortune just to find out in which concentration camp poor Uncle Leopold was kept before they could try to get through to the Nazi hierarchy and appeal for his freedom.

Uncle Leopold – there he was, suddenly, in his soiled uniform, a once good-looking man with a straight, erect figure, now almost bent double from his burden, ladling out soup for us in "protective custody." He gave me a few quick tips for survival... There was not much time for greeting. He wiped a tear from his eye, and then another prisoner pushed us apart in the big throng.

It took his good wife, Aunt Thekla, another half year and countless bribes to petty Nazi officials to get Uncle Leopold out of Buchenwald, Dachau, and other places. His eventual liberation was miraculous. Uncle Leopold was rushed to Munich before September 1939, and quickly put on a train to Trieste for the voyage to Palestine with his wife and children. He stayed there as a chicken farmer for the rest of his life.

Uncle Leopold was a decent, simple soul, a super-loyal German who had distinguished himself during World War I by fighting for the Fatherland on the eastern front. He had caught a Russian rifle shot in his left shoulder – luckily it missed his heart. Uncle Leopold used to display his wound proudly on many occasions although he was never able to lift his left arm in a normal fashion. Once I saw him running with his work detail during a penal exercise, puffing and sweating after the day's grueling work, dragging along behind the other men. This was one of those "specials" we had to witness almost every evening, thought up by the inventive Nazi commandant who probably would claim today that he had been forced to do this or else that he had completely forgotten that those "specials" took place at all.

Stragglers who fell to the ground from exhaustion were beaten mercilessly by the guards. Most of them, but by no means all, somehow found the strength to get up again and hobble along. We had to watch it all through the fence separating us from the "regulars," just as we had to watch the special lashings and floggings on the "bok," as well as one or two hangings. But I do not want to go into more details.

Uncle Richard Tuch, Henny's brother, was in Buchenwald, too, not far from my own barrack. He was a cheerful fellow, always joking, forever trying to pep up those around him. He slipped me many a piece of bread and he lifted my morale and that of many others with his funny stories. He used to say: "Let the others get out of Buchenwald first, I can wait, this stay is good for my health since I am too heavy anyway; I used to pay good money to the doctors to make me lose some weight, and here I get it for free." To have found Uncle Richard and to gradually have gotten our group from Ellguth together – that gave me strength to go on. The first loneliness in that big crowd of prisoners had been the worst experience. After a few days I somehow became used to the situation. It is amazing to me, even today, how much my young body could withstand. Of course, the situation in Buchenwald took a drastic turn for the worse as soon as the war started in September 1939, but we had been freed by then.

I was the last one of our family to see Uncle Richard alive. A few weeks later, the Nazis took the trouble to inform his wife, poor Auntie Susie, that he had died from a fever and that his ashes could be picked up, for a large fee of course. My good Father, fresh out of Dachau himself, had the courage to perform the great mitzvah of going to Buchenwald and claiming the urn for burial. All of us in the family trembled with fright when he undertook that trip.

What did imprisonment in Buchenwald teach me? First, to expect *violence from Nazis that could easily lead to death. To always expect sadism. That I should stay away from Germans at any cost and get out of the country as soon as possible. To expect help from relatives working behind the scenes. To expect some generosity but also theft from fellow inmates. But finally, to recognize that I was on my own. I had to make decisions by myself. All of these "Buchenwald lessons" contributed to my survival in The Netherlands.*

Dad did not describe everything that occurred in Buchenwald. He omitted, for example, the work detail to which he was attached. Instead, he focused on the humiliation, the stupidity of the Nazis, the irony of their actions and the disorganization of the camp.

It took three weeks before I had to submit to the bursary the 30 Reichsmark I had taken into the camp, something that was supposed to be done upon entry. Forty years later, I understood how much worse it could have been, and that Buchenwald when I was there was not as bad as later when "protective custody" camps were repurposed as extermination centers. I even had some free time, time that I spent with my friend Shushu studying Hebrew poetry.

For my friends and me, it was somehow unreal. We suffered, it is true, but we were young and could stand a great deal. There was none of the mass killing that occurred later during the war. Indeed, we believed that we would not be killed if we did exactly what the SS ordered us to do.

Out of Buchenwald

It turned out that our group was freed from Buchenwald on a Saturday morning. We had been brought there – not counting the two-day trip – on a Saturday morning as well.

There are at least four explanations for Dad's being released at all. The first is that the Germans had planned to keep prisoners in Buchenwald for only a "short" time, because the Nazis' intent was to frighten Jews into emigrating and not to have to keep "feeding" these prisoners. Thus, the powers-that-be decided to release 10,000 Jews by the end of 1938. The Nazis had not yet planned to exterminate the Jewish people. That project, euphemistically called the "Final Solution," was agreed upon four years later, on January 20, 1942, when Reinhard Heydrich, the chief of Germany's Security Police, convened the secret Wannsee Conference at which the participants decided to murder all the Jews of Europe.

The second possible reason for Dad's release is that as the camp filled up, the Nazis wanted to release some prisoners and incarcerate others to frighten them.

A third possibility stems from the fact that Dad had just been accepted as a student at the Hebrew University of Jerusalem. The acceptance letter might have been mailed to his mother in Munich and she could then have shown the proof of Hebrew University admission to some Nazi official who arranged for his release. But then, Dad may have rejected his offer to enroll because he would have had to leave Ilse behind. Or, he might not have been able to go because he lacked a British Certificate to enter Palestine. In addition, tuition was costly.

The fourth possibility, which Dad mentioned with gratitude countless times, was Zionist: he believed that the tireless work of German Zionist organizations orchestrated his release.

Ilse strongly advocated a fifth theory: that Wilhelmina, Queen of the Netherlands, had "invited" 300 young Jews to enter her country. I have explored this idea as deeply as I can. In my discussions with historians, my reading of research on this topic and examining archives, no support for this hypothesis has ever appeared. In addition, for Queen Wilhelmina, the head of the Dutch government, to have taken this action would have been completely out of character. Experts concur that Queen Wilhelmina felt no responsibility toward Jews, Dutch or otherwise. Dad wrote, "*All my life, I reiterated my gratitude to the Zionists who freed me, and Ilse reiterated hers to Queen Wilhelmina.*"

I always attributed my release to the coordinated effort of the Zionist organizations in Berlin and Deventer, a small city in the Netherlands. Had it not been for these groups, I believe I would not have been saved from Buchenwald in 1938, together with dozens of my chaverim. I owe my liberation from the concentration camp exclusively to the tireless efforts of those leaders of the Hechalutz movement in Berlin [i.e., the

German national umbrella Zionist youth organization that included Habonim] *who worked day and night to get us out. During the weeks of November 1938 immediately following Kristallnacht, the Zionist top leaders in Berlin secured permits so we could enter The Netherlands as "Palestine Pioneers," and on the strength of those documents we were released from Buchenwald, Dachau, and other places.* Of the 10,000 or so Jews released from Buchenwald in December 1938, approximately 300 were promised entry into the Netherlands as "Palestine Pioneers."

Dad's statement is extremely important for the ultimate framing of his survival. True, he chastised the Zionist establishment for delaying immigration to Palestine and branding as "traitors" those who chose America. But he always balanced those shortcomings with gratitude that the Zionist establishment liberated him from Buchenwald. To understand the extraordinary nature of Dad's being able to leave Germany and enter the Netherlands, consider the following from historian Bernard Wasserstein, who described the weeks following *Kristallnacht*, exactly the time when Dad was imprisoned in Buchenwald:

> The [Jewish Refugees Committee in The Netherlands] was inundated with over 11,000 letters from Jews in Germany seeking help in emigrating.[29] The Dutch government agreed to admit up to 1,500 children [or 13 percent of the requests], provided they not become a permanent charge on [Dutch] public funds and would remain no longer than necessary to meet requirements for immigration to the United States… Initial discussions envisaged the admission to The Netherlands of 326 children. But reports indicated that as many as 5,000 were massing 'on the Dutch border.'[30]

Once again, there was an ironic twist, in this case related to my release. Sometime in the late 1970s, I applied to the Germans for "Wiedergutmachung" [German: restitution]. *Among other items in my application, there was the four-week imprisonment in Buchenwald that would entitle me to compensation. The new German authorities did not contest my claim but responded that I had been in Buchenwald for 28 days minus two hours, thereby disqualifying me from compensation, because the minimum stay, as per paragraph so-and-so was four weeks, i.e., 28 full days!*

Getting Home from Buchenwald

Upon my release, my group and I returned to the Hachsharah camp in Ellguth, using the 30 Reichmarks I had with me when I arrived at Buchenwald and that were returned to me on my departure.

To my dismay, no one and nothing was left of the Hachsharah camp! The leaders had fled to Palestine and the girls had been sent home. At the train station near Ellguth, we stepped out into a beautiful day and marched through the fields, which only a few weeks earlier we had worked with rake and hoe...We sang our Zionist songs, we forgot our dirt, our shaven heads, our misery, and we were oblivious to the fact that all of us had severe colds. There was even a doctor in Ellguth, a non-Jew, who acted as though he knew nothing about our [shaved] heads, our general condition and how we had gotten to the physical state we were in. He examined us and urged us to "dress warm."

We were given clean clothes by some friends who had remained out of Buchenwald and who helped the [Zionist] movement take care of us. We were fed royally – no food has ever tasted as delicious as those first bites outside Buchenwald. We packed our few belongings and called our families with the good news that we were free and would soon be home. We travelled back to our hometowns and hoped to be reunited with our girlfriends. We knew that the Zionist movement, which had worked so diligently to get us out of the concentration camp, would secure a new life for us in the Netherlands.

Gunzenhausen Vice Mayor, Peter Schnell, addressing residents of town plus descendants of former Jewish residents, July 2023, about townspeoples' action against the Jews during Nazi period.

Gunzenhausen, Marketplace, 1860.

Gunzenhausen Synagogue with onion dome towers.

Dad's Father, Dr. Karl Rothschild, as a physician in the German army during WWI

Dad's Mother, Thekla Katzenstein Rothschild.

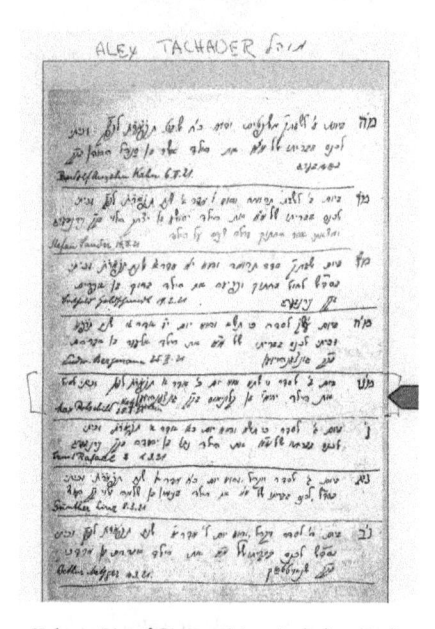

Hebrew List of Circumcisions including Dad's.

Thekla with her three living children.

Thekla's grave (right) now vandalized and remnants removed.

Engagement of Dad's Father and second wife, Henrietta Tuch.

Shushu in Elguth Hachsharah, 1938.

Jewish Male Prisoners Line up in Buchenwald Concentration Camp for a Roll Call. American Jewish Joint Distribution Committee, Courtesy of United States Holocaust Memorial and Museum Photo Archives.

---

1. https://www.ushmm.org/online/hsv/source_view.php?SourceId=49933
2. Soon after Hitler seized power, teachers throughout the country had to be vetted by local Nazi officials. Any teacher considered disloyal was sacked. Teachers attended classes in which a new recognized Nazi curriculum was spelled out. A full 97 percent of all teachers joined the Nazi Teachers' Association. Children were encouraged to inform the authorities if a teacher said something that did not fit in with the Nazi's curriculum for schools.
3. Habonim, founded in 1929 in Great Britain, is a Jewish Socialist-Zionist Youth Cultural Movement for teens between the ages of 12 to 18 years.
4. An assimilated Viennese Jew, journalist and playwright, Theodor Herzl brought worldwide political Zionism to life in the late 1890s. His basic message was that Jews should return to the Holy Land, create an independent Jewish state, and not delude themselves into thinking that they were welcome in Europe. At the time, the Holy Land was part of the Ottoman Empire. At first, the Zionist movement was quite weak among German Jewish youth and their elders. Its main opponent, Orthodox Judaism, argued that Jews would return to the Holy Land only when the Messiah arrived. Thus, Orthodox Jews believed it was sacrilegious to engage in political Zionism, an ideology that undermined reliance on God.
5. Probably the RJF (Association of Jewish Frontline Soldiers), whose purpose was to combat Nazi propaganda by highlighting the military contributions of German Jews in World War I.

6. The United States Holocaust Memorial Museum defines Gestapo as follows: a secret-police organization employing brutal, underhanded, and terrorist methods against persons suspected of disloyalty.
7. Leonard Gross, *The Last Jews in Berlin* (New York: Simon & Schuster, 1982), p. 62.
8. In case Dad thought he could escape the tightening noose by changing his name from Max Rothschild to something that hid his Jewish identity, the Nazis prevented this through *"The Law on the Modification of Family and First Names" (January 5, 1938)*.
9. February 3, 1933, pp. 45-46, reprinted in Jurgen Matthaus with Emil Kerenji, *Jewish Responses to Persecution, 1933-1946: A Source Reader* (Washington, D.C.: United States Holocaust Memorial Museum, 2017), p. 9.
10. See Jonathan Kirsch, *The Short, Strange Life of Herschel Grynspan: A Boy Avenger, a Nazi Diplomat, and a Murder in Paris* (London: Liveright Publishing, 2013).
11. Josephthal, Senta, "Sketch of Giora Josephthal's life," in Ben Halpern and Shalom Wurm (eds.), *The Responsible Attitude: Life and Opinions of Giora Josephthal* (New York: Schocken Books, 1966), p. 10. Senta claimed they left in September 1938, but I believe they left in October shortly before the events in Munich.
12. Snyder, Louis L., *Encyclopedia of the Third Reich* (New York: Paragon House, 1989), p. 201.
13. *The New York Times*, November 18, 1938. "Thousands of Jews arrested in Germany." It took *the New York Times* nine days to report this story.
14. Although "having their breasts handled in a clumsy way" may not have been serious abuse in Max's eyes, the girls probably saw it differently.
15. Untitled essay by Ilse Rothschild, March 1996, 3 pages, p. 1. Author's archive.
16. Transcript of Lenore Weitzman's interview with Ilse Rothschild, p. 6. Author's archive.
17. "Buchenwald," *Encyclopedia of the Holocaust* (New York: Macmillan Library Reference, 1995), p. 254.
18. Allied High Commission for Germany, Certificate of Incarceration, No. 038461. Author's archive.
19. Reinhard Rurup (ed.), *Topography of Terror* (Berlin: Verlag Willmuth Arenhovel, 1989), p. 99.
20. *Encyclopedia of Camps and Ghettos, 1933-1945.* (Bloomington, Indiana: Indiana University Press, 2009), Vol. I, Part A, p. 185.
21. See Jeremy Dronfield, *The Boy who Followed His Father into Auschwitz* (U.K.: Penguin Books, 2019), p. 47.
22. See fn. 20, Jonathan Kirsch *Ibid.*, p. 221.
23. On Nazi use of photography to create hideous photographs of Jews see Nina Siegal, "Propaganda Became Evidence," *The New York Times,* July 30, 2022, pp. C1-C2.
24. jewishvirtuallibrary.org/propaganda-and-children-during-the-hitler-years
25. ITS (International Tracing Service)'s Buchenwald Individual Documents – Male section 1.1.5.3, Geldverwahrungskarte from Buchenwald, indicates his inmate number.
26. Arthur B. Shostak, *Stealth Altruism: Forbidden Care as Jewish Resistance in the Holocaust* (New York: Routledge, 2017).
27. Primo Levi, *Survival in Auschwitz or If This is a Man* (Scott's Valley, CA: CreateSpace Independent Publishing Platform, 1947/2013), p. 39.

28. Yvonne Abraham, "Retelling the horror for future generations," *The Boston Sunday Globe*, November 20, 2016, pp. B1, 3.
29. Wasserstein, Bernard, *The Ambiguity of Virtue: Gertrude van Tijn and the Fate of the Dutch Jews* (Cambridge, MA: Harvard University Press, 2014), p. 49.
30. *Ibid.*, pp. 50-51.

2

RESISTING AND HIDING IN HOLLAND

Ilse and Max's names were part of the daily requests from *Hechalutz* headquarters in Berlin to the Dutch Zionist authorities in Deventer, Holland.

Our acceptance was one of the many miracles in our lives. But our situation was still precarious. The Dutch government wanted to be sure that incoming Jews would not be a financial burden and would leave the Netherlands as soon as possible. In response, the Dutch Zionist organization, called the Deventer Group, promised the Dutch authorities that these temporary refugees would leave the Netherlands after completing two years of agricultural training during which time they would learn from and help Dutch farmers. The Deventer Group had been working on such a plan since at least 1937. The imprisonment of German Zionist youth in Buchenwald during Kristallnacht propelled the Deventer Zionists to act even more quickly and emphatically.

Kristallnacht showed the Dutch Zionist organizations how important it was to bring Jews into Holland, and it propelled Jews in England to work with their government to set up the Kindertransport program. Eva and Hannah, Dad's sisters, were two of the fortunate Jewish youngsters to get out of Germany and enter England on the Kindertransport in spring 1939.

A day after my release from Buchenwald on December 13, 1938, an official sitting in his office in Deventer typed a document that saved my life. Ru Cohen, Secretary of the Deventer Zionist Group, was a very capable person who took responsibility for bringing into Holland those young Jews who already had obtained agricultural training at a Hachsharah camp in Germany.

> We declare herewith that you, Max Rothschild, born on February 20, 1921, in Munich [sic], a German citizen [no longer true], have been accepted as a student in our organization, the Agricultural Educational Association, with the provision that after intensive training which will last at least two years, you will emigrate to Palestine.
> We await your arrival as soon as you obtain the necessary papers we have mentioned in our previous letter as part of the conditions of acceptance.
> Organization of Palestine Pioneers, Ru Cohen, Secretary
> Before a notary. Deventer 14, 1938

The Deventer Group had obtained entry permits from the [Dutch] *government for 200 to 300 Jewish boys and girls and thus had facilitated the ability of Hechalutz to bring about their release from Buchenwald. These are the basic facts, and they tower over all the criticism and all the complaints about the Zionist movement that would arise when we settled in the Netherlands.*

The only condition to admit these Jewish refugees, as far as the Deventer Group was concerned, was that they had to be placed as a single individual with individual farmers. It turned out that this individualistic philosophy also contributed to saving Dad's life. The facts are that "a much larger percentage of these individual *Hachsharah* placements survived hiding (over 80 percent) than either in the Jewish population at large or in the entire *Hachsharah* movement."[1]

A few of us [including Ilse but not me] *were sent to the* [Dutch] *Jewish group training farm in Wieringen rather than to an individual farmer. This distinction had grave consequences. According to testimony given in May 1944, the Germans deported to Amsterdam all the boys and* girls living under the supervision of the Jewish manager of the Wieringen on March 20, 1941. Sixty pupils and 20 staff members were allowed to remain on the group farm to finish the harvest. Another 60 were sent to the concentration camp Mauthausen. A hundred were deported to Poland; 50 are still in Westerbork and Bergen-Belsen; and 60 are in hiding.[2] Fortunately, Ilse left Wieringen before March 20, 1941.

Goodbye Munich, Germany, and Family

I quickly returned to Munich. Desperate to say goodbye to my family, I had to apply quickly to get a passport to Holland through the Hechalutz organization. But my return to Munich was not what I had expected. What I felt most strongly during the weeks between my release from Buchenwald and the trip to Holland was the total breakdown of the old order in our Jewish community. Any semblance of authority ceased to exist. Rabbis, teachers – nobody counted any longer. I had little respect for anybody at that time. I started eating non-kosher food on the sly.

It is strange, but for me, the return home to Munich from Buchenwald was, in a way, as difficult as having been in the concentration camp! There was nothing to hold on to anymore. Everything had been shattered. Some of my uncles and cousins were still in Dachau. There was no synagogue, no youth group, no Jewish leadership. People were on their own, running back and forth in search of emigration possibilities. Father looked so strange with his head shaven.

The family were holed up in the apartment, eating, sleeping, fearing together, scurrying around for news, for emigration papers, for mail, clinging to rumors. Some old friends had not come back from the camps, and word had gotten out that they had died in Dachau or Buchenwald. The family exchanged experiences, Father told stories of his five weeks in Dachau, where he so loyally tried to minister to some of his dying fellow Jews, while I told my stories of Buchenwald.

A few days after arriving in Munich, I registered at a police station. There I swore that I lived on the second floor of 19 Thierstrasse with Dr. Karl Rothschild, having previously lived in Ellguth-Steinam O.S. [i.e., Upper Silesia]. I declared that I was single, that Father was a "Federal Physician," that my birthdate was February 20, 1921, that my nationality was German and my religion Jewish. I stated that the expected remaining length of my stay in Germany was four-six weeks.

A second registration document had the ominous stamp of an eagle holding a swastika in its talons and the words, "County of Klein Schnellendorf, District Falkenberg E." This paper used my altered name – Max Israel Rothschild. On the back of the form, there was a lengthy, complicated set of instructions about who had to register when moving in or out of the country and what forms to bring to the police. This material is titled "Excerpt from the state reporting ordinance of January 6, 1938 (State law 1 & 13)."

Clearly all these procedures were time-consuming, complicated, prone to mistakes, and energy-wasting. One would have thought that the Germans would have made the emigration process as streamlined as possible given that they were interested in having all the Jews leave. But the Germans were devious. They recognized that Jewish efforts to emigrate were an opportunity for Germans to collect or steal their money by charging for these forms and levying departure taxes.

On January 16, 1939, with his 18th birthday a month away, Dad finally had an appointment with the Munich Office of Finance and Foreign Currencies, where he received another form bearing several stamps with the familiar Nazi eagle holding a swastika. This document stated that as an emigrant from Germany, Dad was allowed to take a maximum of ten Marks out of the country. The forms were countersigned by a bank in the German city of Bielefeld where he later exchanged this paltry sum for Dutch guilders at a train stop on the way to Holland. Dad received a Dutch visa in Munich on the same day, a little over a month after his release from Buchenwald.

Thirteen days later, on January 29, 1939, Dad left Munich, arriving nearly penniless in the Netherlands. Little did he know that 16 months later, only one aspect of his new identity would matter, the fact that he was a Jew.

Since infancy, Dad had benefited psychologically from having a warm, loving family. Now he had to separate from them for the unknown. *Given all the violence I had witnessed, it was heart-*

wrenching to flee to Holland knowing that the rest of my family could face similar violence and I would not be there to help. As difficult as this was, I was prepared to abandon them to save myself because I harbored the hope that although I was the first member of my family to obtain a legal means of emigration, I wouldn't be the last. And, as always, my compassionate Father was willing to let me go to Holland, even if the rest of the family was stuck in Germany.

By moving to the Netherlands in January 1939, Dad joined the history of Jewish immigration to that area that had begun in Roman times. For example, at the end of the 16th century, northern Dutch provinces declared independence from Spain in order to practice Protestant Christianity. This declaration of independence instituted religious tolerance as a central principle of Dutch law and culture, a principle which continued to attract Jews persecuted elsewhere. But the Dutch people's vaunted tolerance was a myth in 1939.

To leave Germany and enter Holland in 1939, one needed authentication of an entry permit by the Dutch national government in The Hague, the capital of the Netherlands. Dutch "immigration policy," more accurately labelled "Dutch anti-immigration policy," was restrictive, as was the policy of almost every other government in the world. No country wanted a massive number of refugees and, because of antisemitic prejudice, they particularly did not want Jews.[3] The few countries that accepted Jews imposed specific requirements, e.g., Ecuador took Jews only if they were farmers.[4] A rare exception was the open city of Shanghai that did not require a visa.[5] The Dutch "anti-immigration policy" stemmed from antisemitic attitudes that cast doubt on its reputation of being friendly to Jews. The policy also reflected seeming self-interest, i.e., protecting the jobs of Dutch people and not increasing the Dutch welfare burden.

I was taking a big step for a person so young. From now on, I had to take care of myself and make my own decisions. Soon my new "family" would consist of my peers, i.e., Jewish Zionist teenagers in Holland on whom I would need to rely. Ilse had gotten an invitation from the Deventer Zionist Organization to enter the Netherlands as well. It is unclear what I would have done if I had had to leave Ilse behind. As it turned out, she crossed the border into Holland two months after I did. Having a girlfriend who would soon join me in the Netherlands was a great boon. Ilse was a stand-in for my loving family and a person who shared my values.

As a young socialist Zionist, and with the Munich Jewish community disintegrating, "I was ready to change [my life] completely." [6] *Everything was different. Father and I had our heads shaved in the concentration camps and were branded. Jewish organizations no longer existed, lots of people had simply disappeared and all Jewish money had been confiscated. We had to live on what the authorities apportioned to us from our own savings!*

Dad stayed in Munich for a few weeks amid feverish preparations for emigration. Then he, and later Ilse, became part of the approximately 35,000 German Jews who moved to the Netherlands after the Nazis took power in Germany in 1933, 22,000 of whom had already arrived by 1937. German Jewish parents tried every possible trick to send their children into the Netherlands, even if they themselves could not enter. But their efforts were nearly always futile.

The Dutch government policy was to minimize the number of entry visas by prioritizing people who would pass through to a new destination. The best way [for the Netherlands] to do this was through the encouragement of training and agricultural education schemes so that [these foreign Jews would] emigrate to countries where they could settle.[7] It was remarkable that Dad was admitted into Holland at that moment. A confluence of events gave him a tiny opportunity. And he grabbed it.

The Journey

Unfortunately, Dad didn't describe his actual departure from Munich or his train ride into Holland, but I know that his train traveled north for six hours almost as far as Berlin, and then west for five and a half hours toward Bielefeld where a group of Zionist teens from throughout Germany was assembling. From there, it was another three-hour train ride to the Dutch border, plenty of time to deal with memories, thoughts, and fears, but apparently not to write them down.

The single aspect of the momentous journey that I remember concerned my feelings as the train chugged past my hometown of Gunzenhausen. As a child I had stood near those tracks with my friends and watched the glorious trains speed by. Now I was on the train! And as I caught a blurred glimpse of the little town, I assumed I never would see Gunzenhausen again or even set foot in Germany once more.

Dad didn't write about this life-saving voyage between one country and the other, between family and aloneness, between danger and safety. But had he described himself, he likely would have recorded that he was a German Jewish late teen, the product of a good home, the graduate of a Jewish elementary school, a rural junior high school, and an urban high school in which he was one of very few Jews. He might have labeled himself facetiously as an "alumnus" of a concentration camp and proudly added – an avid member of a Zionist agricultural training group. He crossed into Holland with a strong Jewish identity rooted in his solid Jewish education at home, schools, and synagogues. He might also have expressed confidence simply by being a male. Even though he was traveling alone, he did not fear sexual assault.

Dad did leave a description of his physical appearance at this time: *my stereotypic "Jewish-looking hair, nose and face" especially in contrast with the German or Dutch male physique, as well as my circumcision, endangered me. My hair, crudely removed in Buchenwald, left me nearly bald, and my weight, already low on a thin frame, had plummeted. I was not much to look at.*

On his journey, Dad might have reminisced about a recent evening, the final time he spent with the family in Munich.

The night before I left for the trip, I had the feeling that a time would come when I would see my parents and sisters again, but I also knew instinctively this was the last time I would see my grandmothers and uncles.[8] *Both predictions were true. The intuition that I would see my parents and sisters in the future was more than a prediction. It was a thought that sustained me.*

When the family came together in Munich for the last time, I played the piano parts of some of our favorite Schubert and Schumann songs on our gorgeous Bluethner – yes, that piano, saved miraculously during Kristallnacht, would be gone forever. Those songs were so dear to me. Sadly, Henny did not want to sing anymore. [So] I whistled and hummed the "Nussbaum" and "Lotosblume" and a few others that I had always loved. And that was the end of that part of our life, of our family as it had existed until then.

A Tiny Window of Opportunity

As predicted, things in Germany deteriorated even further after *Kristallnacht*. Fearing an onslaught of applications for legal immigration and perhaps a rush of illegal immigrants in early 1939 just as Dad was entering the country, the Dutch authorities constructed an internment camp near the town of Westerbork for existing and future refugees and passed the costs on to the Dutch Jewish community.

Because the Zionist program vouched for his commitment to work and leave, Dad was not interned in Westerbork when he arrived. Later, Westerbork became the notorious collection and deportation site for the trains bringing the vast majority of Dutch Jews and German/Dutch Jews to their deaths in extermination camps. The last train, the 94th, left Westerbork for Auschwitz on September 3, 1944, with Anne Frank and her sister Margot among its passengers, along with all the others in their former hiding place.

Dutch Residency Permissions

In January 1939, when Dad finally crossed the border from Germany into the Netherlands, he was about to receive refuge in a country of 8.9 million people, where only 1.6 percent, or about 140,000, were Dutch Jews. Among these were 24,000-25,000 German Jewish immigrants who had fled Germany in the 1930s. The Frank family, for example, moved to the Netherlands from

Frankfurt in 1934 after Hitler's rise to power the previous year. The 1947 Dutch census reported that of the original approximately 140,000 Jews in the Netherlands in 1940, at the end of the war there were only 14,346 or about 10 percent of the prewar population. Although the newcomers to Holland were identified primarily as German or Polish Jews, they should have been called "stateless Jews" because their citizenship had been revoked.

The town of Borne was the population center of the easternmost section of Holland and the area in which Dad would soon work as a farmer. In Borne, Dad received a "Temporary Residence Permit" allowing him to stay for half a year through June 30, 1939. On June 26, four days before his residence permit ran out, he received permission to stay another month. On August 1, 1939, he received a permit to stay two more months. Another residence permit allowed him to reside in Holland until June 1941. The final residence permit authorized his stay in the Netherlands from March 15, 1942, to September 15, 1942, by which date Dad had already gone into hiding.

On October 20, 1939, nine months after his arrival in Holland, Dad left the farm on which the Deventer Zionist group had placed him and moved to Amsterdam to learn to be an auto mechanic. Because of this move, Dad had to obtain a long series of permits from the City Police of Amsterdam at the Aliens Registration Office, allowing him to live in that city through June 1940, a month after the German Occupation of the Netherlands began. Dad soon assumed correctly that it was not prudent to stay in Amsterdam, but much better to return to the relatively remote eastern town of Almelo, where he had worked as a farmer's helper.

Once again, he had to go to Borne, this time to receive a document permitting him first to stay through June 30, 1940, later extended until December 31, 1940. But then his residence permit to live in Borne was withdrawn because he moved to Vriezenveen, where he was added to the registry of the town's population on December 12, 1940. In Vriezenveen he received a permit to reside for three months until March 1941, and then to stay for another three months until June 1941. The final permit allowed him to stay in

Vriezenveen until September 10, 1941. From that date until August 16, 1942, he did not have a permit to live anywhere in the Netherlands. Simply put, he was counting on luck to keep him safe. And then, from August 16, 1942, until the end of the war on May 5, 1945, he hid. Perhaps for the first time since the Nazis came to power in 1933, neither the German nor the Dutch government knew where he was or if he still existed.

I have included this tedious list of permits, places, and dates to illustrate how carefully the Dutch authorities monitored the German Jewish emigrants even before the German invasion of the Netherlands on May 10, 1940.

At all times, I had to carry a passbook later issued by the Nazi occupiers identifying me as a Jew. To undermine the system of tracking people under the German Occupation, the Dutch Resistance forces bombed the Amsterdam Public Records Office on March 27, 1943. This successful raid hindered Nazi attempts to compare forged documents with documents in the registry, but by then almost all Jews in the Netherlands had been killed.

The Dutch government, like all the others that closed their doors to Jews or kept their doors only slightly ajar to "protect jobs," never even entertained the idea that Jewish refugees were more likely to be educated than Dutch peasants and thus more able to create new employment opportunities for others than they were to rob the Dutch population of current employment opportunities. To some minds, the protection of native Dutch people's jobs was necessary because the Netherlands had not yet recovered fully from the stock market crash of 1929 and the catastrophic international economic depression that followed. Humanitarianism, in this case saving the lives of innocent persecuted Jews from another country, was apparently not part of the equation. "How could the Dutch be expected to deal with a refugee crisis and an economic crisis at the same time?" Hollanders asked.

The Dutch also had a unique attitude that undermined their willingness to help Jews. They defined "paying special attention to Jews, as a form of discrimination or special treatment," which did not align with their outlook that all people should be treated equally. According to this way of thinking, Jews should not be treated differently from anyone else, no matter what was happening to them. No "affirmative action" should ever be in place for Jews regardless of the Nazis' murderous intent. The Dutch government recognized people based only on nationality (e.g., German, Dutch, French) and citizenship. Jewishness was subsumed under nationality.

Thus, the Dutch government regarded German Jews and German non-Jews as part of the same category, i.e., Germans. These dangerous "identity-blind" and "anti-discrimination" attitudes of the Dutch continued after the war's end in a shameful and extremely callous way. In the words of Dutch historian Dienke Hondius, "The Dutch government's refusal to make a distinction between Jews and non-Jews – to help Jewish refugees in the 1930s, to support deported Jews during the years of persecution, or while repatriating or providing relief for Jewish survivors – arouses both astonishment and bitterness... Foreign observers pleaded for recognition of the Jews' specific circumstances [to no avail]."[9]

The only people who helped German Jews in the Netherlands before the invasion were Dutch Jews. Although native Dutch Jews did a great deal to help German Jewish refugees, they also displayed ambivalence. "[Jewish] philanthropic concern for the victims of pogroms and antisemitism was often coupled with a desire to avoid negative repercussions in the Netherlands. There were fears that the arrival of large groups of Jewish refugees, possibly with very different, conspicuous customs, might contribute to the growth of Dutch antisemitism."[10] The same attitude pervaded Great Britain and served as an argument against setting up the Kindertransport. The idea was that one could prevent antisemitism by not admitting Jews. But not admitting Jews, of course, was itself an indicator of antisemitism.

An exception to the Dutch government's "rejection policy" was the small number of young German Jewish refugees who were allowed entry into Holland as "Palestine Pioneers," i.e., people who would reside in Holland up to two years and then leave for

Palestine. While in Holland, they would work as very meagerly paid farmhands. As begrudging as this welcome was, at least it was something.

From the Dutch perspective, the Palestine Pioneers could be an "exception" because these young people would provide cheap, nearly free labor to farmers who were short-handed [or, as I sometimes discovered, lazy]. The Pioneers were young, healthy, and motivated to work hard. What's more, they had no dependents. They were the ideal pass-through immigrants, particularly since, as Zionists, they were committed to go to their Promised Land.

Dad did not know the Dutch language when he arrived in Holland, but this was not a problem. Learning languages came easily to him, and for all his adult life he was fluent in German, English, Dutch, and Hebrew, with a smattering of Yiddish, French, Latin, Spanish, Aramaic (the language of the Talmud), and who knows what else. Later, in hiding, he studied Russian on his own.

But despite my facility with languages, I had major shortcomings as I crossed the border. I had not visited the country before; I knew little or nothing about its culture; and I knew no one there except one family of relatives, the Steins, who lived in Amsterdam and were quite a bit older than me. Even before I left Germany, Fritz and Ruth Stein were eager to help me. But, as it turned out, Fritz, the father of three young boys, had troubles of his own.

I also had a few assets when crossing the border. Being young helped me face physical challenges. Having been a "rascal" reduced my fear of taking risks. Being single meant there was no one I had to take care of. And I seem to have been in relatively good health based on later comparisons with friends who were too physically weak and could not withstand the rigors of this new life. My girlfriend said I had "boundless energy." Membership in a socialist youth organization and being part of a web of reliable, like-minded friends who were acquiring agricultural skills and deepening their knowledge of Hebrew – all of this was invaluable. As was being backed by a Dutch Zionist organization.

At the time, Dutch Jews were not particularly sympathetic to Zionism. At Passover Seders, some Jews sang "Next year in Amsterdam" instead of the traditional "Next year in Jerusalem."[11]

Nevertheless, by the time of the founding of the first World Zionist Congress in 1897, two individuals were elected to represent Dutch Zionists.

Twenty years later, on November 2, 1917, Lord Arthur Balfour, the British Foreign Secretary, gave international Zionist leader, Dr. Chaim Weizmann, a simple letter, subsequently labeled the Balfour Declaration, stating:

> His Majesty's government view with favor the establishment in Palestine of a national home for the Jewish people and will use their best endeavors to facilitate the achievement of this object, it being clearly understood that nothing shall be done which may prejudice the civil and religious rights of existing non-Jewish communities in Palestine, or the rights and political status enjoyed by Jews in any other country.

This letter awakened Zionist dreams throughout Europe, including in Deventer. Taking advantage of the British Mandate, Deventer Zionists created organizations to facilitate *Aliyah* [immigration to Palestine]. One was The Deventer Society, a vocational school to provide agricultural training for Dutch youngsters. Deventer's Ru [Rudolf] Cohen and his brother, Isaac (nicknamed Chi), played important roles in founding and leading the school. In the period between the two World Wars, hundreds of young people, calling themselves "Palestine Pioneers," from the Netherlands, Germany, Austria, and Czechoslovakia, received training in the Deventer area.

The Balfour Declaration had simply announced British governmental sentiments. But one year later after World War I had ended, the newly created League of Nations granted Britain the official Mandate for Palestine, meaning Britain was responsible for governing the area. This Mandate generated a lot of trouble for the British government which had to find a way of balancing the needs and demands of the Jews and the Arabs. On the other hand, for Jews, the mandate made real the possibility of moving to Palestine – *Aliyah* was now possible, or so Zionist Jews thought.

The Deventer Jewish community created an organization to provide German and Dutch Jewish youth with paid internships on local farms. The Deventer group named this organization Vereeniging Tot Vakopleiding van Palestina-Pioniers or The Organization for the Preparation of Pioneers for Palestine. To set up training opportunities, Ru Cohen turned to Emile (Miel) Visser, who had served as secretary or treasurer of the Deventer Zionist organization for several years. Mr. Visser's father, a local butcher, knew the local farmers well.

Years earlier, a Zionist friend of Ru's had approached the butcher to ascertain if any of these farmers might be willing to accept young Jews who had fled Antwerp, Belgium after the German invasion into that country at the start of World War I. This was no easy task since Dutch farmers believed the stereotype that Jews were poor manual workers. The farmers' fears were upended, however, when it became clear that the Jewish youth were highly motivated and did an excellent job on the farms. After this successful experience, Jewish youth became a sought-after manual work force, especially since they were willing to work for practically no pay.

The somewhat positive conditions for *Aliyah* in the eight years between 1934 and 1942, however, enabled only 36 Dutch "Palestine Pioneers" to move to Palestine, a number that did not reflect all the people who wanted to emigrate.[12] The sticking point was the lack of British Certificates allowing Jews to enter. Even after the end of World War II, British policy hindered the issuance of certificates. "Only in May 1948 with the creation of the State of Israel did Dutch Jews immigrate to Israel in substantial numbers because it was possible to do so." At that point, "Dutch Jewry, as a whole, chose a Zionist direction."[13]

The Cohen family played a public role beyond Deventer. In December 1940, half a year after Germany invaded the Netherlands, the Jewish community of Deventer established a leadership group, The Jewish Coordinating Committee, chaired by Emile Visser, to deal with the Nazis. Two months later, the Germans imposed a Judenrat [German, Jewish Council] called the

Joodse Raad voor Amsterdam, chaired by Abraham Asscher and David Cohen (another of Ru's brothers). Its purpose was to inform Jews throughout Holland of new Nazi-imposed restrictions. It also controlled the distribution of exemptions allowing some Jews to avoid deportation to the Westerbork transit camp. But most terrifyingly, it provided lists of Jews for the Nazis as required. To this day there is a disagreement about whether the Judenrat was collaborationist, ineffective, or essentially helpless.

The Joodse Raad staff believed that if they carried out the Germans' directives, they would be spared deportation, but in September 1943, they, too, were transferred to the Westerbork transit camp. From there, they were sent to dreaded camps in the east. Five members of the Cohen family of Deventer – three brothers, one sister and their mother – were murdered in Bergen-Belsen, Auschwitz and Sobibor. The one survivor, David Cohen, the controversial co-leader of the Jewish Council, was deported to Theresienstadt. Until their own deportation to Nazi death camps, the commitment of Ru Cohen and his wife, Eva Cohen-Koningsberger, to the welfare of the young Zionists was legendary. Ru's brother, Chi, oversaw British Certificate applications to Palestine and functioned as editor of the Zionist publication *De Joodse Wachter* [The Jewish Watchman].

Dad's First Placement: The te Riet Farm

When I arrived in Deventer in 1939, The Deventer Zionist Organization informed me that I would be working for a non-Jewish farmer, Hennie te Riet, in the Almelo area near the German border. My job description was concise: to assist the farmer without any other Palestine Pioneers working with me. Even though I had never had a job before and didn't know Dutch, I realized immediately that I was not going to be trained. I was going to be used.

My first farmer, head of a very decent and honest family, was about to have a big wedding on his homestead, that of his only daughter. There was lots of extra work to be done and extra hands were needed. And so in line with the cleaning and scrubbing of the entire house and all the barns and outbuildings, a lot of painting had been planned. We painted everything from top to bottom. The eaves and trimmings on the old-fashioned roofs had to be shined up and who but me would be sent up there with two or three ladders strung together, to do the job?

I stayed with te Riet, "my farmer," for less than a year... I was one of the lucky fellows. I had my girl on a farm close by. And although she, too, had to work hard, we could at least see each other on an occasional evening when we went to *Snif* [Hebrew: branch] in this case the meeting of their Zionist group. As I worked out in the field, I could sometimes spot Ilse raking hay. We were each other's support. I am not sure that either of us could have adjusted so well to the new life, had we not been together. It was not only the hard physical work, the long hours, the strange language, and unusual customs, nor even the food or the hard wooden "klompen" [Dutch: wooden shoes] we had to wear but being away from home and the uncertainty concerning the fate of our loved ones we had to leave behind...all combined to make life difficult.

These hardships were balanced by the positive features of our situation. We were young. We could be together, walk in the woods or study a Hebrew book together into the night. Sometimes I read Bialik's poetry with [my best friend and fellow Buchenwald inmate] Shushu who was placed on a nearby farm. Shushu was my spiritual and intellectual partner. In Buchenwald we had studied the Bible together! On the Dutch farm, studying Bialik with Shushu became a magical experience, and later, a comforting memory when Shushu killed himself. The cows were munching their cud a few feet from where we sat, and somehow for a long time Bialik was connected in my memory with the smells and warmth of the stable. A few hours later, between 05:00 and 06:00 a.m., we would sit again under our cows, milking away, trying to wipe the sleep from our eyes. Poring over Bialik's poetry with my beloved friend from dusk to dawn was worth the fatigue.[14] Fortunately, my farmer was a kind man as well. The te Riets were friendly and understanding. They liked to show off their Jewish trainee with the shaven head to their neighbors.

My bed was a sheaf of straw; and I had to eat out of a shared single pot with this family of strangers. But living with the te Riets was also advantageous. I began to learn Dutch by listening to various people speak. Some of these people were neighbors, others were friends of the te Riets. Moreover, having te Riet "show me off" meant that he was vouching for me. This status became crucial later when I sought people to hide me. But it also could have endangered me because some of these neighbors were pro-German.

We trainees had little contact with the outside world other than one afternoon every second Sunday when we were allowed to be with our chaverim [Hebrew: friends]. The Vereeniging leaders understood that young people needed at least a little time to cheer each other on. So they rented a room for us. We would bicycle to the café in Hengelo and gather as a "snif" of our Zionist youth organization. Those gatherings meant everything to us. We compared living conditions on our farms. If somebody had his own bed or was allowed to read for 15 minutes each night, he was looked upon with envy. Some of us who received a few extra pennies of pocket money were better off than others.

We also listened to an occasional lecture, sang songs, learned Hebrew together, and above all, exchanged experiences. Those visits were perhaps the only contacts we had off the farms, but they were a bright spot in our difficult existence. Just being together with our peers helped us adjust.

The farmers believed they were doing their nearly cost-free laborers a favor simply by employing them. And the Vereeniging was unable or did not try to enforce better working conditions. Some of the young people might have an especially nice and understanding family to live with. But there were also notorious slave drivers who would squeeze the last drop of sweat from a "Palestine Pioneer" whom they were supposed to train. Why weren't the "slave driver" farmers removed from the list of potential placements? Perhaps the Vereeniging didn't have enough farms to choose from. Perhaps they thought that rough training was good for male pioneers. Or perhaps the organizers in Deventer had not visited the farms. Middle-class Jewish Deventers were certainly not working on these farms! Some of the young workers had an easier time than others. A few were too weak physically and could not withstand the rigors of this new life.

These young men were constantly threatened with being returned to Germany if they wouldn't shape up, heart condition or not. Yet most of us *were strong. We were more than willing to work, and we believed that this was the only sure road towards salvation in Eretz Yisrael. It was only on the presumption of being trainees that our work on the farms could be socially and legally tolerated. We received practically no wages, although many of us produced as much as, and frequently even more than, non-unionized farm workers. We had no health insurance, but there were hardly any cases of illness or accident. The reason why many of the farmers could be sold on the idea of taking in one of those strange Jewish boys or girls was...getting cheap labor.*

Although agricultural training in the Zionist *Hechalutz* camps throughout Europe was intended to prepare Jewish youngsters to emigrate to Palestine, as it turned out, it was more than that. It was one of the few institutions through which Dad could be trained to do anything worthwhile. From 1934 on in Germany, Jews were excluded from training in medicine, dentistry, pharmacy, and the law. They could work in agriculture as provided by the Zionist groups or as apprentices with Jewish piano teachers and other music teachers. Jewish businesses were being seized and could not take on young Jews as employees.

The Zionist Organization of Deventer

The Deventer Vereeniging had its hands full. It had to identify appropriate Zionist youth in Germany and bring them safely and legally into Holland. It had to be in touch with the Zionist organizations in Palestine who were negotiating with the British to acquire certificates that would allow these Jews to emigrate to Palestine within two years. It had to find farmers who would take on these non-Dutch-speaking newcomers. Once the youth arrived, the Vereeniging had to make sure the young people were placed, were receiving actual training, and were not getting into trouble. They had to be certain that the training would equip the "Pioneers" "to cultivate undeveloped areas in Palestine," which was almost never the case. The agricultural conditions of canal-rich Holland had nothing to do with the swampy, malaria-ridden or arid conditions in Palestine. All of this had to be in place because agricultural skill was a prerequisite for obtaining a British "Palestine Certificate." Finally, sufficient funds had to be raised to undertake these activities.

"Palestine Pioneers" in Holland had a harder time getting certificates for immigration than Zionist youth in other countries because before the German occupation, the British considered Jews in the Netherlands to be living in a country that was not persecuting them. Using a triage system, Dutch Jews were classified as non-emergency cases in contrast to the Jews of other countries such as Poland. After all, Holland was a free country and had a neutrality promise from Hitler.

The Deventer Zionists – whom Dad sarcastically and perhaps unfairly labelled "well-intentioned ladies and gentlemen" – were governed firmly by two overriding principles. First was that each Zionist girl or boy must be placed in a separate farm, and second, that the agricultural work should be done on an individual, rather than a collective, basis. This was the opposite of Dad's Ellguth experience. I suppose the Deventer Zionists tried to keep girls and boys apart to prevent pregnancies.

Attitudes toward gender underlay the Deventer committee's desire to control the sex lives of the young people. In general, women's emancipation was not highly advanced in the Netherlands. In 1917, women were granted the "passive right to vote," meaning they could be elected but could not vote! Two years later, in 1919, Dutch women did win the right to vote, but even then, equality in the voting booth did not mean equality elsewhere. And even if they were technically "equal" to men, women were still "different."

Dutch people – including the Deventer Zionist organization leaders – believed that middle-class women should not engage in heavy agricultural work. Zionist groups, by contrast, believed in gender equality even if it wasn't fully defined or realized. Thus, although Dad clearly acknowledged owing his life to the Deventer group, he ridiculed their philosophy. To him, they were not bold; they were old-fashioned.

The [organizers in Deventer] were convinced that life with a Dutch farmer for the boys (or for our girls, life as a domestic in some luxurious household or hotel) would prepare us for the pioneering life in Palestine.

The emphasis on training the individual – the second condition imposed by the Deventer Organization – brought about a new label, *Einzel Hachsharah*, or agricultural training of an individual person [German: *Einzel*, single]. Whereas other Zionist pioneering groups in Holland supported the idea of cooperative work, the Deventer-based program emphatically did not. These other groups arranged dormitory-style housing for 30-50 youngsters or more in various places around the country especially in the north. A kibbutz-style autonomous settlement was referred to as a *Werkdorp* or "work village." Although Ilse decided to join a *Werkdorp* for a while, Dad never did. As it turned out, those working on the group farms and in the work-villages were much more vulnerable after the Germans invaded than were the *Einzel Hachsharah*, because the Jewish youth living in groups were already "rounded up" for easy capture.

Bernard Natt, a young German Jew, wrote that the *Hachsharah* organization placed him in the large Jewish *Werkdorp Nieuwesluis*. "When living [there], I had very little contact with Dutch people. In the Werkdorp we spoke only German, and we were not encouraged to learn Dutch."[15] [I presume this was the case because] "the Dutch authorities had given us permission to set up this training farm on condition that after training completion, everybody would leave Holland to emigrate to another country. For this reason, mastering Dutch wasn't necessary." By contrast, when Dad came to the Almelo region, he learned Dutch from his farmer and got to know many local people.

I befriended non-farming families, both Jewish and not. These were highly cultured individuals who had interests outside their own little world. Whenever I could manage it, I would visit these people after work. In addition, living with non-Jews on their farms contributed to my ability to adjust to living in their homes when I later hid.

In general, agricultural training of Jewish Zionist youth had two divergent, and sometimes conflicting, long-term goals. The first focused on a particular refugee. The goal for such a person was to emigrate to Palestine, find work with farmers who had already settled there, and later perhaps establish a farm of their own. The other orientation focused on the group. In this variation, young Jewish Zionists were trained for *Aliyah* to Palestine as a group of like-minded youngsters who would join an existing kibbutz together or start a new kibbutz of their own. The Deventer Vereeniging advocated the first alternative strenuously. In a sense they wanted to create in Palestine a society that mirrored the Netherlands, where people lived as individual families, not on collective farms.

Antipathy to Collectivism

The Vereeniging's antipathy to collectivism – even in distant Palestine – was rooted in the Dutch people's rejection of socialism and their fear of communism. Dutch society preferred stability. They shunned radical actions and revolutionary movements. "Communism remained politically and culturally a marginal phenomenon.... The political failure of communism in such a stable community was only to be expected."[16] For this reason, "socialism came relatively late to the Netherlands. Because of [the country's] slow industrialization...a socialist party was not established until 1881."[17]

With my positive background in Ellguth, I advocated living on a kibbutz, of course, even if I was now benefitting from living alone with a family on a Dutch farm. My allies in the critique of the anti-collectivism of the Deventer Zionist Society were a few open-minded Deventer Zionists, my fellow refugees including Ilse, and some of the farmers who perhaps wanted more workers.

Prior to encountering this strongly held difference of opinions, I had not had to deal with the variations among Zionists. But now the conflict between points of view was real. We had many arguments with the Vereeniging. The question of collective vs. individual training was a running sore between us. But I cannot dwell on criticism of the Vereeniging because the fact remains that our lives were saved through their efforts. The Vereeniging didn't care much about our Zionist politics.

If we did our work on an individual basis, the Vereeniging was for it, while anything smacking of collectivism was anathema.

We worked long hours in the field, sometimes until the moon was out, and the work sometimes could be quite boring. But our life with the farmers' families had some educational value for us spoiled boys and girls. We knew we were a world apart from the well-intentioned leaders of the Vereeniging. We were, first and last, refugees. And we did learn physical work thoroughly. I am grateful for that. Differences aside, it is impossible to exaggerate the significance of the local Deventer Zionists in saving young Jews from Germany by placing them as worker/trainees with non-Jewish farmers who could use their help.

Because the Dutch government did almost nothing to help the thousands of Jews wanting to enter Holland, a group of Dutch philanthropists and social workers had established The Committee for Jewish Refugees (CJV) six years earlier, in April 1933. The CJV had to deal with challenges imposed by the Dutch government. Many of these read like Nazi policies but were new Dutch rules. Money problems, the flow of refugees, and the increasingly stringent policies of the Dutch government made the work of the Committee difficult.

For example, in May 1934, obtaining a work permit was no longer possible for refugees whose work could be performed by a Dutchman. By the end of 1937, the government had made it virtually impossible for a refugee to start a business. Ultimately, refugees could no longer get work and residence permits at all. Consequently, more and more refugees could no longer provide for themselves, and the Committee's expenses to assist them climbed ever higher. A year after the German invasion in May 1940, the CJV was no longer allowed to operate. But while it was in operation, it took responsibility for direct services to Jewish refugees without receiving financial support from the Dutch government. The government never perceived Jewish refugees as its problem or responsibility.

British Certificates to Enter Palestine

The Vereeniging's mission to train German Jewish Zionist youth and later send them to Palestine was stymied by Britain. Bowing to Arab pressure, the British government issued a grossly inadequate number of certificates for Dutch Jews who wanted to enter Palestine. The Immigration Department of the Jewish Agency in Jerusalem was responsible for distributing the certificates that the British allocated. In an impassioned letter of July 1, 1938 (four months before *Kristallnacht*), Ru Cohen in Deventer wrote to Eliyahu Dobkin in Jerusalem beseeching him to provide more certificates than the two (!) assigned to Dutch Zionist youth. Cohen explained to Dobkin that trained pioneers had been in Holland since 1935 or even earlier. By agreement, they were required to leave when two years had passed. Poignantly, Ru Cohen wrote, "We're not asking for the maximum number of certificates, but certainly not less than the minimum."[18] Basically, hardly any Jews could get into the Netherlands, and once there, hardly any could get out to Palestine.

During the Evian Conference (July 6-15, 1938) convened by American President Franklin Delano Roosevelt, 31 nations refused to raise the number of Jewish refugees they would accept, one exception being the Dominican Republic, which saw an influx of Jews as an economic advantage. Every other country wanted someone else to take in more Jews. The Dutch government shared this anti-Jewish-immigrant attitude. As a result of the Evian conference, Hitler surmised correctly that the world was indifferent to Jewish suffering. He reasoned that he thus had proof that he could persecute Jews without interference from foreign powers.

Planning to Leave Holland

After seven months on the farm, the mail brought Dad a welcome surprise.

My parents and I were going to be able to meet in Holland! Father's letter told me that a near miracle had occurred – Henny and he had obtained the necessary permits to leave Germany and enter England! And then, when their actual plans for the trip were finalized, another stroke of good fortune appeared – their itinerary included a stop at a railway station in Holland not far from where I was working. With all the details settled, Ilse and I arrived at the train station for the rendezvous. It was August 1939, and I had not seen my parents since January.

My farmer gave me time off to meet my parents in Hengelo, the first station on the Dutch side of the border. Ilse also received an afternoon off. It was a good reunion. Holland was still free. And my parents were beginning to unwind for the first time since leaving Germany. During our brief meeting, Father impressed on me the need to re-apply for my American immigration visa. And so I made up my mind to try again. I was ready to be a traitor to the Zionist cause, as [the cause] had been taught to us.

Seen in retrospect, my action [of rejecting the first visa] *had been quite frivolous and unforgivable. How many people would have given their right arm to get an American visa! After high school, I had permitted my visa to lapse quite cavalierly. I always thought that there was still plenty of time, and that time had to be used for training as a "Palestine Pioneer." It is true that in my own case, my attachment to Ilse played a big role, but it was not the exclusive factor that influenced my decisions. When we met with my parents, I wasted too much precious time complaining about my farm placement, even though the family with whom I was staying was kind. It bothered me that I wasn't learning anything. It would take eight years and many miracles before my parents, Ilse, and I would see each other again.*

Moving to Amsterdam

It was around that time that I felt I could just not work on the farm anymore. Ilse also had had enough and was accepted in the Wieringen Werkdorp [the large group collective training farm mentioned above]. *After she moved, I tried as hard as possible to transfer to Amsterdam to be nearer to her. With permission from the Vereeniging in hand, I was allowed to leave my farmer and move to Amsterdam for additional "training," this time as an auto mechanic.*

Within the non-farming Vereeniging options, auto mechanics was the best. But I had to find my own workplace, i.e., a garage where the boss was willing to take me on as a trainee without official working papers and naturally at an undetermined or non-existent salary. I found such a place! It was an unheated garage in Amsterdam that rented private cars to traveling salesmen and did small repairs to keep the cars running. One of the bosses was a decent fellow. The other tried to exploit me in the worst possible way. I owned one set of overalls, which got so greasy after a week that I could hardly move in them. My position was tenuous at best. I did learn a few tricks in automobile mechanics, but it became obvious to me that I was used mainly as a cheap errand boy, car washer, cigar-getter and so forth. So just as was true on the farm, I hardly learned anything in the auto shop.

By then, I had become accustomed to living on very little money. So despite being paid on the cheap in the auto-shop, I earned enough to get by. Money wasn't important to me. I soon discovered that life in Amsterdam was much more interesting than at the farmer's – although a great deal less healthy. I had my own small room as a sublet from a Dutch couple, and I ate my main meals in a little café, frequented by German Jewish refugees.

That café became the target of one of the first German police actions against Jews shortly after the Nazi invasion in May 1940. A few Jews were shot on the spot, sparking a famous episode. Later, in January 1941, eight months into Nazi rule, violent Dutch Nazis provoked Jewish youth on the streets. In February, some Jews fought back, perhaps constituting the only instance of Jewish armed resistance during the German Occupation of the Netherlands.

Young Amsterdam Jews of working-class background formed rowdy Action Groups (Dutch: *Knockploegen*) in response to the provocative marches of the Nazi storm troopers. These Action Groups secured primitive weapons and fought pitched (street) battles with members of the N.S.B., the Dutch Nazi Party, wounding a number and killing one.[19]

On February 19, German police entered the popular eating establishment in the major Jewish residential area of South Amsterdam, a café owned by German Jewish refugee Erich Cahn. The Nazis attacked the patrons. I had eaten at this place regularly, and because of yet another miracle, I was not in the café when it was attacked.

The Germans arrested, tortured, and sentenced Cahn to death by firing squad. Moreover, the audacity of killing a Dutch Nazi (as the Jewish resisters had done) led the occupation government to seize 425 Jews from the streets of Amsterdam and send them to Buchenwald. 389 people from this group were then sent to Mauthausen; only a few survived that notorious camp.

Later, I moved to the Beth Chalutz, a large communal apartment where several of my friends had rooms and where all our meetings and cultural activities took place... Since Ilse and I were now geographically closer to one another, we had more time for each other. I also had more time for myself. Ilse then moved to The Hague [about an hour south of Amsterdam] where she worked in the kitchen of a fashionable vegetarian restaurant that counted the royal family among its clientele. All of this went under the guise of "training for 'Palestine Pioneers!'" The atmosphere in that restaurant was stone-age pre-Victorian. Male visitors were not permitted. However, among our girls' duties was serving breakfast in bed to Dutch gentlemen and their mistresses since this establishment was a favorite for such purposes. I didn't really care if Dutch gentlemen had mistresses or that I was being exploited in the garage. My concern, instead, was longing for Ilse who now lived in The Hague and for my parents who were on their way to England.

I still wrote to Munich a few times during that period. Grandma Betty and my uncles were already housed forcibly in barracks on the outskirts of the city. They thought that from then on, nothing worse could happen to them. "Bear up," Grandma Betty replied in her last letters when I sounded so pessimistic... "Bear up," even after the Germans had invaded Holland, as though I was the one who needed moral support.

Almost Leaving Holland

As I have written repeatedly, my admission into the Netherlands was predicated on leaving that country within two years. Given that I had no idea what measures the Dutch government would take to expel me when the two years ended, I was forced to plan an exit strategy from Holland on my own. Clearly, it was nearly impossible for Jews to enter any countries, so my decision boiled down to two inaccessible options: Palestine and the US.

My parents had by then joined my sisters in England and had no exit plan either. But after a short stay they were on their way to America, while I was stuck in Holland actively pursuing a new immigration visa to the US. Perhaps we could be together again, I thought, even though I had missed my first opportunity to go to America when I chose the Ellguth Hachsharah instead of using my visa.

True, the visa from the Netherlands to the US could have been given to me earlier had I pursued the matter with more energy. I never thought of myself as a worse Zionist at the time, for doing what I did or attempted to do in early 1940, i.e., go to America. I began to believe that I could be a good Zionist without going on Aliyah, an idea that Father endorsed but which was not generally accepted by Zionist leaders or ideology.

Although I had seen my parents when they passed through Holland, it took until March of 1940 – a full seven months! – for me to dedicate significant time to obtaining a US visa. In the interim I casually organized documents demonstrating my suitability as a prospective American immigrant. I already had one formal letter attesting to my good character and mastery of English from Professor Joseph Lorenz, my former high school teacher. I believed this letter could be helpful in showing the US immigration officers that I could read, write, and speak English adequately.

Professor Lorenz wrote:

> Max Rothschild was for several years one of my pupils. His well-bred, attentive, and irreproachable behavior, and his keen application to study, made him one of the most sympathetic boys of his form. With a considerable talent for all sorts of studies, he displayed a particular interest in English, in which he obtained remarkable success. Altogether, he proved a clever, well-educated boy. As far as I can judge by his efficiency in younger years, he will be apt to vigorously put his shoulder to the wheel, whatever the task he is entrusted with.

Munich, June 20th, 1939
Jos. Lorenz, Prof. of Humanities

Dad also had two professional photographs taken for eventual visa applications: a chest-and-headshot of himself and another of Ilse taken in the well-regarded Gordon Studios Holland. These are not the tiny, glossy snapshot passport photos of today, but rather are carefully composed and produced. Ilse looks well-fed, Dad's hair has grown back. The Deventer Organization probably lent him the tie and paid the bill.

Gradually, I found rewarding ways to spend my free time after the daily "work" in the Amsterdam auto repair shop. Following the German invasion of Holland in May 1940, I became engaged in Jewish education, and youth- and community-work. I was a member of the Board of the Federation of Zionist organizations in Holland, served in its youth and education departments, and was a member of the Hebrew language examinations commission. I led Zionist youth groups and published translations from Hebrew literature as aids in education and programming.

I was deeply engaged in Zionist activism even if I planned to go to the US. In addition to arranging exit documents and obtaining an American visa to the US or a British Certificate to Palestine, I also had to demonstrate proof of having ship passage. All of this became more difficult when I moved back to Almelo from Amsterdam.

Immediately after my parents arrived in England in late August 1939, they began working on acquiring American visas for themselves, Hannah, and Eva. A few days after their arrival in England, Germany invaded Poland. Because England had a defense pact with Poland, England declared war on Germany. The world changed that day. World War II had officially begun, and I was in limbo.

There is an unverified but heroic story in our family that after World War II erupted and casualties began to mount at sea, Henny announced that the family had to leave England – they were physically too close to Germany. "I'd rather die at sea," Henny allegedly said, "than at the hands of the Germans when they invade England." Henny quickly convinced her husband, and they were able to secure passage to the US on the *SS Nova Scotia*, a British ship. Although she had been warned that the trip was not safe, Henny insisted they take their chances. Fortunately, the family arrived in America without incident, but future passengers were not so lucky. In 1942, a German submarine sank the Nova Scotia in the Indian Ocean with the loss of 858 of the 1,052 people aboard.

It is unclear how Henny and her husband purchased the tickets given that the Germans strictly limited the money that Jews could take with them when leaving Germany. Perhaps German-Jewish refugees in England received financial help from American relatives or from Jewish organizations. Perhaps they found a way to smuggle money into England. In any case, the story about the risky voyage across the Atlantic was repeated regularly, with Henny as the heroine.

Pleading for Help

Once I concluded that it was morally permissible to abandon my Zionist plans to move to Palestine, I tried hard to join my family in the US. But to accomplish this, I needed help. The only way to get help was to write to people abroad, especially to Father who had found a home and medical practice for sale in Malden, Massachusetts.

As it turned out, the postal service between the US and the Netherlands was unreliable, beset by delays and even non-delivery of mail. International phone calls were rare. In an undated letter from this period to someone Dad knew in Switzerland, he wrote:

I have not heard directly from my loved ones in the US, although I have written to them again and again. Now I would like to ask you to write to my parents on my behalf, since the mail seems to reach its destination when it is sent from Switzerland. Please tell them that I need all the papers and affidavits to be submitted to the consulate again, urgently, as I will not be able to get my visa extended without them.

In addition, I also need 200 dollars – to be made available to me, in accordance with the new requirements... I have already written all of this to my dear parents. If only I would receive a response. I should be able to leave by way of Lisbon, and since the departure date is very soon, I am quite nervous. If possible, please write on "reply cards" or include cash. I am in such a poor financial situation that just a few cents could make all the difference. Otherwise, I am doing great... Write back soon. Sending my love, Yours, Max

Finally, on January 3, 1940, four months after the start of World War II, I heard from my parents. Two days later, approximately a year after I had arrived in Holland, I responded to them, explaining the Kafkaesque situation in which I found myself re the visa: "You can hardly imagine how happy I was with your collective letter of 12/3/39. It was underway for four weeks from Boston! I didn't dare hope that letters would still come through now because of the war. I would like to report first about my emigration matters, because this is of utmost importance for you and me. Your charge, dear mother, that I do not devote myself sufficiently to the cause, makes absolutely no sense."

The American consul in Rotterdam issues visas only under very strict conditions. Thus, for me, as I have already written to you a few times, an additional document is required (Form 575). Yesterday the consul told me that the affidavit of Carry [perhaps Henry] Morgenthau has still not arrived. This disturbs me very much, because, had it arrived, I possibly would have obtained the visa already. Moreover, we cannot go to the consulate in person anymore. Now the Committee [for Jewish Refugees] is the sole official authority. My case, as it was told to me, looks very favorable. As soon as I have the additional document, the consul will give me the visa, and the German authorities will evaluate my request favorably, which means that I can travel.

Everything therefore depends on the speedy arrival of the documents without which it is useless to entertain any hopes. The expenses for the new request, photocopies, etc., I must obviously meet with Siegfried's money. [Siegfried was Siegfried Kellerman, a businessman and German-born relative who was already in the US. Siegfried had sent about $200 for Dad to use as he saw fit.]

Then I switched gears and asked about the family: I am curious how you are doing, dear Father, on the exam [for a medical license to practice in Massachusetts]. Why are you so nervous?"

In hindsight, that question was easy to answer. Max's father was required to take medical exams in the US even though he had practiced medicine successfully for many years on the German battlefield, in the small town of Gunzenhausen, and in the large city of Munich. The US medical establishment, on principle, did not accept a German doctor's license. Not only that, but new licenses were unobtainable in many parts of the country. "In 1940, only 15 American states permitted foreigners...to take licensure examinations. Of those states, five deliberately discouraged such persons from applying."[20] In other words, the challenge was to be allowed to take the exam, not just to pass it. Still, Max's Father overcame the challenge and passed the exam on April 28, 1941.

Dad wrote: *At present there are attempts, under explicit support of the authorities, to move to the US the education of young people situated here* [in Holland]. *It concerns approximately 200 craftsmen. For several reasons, people in the US have not devoted themselves sufficiently to this plan. Last week, "the first official announcement" came from* [Aryeh] *Tartakover, the leader of Hechalutz in New York, that they have made a start with the issue.*

Next, I pleaded with Father to pressure the organizing group in America to turn the idea into reality. In a subsequent letter, I raised another possibility. "I'm a minor, and you cannot support me. But an American can adopt me. Several people have drawn my attention to this. You must act quickly. Then the American consul can help me with the papers to get out of here. I beg of you to help me with this idea by speaking to an expert. At least we will have tried. I look forward to hearing about this."

Dad was burdened by countless worries, especially the welfare of his relatives in Germany. At that time, he was still hearing from Grandmother Betty who lived in deteriorating conditions in Munich. She wrote, "My dears! Thank you for your letters, which brought such great joy! The consulate's procedures have been narrowed to such a degree that the hope I feel regarding seeing you again is diminishing. I am very concerned about Paul [her son with Down Syndrome]. If his visa is denied, then I can't leave, either. We will continue to hope for the help of God and wait patiently. Heartfelt kisses and greetings to everyone. Your faithful, Oma Betty."

Pleading for help was the common theme in the correspondence between European and American Jews at that time. It was the subject of Ilse's parents' letters to everyone they contacted, begging to be rescued from the barracks of the Gurs Concentration Camp in France. Dad wrote again, in German, with great concern.

Although I have been waiting for five weeks in vain for news from you, I would still like to write to you today about an urgent matter. I received your two last letters with all the papers ... Now that I have all these documents, I have deposited the emigration request with all the appropriate officials. Unbelievably, the committee tells me that the consul still needs an affidavit from you as the next of kin, like form 575. This is very urgent, and the committee has notified HIAS [Hebrew Immigrant Aid Society] *in New York by return mail so that they can help you with this document. Therefore, write your affidavit for me as soon as possible. And try to get a formal guarantee* [for financial support] *from the Rosenfelders* [friends from their hometown of Gunzenhausen who were already in the US] *for this purpose.*

In addition, I was asked whether Ernst Katzenstein [Mammiah's brother and my uncle] had given me an affidavit, and where it is, and most of all, where the affidavit of Morgenthau is... I hope you will manage to get these papers, because I want to be with all of you as soon as possible.

The Committee is working on emigration plans for young people to Santo Domingo [capital of the Dominican Republic]. *Therefore, it is possible that there will be other opportunities for me. Now I would like to ask you, dear Father, in the name of all my friends, to campaign for the cause, which means to appeal to the people involved, with help from people in positions of power. You can also exert pressure simply through a letter of request. Please try all that you can.*

On February 29, 1940, while Dad was frantically engaged in trying to get a visa, he received a document he had requested from the office of the Mayor of Amsterdam.

The Mayor of Amsterdam Declares, in accordance with the received office bulletins, that I, Max Rothschild, was born in

Gunzenhausen on February 20th, 1921, occupation Auto Mechanic, Residence Deymanstraat 12, and have been a member of the community since October 20, 1939. Thus far the aforementioned has shown good behavior. The holder of this document may use this abroad.

Signed Amsterdam, February 29, 1940, The Mayor

In addition to the mayor's generous reference to Dad as an actual auto mechanic, this document is interesting in other ways. It shows that the Dutch kept good records on people's comings and goings, a practice that could be used for innocent or nefarious purposes. Second, no question was asked about Dad's religion, although anyone would be correct in assuming that someone named Max Rothschild was a Jew, and that someone born in Gunzenhausen was a German. And third, the mayor's office agreed to add the lines about good behavior. The mayor knew nothing about his behavior, but Dad couldn't care less. If this document helped him gain passage on the ship to America due to sail on May 11, 1940, he was content.

The Mayor's letter was a godsend. Four months later, on June 14, 1940, one month after Germany invaded Holland, the US State Department established a new regulation that they communicated to the American consulate in Rotterdam. Any Dutch person applying for entry to the US would have to provide "affidavits of good conduct" – meaning sworn declarations that confirmed the good behavior of the visa applicant.[21]

In another letter to his family in Malden, Dad wrote with gratitude that the newly required affidavits were on their way.

I believed that even though this piling on of red tape was tedious, the Americans were fair. I wrote to my parents that everything that's possible is being done. I have filled out all the forms. Soon the passage to the US will follow.

The Cost of Delay

But I was wrong. My earlier delays in applying for a second (or replacement) visa were costly, first, because the Germans were getting closer to invading Holland and second, because American visa availability was on a steep decline.

After Germany annexed Austria two years earlier in March 1938, President Roosevelt suggested liberalizing immigration procedures and combining the German and Austrian quotas to make it more likely for Jews in Austria to obtain visas to the United States. That decision quickly led to the full use of the quota. After the world war began in September 1939, however, State Department officials instructed consuls general in Europe not to admit anyone to the United States if there was any doubt about their political reliability. Fear of Axis spies entering the United States led to a significant reduction in the number of visas issued in 1940.

The State Department instructions applied across the board and decreased my chances of obtaining a visa from Holland to the US. On the other hand, in March 1940, when I'd been in Holland for a little more than a year, my chances for a visa [to the US] looked promising. I told my friends, and I told the heads of our organization, that I was going to America. I had to fight the "still small voice" that wanted to call me a traitor. The moral compunctions were still so strong that even then, early in 1940, I had moments of hesitation in pursuing that visa, which lost me some precious days and perhaps weeks.

Many lessons can be learned from this part of Dad's recollections. From January 1933 on, two major factors (among many others) separated Jews who continued to live from those who were killed. The first was that people were vulnerable if they did not act as quickly as possible to improve their situation. The second was that an ability and willingness to be persistent in dealing with bureaucracy were essential. That is not to say that acting immediately and coping effectively with bureaucracy always led to good outcomes. But delaying and "hoping for the best" were neither wise nor effective.

The time I lost, namely the delay of between three or four weeks, was precisely the time which made all the difference. It was the time when the Nazis finally invaded Holland and everything changed. There is no doubt that my life would have taken an entirely different turn had I acted more vigorously during that crucial period.

Had I "acted more vigorously," I would have made it to the US before the invasion of Holland and would have avoided living under the Nazi occupation for five additional years. On the other hand, if I had gone to the US earlier, I might not have married Ilse. Because of my persistence when I finally dedicated myself to the task, and because of Father's help with all my requests, I did receive a new American visa. Next, I quickly booked passage on the S.S. Veendam, due to sail from Rotterdam on May 11. But, ironically, on May 10, one day earlier, the Germans invaded. My trunk was already on-board. I got it back a few weeks later with some bullet holes and dents... I literally had missed the boat by one day.

The Dutch American Line reimbursed me $179.67 for the cost of my one-way ticket and the near destruction of my trunk. I loved telling this story. Perhaps it represented some sort of victory on my part. I certainly enjoyed the fact that the now-Nazi controlled shipping line responded to a refund request from a Jew. The story was the only good thing that came out of the German invasion.

When I arrived in peaceful Holland in January 1939, I assumed that I would no longer be persecuted as a Jew. I also believed I would develop agricultural skills. I did not enter Holland to become a Dutch citizen; I fully accepted being a "pass-through." For me, Holland was a stepping-stone to Palestine. My belief that by leaving Germany I could live in peace lasted one year and four months, from my arrival in Holland in January 1939 until May 10, 1940, when the Germans invaded. Tragically, once the German Occupation began, I lived under the same conditions in Holland that I had fled in Germany. German Nazi murderers and Dutch citizens with similar attitudes would seek to kill me.

Strangely, Zionist leaders in Holland did not alter their approach to Jewish youth even though circumstances had changed so dramatically. Despite the ever-growing German threat during the fall of 1939 and early spring of 1940, despite several visits by special emissaries of our movement from Palestine, we did nothing, absolutely nothing to prepare *for the possibility of a German invasion. Holland was extremely vulnerable. It was merely a question of time before the axe would fall.*

I have never come to terms with the Zionists' narrow focus on preparing young Jews to pursue agriculture in Palestine and not on the greater necessity of saving their lives. These Zionist emissaries from Palestine paid little attention to the situation other than to secure Aliyah for those they deemed adequately trained in agriculture. And an extension of training (Hachsharah) – for the rest of us. Perhaps some of us could have gotten away to several other countries, even some exotic island or other. For young people with agricultural or mechanical training there were still some possibilities. But, as I said before, those thoughts were taboo, totally out of the question.

Underutilized at the auto shop and unimpressed with the "schlichim" [Palestinian-Jewish emissaries] I decided to create a group with whom I could study. As I wrote to my parents, this group met in the evenings for discussions. One evening we talked about the role of Aggadah [non-legalistic debates about religious texts]. So at least I find a balance between work and the evenings, which is an outlet for my needs. A few days before the German invasion, I got up the courage to reveal to my friends my plans to emigrate to the United States. I promised to stay true to the chalutzic ideal and to continue working for the Zionist cause in the US. My main worry was Ilse, although I was much too immature at that time to make plans for saving her as well.

"I was much too immature" is incomprehensible to me as a description for a person who claimed he was "madly in love." Was he too immature or rather too self-centered? Was he ambivalent about Ilse? Perhaps it was Ilse who refused to go to the United States because she was still completely committed to Palestine. *Ilse's two sisters had already moved there, but Ilse was worried about her parents who were languishing in a concentration camp in France. Perhaps Ilse had decided not to leave the Continent without getting them out.* If she had feelings about my "immaturity," she never mentioned it.

My friend, Shushu, with a wry smile, gave me a present when I said farewell to him and told him I was going to the US: the one volume edition of Bialik's selected works from which we had read and studied together in Ellguth and in Holland. Here we were in April 1940, with the world aflame, Polish Jewry had already suffered heavily, German troops were massed at the Dutch border and everywhere else in Western Europe, and yet, my dearest friend inserted a line on the title page of the book criticizing me for abandoning Zionist ideals!

Prelude to the Invasion

As could be expected, there are many accounts of the lead-up to the invasion, the preparedness or lack thereof of the Dutch military, and the strategy of the German attackers. Nearly every element of these accounts is challenged by other accounts. My purpose is not to resolve these disputes. It is simply to reflect on what they meant to Dad.

Clearly, Dad had been naive in believing he would be safe by crossing into Holland. For months, Hitler had been violating borders throughout Europe. In March 1938, Hitler annexed Austria. Seven months later, the governments of France, Italy and Britain bowed to the Nazi demand to take over the Sudetenland, which had formed part of Czechoslovakia. A month later the government–sponsored riots of *Kristallnacht* broke out, showing that Hitler was flexing his muscles both inside and outside Germany. The Dutch government and citizenry hoped, prayed, and even believed that Germany would honor Holland's proclaimed neutrality as it had done during World War I.

But I was not alone in my belief that Holland was safe. The native Dutch population shared this view. The Dutch population's conviction that they would be safe from German harm was bolstered in October 1937, one and a half years before I entered Holland, when Germany declared that "the integrity of the Belgian frontier was a common interest between her and Belgium..."[22] *The integrity of the Netherlands' long borders with Germany was similarly understood to be a common interest of both countries. But this declaration was a lie.*

Because Hitler was making dramatic military inroads into the east, few people expected he would launch a simultaneous invasion into Western Europe. But in a top-secret document of August 24, 1938, Hitler told his Armed Forces Supreme Command that it would be advantageous to capture and occupy Belgium and the Netherlands to launch and sustain an air war against Great Britain and France. The staff officer who prepared the secret document "assumed quite rightly that the leaders of the German nation and the High Command would not pay the smallest attention to the fact that Germany had given her word not to invade Holland or Belgium."

Another deceit concerned the Jews who lived in the countries the Germans planned to conquer. In February 1940, the German government "decided" deceitfully once again that their "occupying forces in Belgium and Holland would conduct themselves according to the dictates of international law and refrain from any acts of violence or pillage so as to avoid the impression that Germany intended to annex these countries." The directives to this effect included the statement, "No initiative should be taken on the racial issue... One must not support special actions against an inhabitant solely because he is a Jew." This led to Jews lowering their defenses. And, as it turned out, it was just another lie.

England and France declared war on Germany when the German military invaded Poland on September 1, 1939. Given Hitler's non-intervention promise to Queen Wilhelmina, Holland did not declare war. But a few days after the German victory in Poland, Hitler ordered his General Staff to prepare to attack Holland, Belgium, and Luxembourg as the first step in a final showdown with France and England.[23] The plan called for an invasion in the spring, when Germans would take the first step to dominate the Atlantic coast. Spring arrived, and on April 9, 1940, the Germans devised a plan to conquer Denmark and Norway. On May 4, 1940, both the Vatican and the Dutch military attaché in Germany informed the Dutch government that an attack on its soil was imminent. They were right, but the trusting Dutch government did not prepare.

Behind its declarations of non-aggression, Germany hid its true goal: to occupy all of Europe, including Great Britain. To accomplish this feat, Germany was interested in capturing France as a springboard for conquering its enemy across the English

Channel. Invading the Netherlands was an early component of Germany's larger Battle of France, an operation lasting six weeks from May 10 to June 22, 1940. During that period the Nazi military overran and occupied the Netherlands, Belgium, Luxembourg and more than half of France, establishing Germany's new Western Front.

The Start of the German Occupation

After the Dutch defeat on May 14, 1940, Hitler sealed Dutch Jewry's fate when he gave Adolf Eichmann, later labelled "the architect of the Holocaust," responsibility for Jewish affairs in all Nazi-occupied areas in Europe. Charged with appointing a Commissioner for the Netherlands, Eichmann chose Dr. Arthur Seyss-Inquart (1892-1946), an attorney who had served as Chancellor of Austria after that country was absorbed by Germany. Seyss-Inquart established civil authority in the Netherlands and revamped Dutch society completely. The Dutch political leadership, called the Secretaries-General, "declared themselves loyal to the highest-ranking German in the new Dutch government."[24] According to oral testimony given by German Jewish survivor Bernard Natt, "In Holland, anti-Jewish policy was enforced much faster than had been done in Germany where it had taken about six years, from 1933 to 1939. We Jews felt this immediately when it became more and more difficult for Jewish people to live a normal life because of nasty anti-Jewish laws."[25]

When the Dutch Queen Wilhelmina fled to England at the start of the invasion, she left an order to her civil servants that they should carry out "business as usual." This strange directive was a major culprit in undermining Dutch resistance; the Queen essentially advised Dutch bureaucrats to carry out the occupiers' foul deeds. Thus, throughout the occupation of the Netherlands, Seyss-Inquart worked with a fully operational and cooperative Dutch civil service. This meant that Jews could not turn to Dutch civil servants for help against the Nazis.[26]

Next in command under Seyss-Inquart was Hanns Albin

Rauter, Senior SS and Police Leader. After he sent approximately 100,000 Jews to their death, Rauter announced: "I will gladly pledge my soul in heaven for what I have undertaken here against the Jews. He who has discovered the meaning of Jewry as a race and nation cannot do otherwise than we have done."[27]

The Commander of the Security Police, SS Major General Wilhelm Harster, set up the German "Green Police," which engaged in raids and roundups, broke strikes, and carried out executions and reprisal murders. Soon "Green Police" became a byword for terror. When Harster was replaced in 1943 by SS Brigadier Erich Naumann, a commander of an *Einsatzgruppe*, terror rose to even greater heights. Naumann was responsible for shooting hostages, extortion, and the mass deportation of more than 100,000 Dutch Jews, mostly to Auschwitz.

To my surprise, nearly every historian of this early post-invasion period in Holland labels the immediate aftermath of the invasion as "quiet." While it might have been the "honeymoon of the occupation" for the general population, it certainly was not a honeymoon for the Jews.[28] In fact, less than a month after the invasion, the Jewish Telegraphic Agency, based in London, reported the following:

The situation in Holland: epidemics, arrests, murders; June 3, 1940

According to the "Jewish Chronicle," a telegram has been received from Amsterdam announcing that the influx of refugees from the provinces has provoked an explosion of epidemics in the ancient ghetto of Amsterdam. The food shortage aggravates the situation. Mass arrests of Jewish journalists, industrialists and shopkeepers have occurred in Amsterdam. Many Jews have been shot. The Gestapo has closed the offices of the Jewish community in Amsterdam, Rotterdam, and The Hague.[29]

This description makes it clear that the war against Dutch Jews began in the Netherlands as soon as the Nazis arrived. There was no quiet period. Exactly two weeks after the capitulation of the Dutch military, Seyss-Inquart issued a deceptive letter to the Dutch people, posted throughout the country in German and Dutch. Part propaganda and part threat, the letter provides a window into Seyss-Inquart's thoughts and psychological strategy to confuse the Dutch people.

[To:] Dutch citizens in occupied territory, May 29, 1940:

As of today, I have assumed supreme control of government and civic affairs in the Netherlands. Already a few days after the catastrophe was allayed [meaning that the Germans stopped bombing Dutch cities because the Dutch surrendered] by the former government [the legally elected Dutch government], the magnanimity of the Führer and the strength of the German armies have made it possible for order to be restored.

The normal situation will be interrupted only if special occurrences justify this. As Reich Commissioner, I shall exercise the supreme command in civic affairs over Dutch citizens, protected by the German armies, to maintain law and order. I shall take all necessary steps, eventually by decree, to complete this task.

In doing so I wish, as much as possible to respect the Dutch law and independent jurisdiction, as well as to consult the Dutch authorities. But I expect all judges, public administrators, and civil servants rigorously to enforce my laws. I also expect the Dutch people to accept the situation with intelligence and self-control. In battle, the Dutch soldier was brave. Dutch citizens behaved in an orderly manner towards the fighting troops, therefore nothing can prevent us from treating each other with courtesy and respect.

Under the leadership of the Führer, the German people are fighting for their existence. They were forced to fight because of the hatred and envy of their enemies. This struggle forces the German people to exert all their strength and gives them the right to attain their goal by any means whatsoever. This duty and necessity will also influence public life in the Netherlands. Therefore, I shall see to it that the Dutch people, being of the same blood as the German people will not have to suffer unnecessarily, owing to the destructive intentions of our enemies.

As Reich commissioner, I must and shall maintain the interests of the Reich in Dutch territory, now under German protection. By accomplishing these tasks, caused by a common fate, the Dutch people will ensure the freedom and liberty of their country.[30]

Seyss-Inquart did not mention Jews in his initial communication to the Dutch public. Rather, he described the new circumstances in terms of good and evil. The "good" included the decision of the Dutch government to capitulate, the kindness of the Führer, the strength of the German armies, orderliness, the German armies as protectors of law and order, respect for Dutch law, Dutch cooperative enforcement of occupiers' laws, Dutch self-control, courtesy, respect, and more. Evil phenomena included "special occurrences," the hatred and envy of the Dutch people toward Germany, and the enemy's destructive intentions. Seyss-Inquart's letter blames "the other" for what the Nazis themselves were doing, starting with the German invasion. The message reads like a letter, with Seyss-Inquart addressing the Dutch population in the first-person singular nine times.

Seyss-Inquart quickly began issuing decrees against the Jews. On the heels of his proclamation that made no mention of Jews, he began to harass them. Several decrees issued in the summer of 1940, right after the invasion, laid the groundwork for first isolating and then exterminating the Jewish population. Seyss-Inquart directed the German occupying forces to treat the Jews living in the Netherlands almost exactly as the Jews living in Germany. In fact, some particularly severe measures imposed in the Netherlands were not applied in other West European countries that had been conquered. Germans planned to integrate the Netherlands into Germany at the war's conclusion.

To the Nazis, Holland was special, "Aryan," and thus, the Germans approached the Netherlands as if it were already part of Germany.

Seyss-Inquart worked at a feverish pace fueled by his personal grudge against the Dutch people and its Jews, who had dared to fight him.[31] As his letter said,

> I shall see to it that the Dutch people, being of the same blood as the German people will not have to suffer unnecessarily, owing to the destructive intentions of our enemies.

French-Jewish historian Leon Poliakov wrote that "The Nazis... experienced their greatest disappointments in the Netherlands. Opinion was unanimous on this. Goering exclaimed: 'The Dutch are unique as the nation of traitors to our cause.'"[32] This idea was grounded in the expectation that the Dutch saw themselves as brothers of the Germans, i.e. fellow Aryans.

Ultimately, Seyss-Inquart paid for his crimes. On October 16, 1946, after being tried and convicted in Nuremberg, he was hanged as a war criminal. At his trial, the prosecutors pointed out that of the 140,000 Dutch Jews, only 8,000 survived in hiding and only 5,450 came home from camps located in Poland and Czechoslovakia. As head of the occupying government, Seyss-Inquart was held responsible.

Rumors and Decrees

On May 29, 1940, the same day that Seyss-Inquart issued his letter to the Dutch populace, as American historian, Peter Hayes, put it, "the hope of surviving was the enemy of fighting back."[33] Dad wrote about the rumors going around.

There were rumors all over that the Germans would not touch the Jews. "We haven't come here to solve the Jewish question" was a quotation from a statement supposedly made by Goering. This widely cited rumor, most likely initiated and spread by the Nazis, was designed to give Jews hope, which, in turn, would lower their defenses and reduce the chances of their organizing against the Germans. The Jews accepted what Goering was rumored to have said and settled into the "new normal."

Anti-Jewish restrictions and requirements intensified during the summer, autumn, and early winter of 1940. The Occupation government closed Jewish newspapers, fired Jewish civil servants, and registered the assets of all Jewish businesses. Jewish students were expelled from schools and universities. Some restrictions cost Jews their jobs, some endangered their assets, and others were simply degradations meant to keep Jews apart from others. The latter restrictions included laws against Jews buying fruits and fish, riding bicycles, and entering non-Jewish homes. Signs declared that a particular area was "Forbidden to Jews" or that "Jews were not Welcome." Textiles and shoes were rationed. But this was not all. Every Jewish male was required to have a physical to screen him for "work camps." No one outside the government knew what or where a "work camp" was.

Next came compulsory relocation: the Nazi occupation government forced all Dutch Jews to move to three Amsterdam districts surrounded by German-controlled bridges over Dutch canals. The relocation decrees funneled Jews into a smaller and smaller, and more easily controllable, space. Dad wrote,

Earlier I proudly commented that Jews behaved in a "dignified" manner vis-a-vis other Jews. Standing in line at the offices of the Joodse Raad, Amsterdam's central Jewish organization, we were Dutch Jews, and German Jewish refugees, and a handful of Polish Jews, with everybody repeating a different rumor, with sadness and fright on the faces of many, but without presenting a picture of cowardice. People behaved honorably and maintained even that little element of personal dignity which helped so many of them to survive, whether it was in a concentration camp or in a hiding place. The question is whether it would have been more useful to band together and rise violently against the Germans. And could that have been done? Fortunately for me, the Germans were focused on Amsterdam. Only later did the Germans scour the countryside in search of people like me working on a farm in Almelo.

Between July 1, 1940, and August 7, 1942, when the final decree regarding Jews appeared, Seyss-Inquart imposed dozens of restrictions. When taken together, these decrees allowed the smooth process of mass murder to occur without it being self-evident to the victims. The impact of the decrees was Jewish isolation, impoverishment, hunger, confusion, humiliation, helplessness, and disruption. As time passed, just as in Germany, Jews lost their subgroup identities and became only Jews.

For me, the decree ordering Jews to register had the most impact. Although from the moment of entering Holland, I had registered with the authorities continuously for the purpose of establishing residency, I never had to register as a Jew.

On July 31, 1940, kosher butchering was restricted. On September 6, 1940, Jews could no longer be appointed to public office, and Jews who already were civil servants could not be promoted. These decrees and others like them were announced only in the newspaper published by the Joodse Raad [The Jewish Council]. This way, Dutch non-Jews could claim they did not know what was happening to the Jews. Ironically, in many countries during the Holocaust, stripping Jews of their national identity led them to focus, some for the first time, on their Jewishness. "Despite all the difficulties, a renaissance of Jewish cultural life occurred... Several monographs on topics relating to the Jewish tradition were published, and a new Hebrew dictionary and a few volumes of Hebrew poetry appeared. There was a resurgence of religious feeling, as evidenced by an increased demand for the religious instruction of children."[34] As Bernard Natt wrote, "Due to the [Nazi] developments, our family and I myself became more interested in Jewish culture and values."[35]

Dad's Post-Invasion Letter

In late September 1940, four months after his aborted departure to the US, Dad wrote to his parents that he had a new plan to leave the Netherlands.

I explained how I was trying to get out of the country with passengers from the ship on which I had planned to travel. My information was sketchy and my concern with finances, paramount. Last week I had to send my passport to the Comité for a stamp. I think I will soon receive the stamp that I need to travel out of the country. If all goes well, the Comité, with approval from different offices, will organize a transport of the passengers from the Veendam of the Holland-America line who ended up being unable to travel.

The trip is supposed to be by way of Portugal. That is literally everything I know about it. We weren't even informed whether papers or money or both will be needed. I had to give the [original] ticket back since it was in a foreign currency. Based on a general ruling, I received only 80 percent of the gulden that Fritz had been safeguarding for me. If necessary, I can use the money to support myself when staying in Portugal.

As you can see, I am terribly worried about the financial side of things. I can probably borrow money from close acquaintances to pay for all the trip-related expenses. But if the authorities require foreign currency and I must ask you for that again, it would be a terrible feeling for me, because... I already cost you such a large amount when I should be helping you. But it isn't my fault. If anything is needed, I will let you know promptly via telegrams. Maybe everything will work out so that we can make use of the old ticket. You can't do anything at all to help, since the Shipping Line returned the money to me on this end.

You'll be happy to know that I have a particularly good relationship with Fritz and Rosl Stein. Often, I bring them a few eggs from the farm in Almelo, which they can really use... If I am not able to make the trip to America after the holidays, I have another iron in the fire: Last week I received a message from the Youth Comité informing me that I could have a job as a civics teacher... I can't accept, of course, but if the trip doesn't work out, then I'm sure I will go and work at that school.

In terms of my health, I'm doing well, and I am not quite as nervous as I used to be either. This work may have made me stronger, so I haven't gotten any fatter. (I am not predisposed to that, after all). I close this letter with love and best wishes for the Jewish New Year.

But Dad soon realized that for Jews in Holland, the High Holidays would bring nothing but sorrow and new decrees. Four days after he posted his letter, Dutch Jews were informed that except for one newspaper, the *Het Joodsche Weekblad* [The Jewish Weekly], which The Jewish Council was forced to use to announce new anti-Jewish edicts, Jews may not publish newspapers.

A week later, on October 5, 1940, all civil servants were required to fill out a form declaring if they were Jews or married to Jews. Only those who signed as not being Jewish and having no Jewish relatives could stay on the job. According to Dutch historian Benjamin Aaron Sijes, "practically all the government employees, among them Jews as well, signed the declaration... Only a few officials refused to sign – as far as we know, only 20 persons of the 240,000 people in government service."[36]

On October 22, 1940, Jews had to register their businesses, thereby giving the Germans information needed to seize these assets. Hiding assets was a punishable offense. Thus, Jews had fewer and fewer resources for daily living and bribes. On November 4, 1940, all Jewish civil servants were told they would be "suspended" by November 21, 1940. The secular new year brought no respite. In January 1941, they were all dismissed without compensation.

After January 9, 1941, Jews were no longer allowed to go to the movies. The next day, any person with a Jewish grandparent, had to register at their City Hall. After they submitted the details of their Jewish antecedents, they received a "yellow card" as a certificate of registration. Most Jews, including Dad, did register, hoping that this decree would be the last.

On February 13, 1941, the Nazis appointed a *Judenrat* for the city of Amsterdam. This was also the day on which the occupiers and Dutch Nazis carried out *razzias* in the Jewish sections of Amsterdam. These violent raids, occurring mostly at night, terrorized the population, and culminated in Jews being forcibly transported to the Westerbork transit camp and leaving their property and homes behind – sometimes with the key in the door.

The Nazi strategy combined decrees with arbitrary terror tactics. Seyss-Inquart appointed Rauter to organize the *razzias* and other public terror. Rauter flexed his muscles against 900 unarmed, hungry young Jews "who had committed no offense whatsoever against the German occupying authorities" by sending them to the murderous Mauthausen concentration camp.

Jewish medical professionals were no longer permitted to treat or perform services for Gentiles, nor were they permitted to be part of non-Jewish health organizations.[37] Jews watched their social ties with non-Jews thin out and then disappear. There were no courts to which Jews could bring complaints because the decrees were the law. Jews had to relinquish their cars. Hotels, inns, and restaurants could no longer serve Jews. Jewish musicians employed in state-sponsored orchestras were dismissed. Jews who were prohibited from work or schooling lost their connections with non-Jewish people who might have helped them. So Jews stayed home, venturing out only to search for food. If they were unemployed, "Jews were forced to go to labor camps, for the time being to labor camps located in the Netherlands."[38]

On February 11, 1941, a "numerus clausus" was announced limiting the number of Jewish students in universities.[39] By the first anniversary of the invasion, Jews had been relocated, robbed, isolated, and converted into obedient, terrified, and confused residents of a crowded ghetto. The center of all this horror was Amsterdam.

Return to Almelo

With Amsterdam increasingly dangerous, I left the auto repair shop and moved back to rural Almelo. Since I was fired in Amsterdam,[40] *I've been here in the old neighborhood on a different farm. It has been very bad, and it still is.*

Thank goodness, I had a basic understanding of what I had to do. I knew that to be safe, I had to disobey the Nazis. I also knew that moving out of Amsterdam was more than disobedience – it was resistance. I resisted by returning to the farms and resuming life as a "Palestine Pioneer." Later I wrote to my parents: Last year, when I was already complaining [to you about my farm placement], *it was paradise compared to how things are now. You really cannot imagine. But I am holding up, and that's the main thing. Farm work also has a calming effect on the nerves. The problem is just how very alone one is, with none of one's friends around anymore. Ilse is working in the kitchen at the Werkdorp. I haven't spoken to her for nearly six months. She wanted to come here, but I couldn't find a position for her.*

On February 17, 1941, only nine months after the invasion and a few days after my return to Almelo, I went to the mayor's office in the nearby town of Vriezenveen to register once again. As required by law and for a fee (!) of about 50 cents, a clerk gave me a small slip of paper that was a crucial step in the Occupying power's ability to murder me. The paper stated that "I, Max Israel Rothschild, was of partial or complete Jewish descent and had paid the fee for one registration form." In Vriezenveen, I also received a permit to stay in the area for one month. On my next visit, my permit allowed me to stay for three months until June 1941, and finally I obtained a permit to reside in the area until September 10, 1941. The authorities were keeping very close tabs on people, particularly Jews. During this time, I was registered as a farm worker.

Paperwork was an important component of the Nazi pretense of legality and a key tool in robbing and endangering Jews. Apparently, all the Jews of Holland – native-born and refugees – registered, for a total of 159,806 people of whom 19,561 were the offspring of mixed marriages.[41] In Germany and in Holland, particularly but not exclusively during the Nazi occupation, Jews suffered from being both integrated and separated, both included and defined as "other." The "integrated" side of the equation is apparent in the large proportion of inter-married couples.

After the start of the Occupation, a Jew's life was better if he or she was married to a non-Jew and if the couple became "voluntarily sterilized." A Jewish person's "reward for sterilization was freedom from wearing the star." Voluntary sterilization was also understood as a guarantee of immunity from deportation, although this was not always the case. "More than 2,500 men and women were sterilized as a consequence of this policy."[42] In other words, there were enough couples to warrant the articulation of Nazi policy. Soon, no Jew was exempt from the plan to murder all the Jews, intermarried or not, sterilized or not.

The False Identity Card

Paperwork also had its flip side. Since so much of Nazi control depended on identity cards and registration documents, one could sometimes trick the system by having false documents. I found such a document rotting away among Dad's papers. Identity passbook A35 No. 14911 has a circular stamp and fingerprint on the first of its six sections. The first page states that the owner of the passbook is Bernard Joseph Israel Natt, born on January 14, 1919, in Frankfurt, Germany. On the next page, the signature of B. Natt appears, under a photograph of Dad (!) next to a large J for *Jood*, the Dutch word for Jew.

The next section of the passbook deals with a later date. It states that "the owner of this document is temporarily released from forced labor." This release, Nr. S4290, was issued in Amsterdam, October 6, 1942, a year after the original stamp. By this time, Dad was already in hiding. Fall 1942 was a terrible time especially because Jews were ordered to report for deportation. Next, the passbook displays a stamp of the commander of the Security Police in the Hague bearing a swastika. The following page has a large J for Jood. The page states only Slaakstr 11, Natt's address in the Jewish neighborhood of South Amsterdam. Then XXX and another fingerprint." It seems worthless to carry a false identity card of another Jew but perhaps the "temporary exemption" was valuable to Dad. Both Dad and Bernard Natt survived the war.

On March 10, 1941, I wrote to my parents that to save postage, I would be sending them occasional long letters rather than frequent short letters. I also mentioned that good news had arrived from the US consulate: The strongly desired form 575 has arrived! Many thanks for that. But to make sure that I would not have any illusions about a visa, the consul wrote to me that I still need the following forms: certificates of good conduct from my places of residence; testimonials from at least three persons about my reputation and such; then, from at least three persons, testimonials about political activities, etc. On top of that, of course, also the transit visa and the emigration visa of the German officials... I am quite certain that it will take a very long time before I have all these papers together.

The granting of my visa will not be guaranteed but will be "taken into consideration." I continued my letter to my parents desperately: "Wouldn't it be possible for you, from over there in the US, to write an application to the Foreign Office, with an exact description of my situation, and that you request an acceleration of the granting of my visa? In addition, someone of importance, like for example Drachmann or Reisser, who know me, might give a statement about me which will surely move the consulate here. One must try everything. Please try everything from your side. I write until my fingers bleed over here..."

To bolster my chances for getting into the United States, I also asked Fritz Stein to provide a reference letter. Stein wrote:

I have known Mr. Max Rothschild since his early childhood. He is part of a well-respected family. His father was a practicing physician in Gunzenhausen and Munich. I can attest to the fact that Mr. Max Rothschild has never been penalized by the police, nor has he in any way been involved in politics. In Germany, he successfully completed his education at the Gymnasium...

He proceeded to qualify as a pioneer in agriculture for Palestine. Mr. Rothschild left Germany in 1939, hoping to develop his agricultural skills in Holland. He has also acquired dexterity as a car mechanic. Mr. Max Rothschild has enjoyed a very good reputation. He is an ambitious young man with great skills, which he will undoubtedly use to full satisfaction for any task that will be given him. March 13, 1941

In case there was any doubt about German intentions, less than a year after the start of the Occupation, Seyss-Inquart stated his new position in no uncertain terms. In a public speech in Amsterdam, he contradicted his initial letter that promised to respect the general population. Now he said, "The Jews are enemies with whom we cannot make a truce or peace agreement. We will hit the Jews wherever we meet them and those who join them will bear the consequences."[43] In other words, Jews were inherent enemies. Their status did not depend on their actions but on their very being. Waiting until March 1941 to give this speech conveniently "hit the Jews" who had become weak, without resources, and probably without non-Jewish friends.

What did Non-Jews Know?

Given all the public decrees, the claim that the non-Jewish Dutch population was ignorant of what was happening to their Jewish neighbors and Jews in general is preposterous, unless one is speaking exclusively about knowledge of extermination. This topic – what the average non-Jewish citizen knew or didn't know – is mired in ongoing debate to this day.

Scholars have examined diaries and memoirs for clues about what people knew.[44] But based on logic alone, it is impossible for non-Jews to have been oblivious to the effects of the decrees. True, they might not have known or cared about the restrictions on kosher butchering or Jewish newspapers, but they would have seen the arrest of Jews who attempted to use parks, go to a swimming pool, watch a movie, or attend a university. They would have seen the large public signs barring Jews from entering various spaces. Non-Jewish children would have been aware that there no longer were any Jewish children or teachers in their classes and schools. Non-Jewish adults would have realized that they couldn't place a phone call to a Jewish friend because his or her phone had been confiscated. By April 1942, one would have had to be blind to not recognize that Jews were wearing large Jewish stars on their outerwear, singling them out for mistreatment.

Dutch historian Bert Jan Flim wrote that "already in the fall of 1941, [Rauter] planned the deportation of Dutch Jews and German-Jewish refugees when he announced his intention to make Holland 'Judenrein.'" He "saw no need to be secretive with the highest Dutch government official concerning his plan." Rauter was "responsible for the repression of the Dutch resistance and was co-responsible for the deportation of the Dutch Jews."[45] "Deportation" was a euphemism for being sent to transit- and then extermination camps. The deportation of all the Jews was a big task that required precise planning and countless helpful Dutch and German non-Jewish participants. More than 100,000 Jews had to be shipped off without knowing what was happening to them. That could not be done without non-Jews knowing.

In April 1941, Reinhard Heydrich, dubbed "a main architect of the Holocaust," sent Erich Rajakowitch, a lawyer who worked for Eichmann, to Holland. His task was "to establish a central office which was to serve as a model for the 'solution of the Jewish question' in all occupied countries in Europe."[46] The features of the model were secrecy, speed, the creation of a Jewish Council to compose lists of Jews to be deported, using the local police to do the dirty work, constant threat, violence and deportation, maximum gathering of spoils, and then total annihilation.[47]

Striking on behalf of Dutch Jews

Israeli author Emuna Elon's complex novel, *House on Endless Waters* (2016) is set in Amsterdam during the first year of the Occupation. One of her fictional characters is a member of the Jewish Council, a banker who sits comfortably with his wife and guests in their grand drawing room. Outside the elegant apartment things are quite different. "In the Jewish Quarter, there was a round-up in which scores of Jews were arrested. The labor unions in the city declared a strike in protest and identified with the arrested Jews, but it was quelled after only three days. Since then, the occupation laws in Amsterdam have been enforced, mainly by the Dutch Green Police."[48] The Jewish Council member and his guests in Emuna Elon's story do nothing. They don't know what to do. But others did. The dockworkers of Amsterdam understood and witnessed the persecution of Jews with their own eyes.

Germans' treatment of the Jews so offended the non-Jewish Dutch dockworkers in Amsterdam that they went on strike. This is yet another indicator that non-Jews were aware of the vicious treatment of the Jews. The then illegal Communist Party organized the famous "February Strike" or "Stevedores' Strike" in Amsterdam on February 25, 1941, the first and only non-Jewish mass protest in all of Europe against the German repression of Jews. Historians have gone even further. They maintain that the uprising in early 1941 was the first of its kind in Jewish history, an instance where non-Jews risked their lives collectively to help Jews. On that day,

300,000 Dutch people stopped work on the trams and in offices, shops, and cafes in protest against the events of Saturday February 22 and Sunday February 23. On those two days the Germans arrested 425 Jews from Amsterdam and Rotterdam. All 425 were sent to Buchenwald and Mauthausen. Only two individuals survived.

The tram drivers' refusal to work prevented a large portion of the Amsterdam population from going about their business. The strike did not put an end to the Occupation; but, on the other hand, it was far from trivial. The strike showed that some Dutch Gentiles were paying attention to what was happening to the Jews of their country and would even come to their aid. It raised the possibility of widespread, effective resistance.

In response to the unrest, civil servants were fired, Amsterdam Mayor Willem de Vlugt was forced to step down, and the city was ordered to pay a huge fine. Soon thereafter, a young member of the Communist Party was caught putting up posters for another strike. He was executed the following day. Three other members of the Communist Party and 15 members of the Geuzen resistance movement were executed later.

On December 19, 1952, more than seven years after the war's end, Queen Wilhelmina's daughter and successor, Queen Juliana, dedicated "De Dokwerker"(the Dock Worker Monument) on Jonas Daniël Meijerplein, the square on which the German police rounded up Jews in February 1941. This famous sculpture has become a symbol of Amsterdam, but it distorts and inflates the Dutch non-Jewish resistance during the war. The sculpture cemented the idea in people's minds that the Dutch were resisters, while burying the idea that it was the Dutch Green Police collaborating with the Germans who were the attackers.

Dutchman Mari Andriessen (1897-1979) was a particularly appropriate choice to create the sculpture. During the Occupation, Andriessen was required to join the Nederlandsche Kultuurkamer [Dutch Culture Chamber] if he wanted to display his work. Created by the occupiers to control artists, this association propagated so-called Aryan art based on National-Socialist philosophy. The

Nederlandsche Kultuurkamer was a Dutch version of the Reichskulturkammer (Reich Culture Chamber) established in Germany in September 1933 under the leadership of Joseph Goebbels, Hitler's Reichminister für Volksaufklärung und Propaganda (Reich Minister for Public Enlightenment and Propaganda).

The Dutch Culture Chamber included film, architecture, visual arts and craft, theater and dance, literature, music, and the press. No one in these fields could work unless they were members of the Culture Chamber. Andriessen refused to join. He also defied the Nazis by hiding Jewish people in his home and enabling resistance fighters to house weapons in his studio. Among his works are sculptures of Queen Wilhelmina in The Hague and in Utrecht. Dutch people are proud of the strike and celebrate its anniversary every year. Five other cities to which the strike spread also deserve credit. These are Zaanstad and Kennemerland in the west and Bussum, Hilversum and Utrecht to the east of Amsterdam.

Recent critics have argued that the sculpture and the conventional story of the strike minimize the fact that Jews themselves were heavily involved in resisting. The sculpture does not portray any Jewish symbols or Jewish people. They are invisible. Thus, the sculpture inadvertently reinforces the erroneous idea that Jews were passive and helpless while the Dutch men were strong and virtuous resisters.[49]

Having moved back to rural Almelo, I felt somewhat distant from the big cities of the west and even from the strike. Amsterdam and Almelo were different worlds. It took some time for us in eastern Holland to grasp the meaning of these events. Shortly afterwards, razzias began all over Holland out of revenge for those bold Kattenburgers who had used their wooden poles to beat up collaborators.

The strikers' courageous action and the Nazi occupiers' vicious reaction raised my consciousness. I concluded that the situation had become extremely serious for Jews in the entire country, and that although armed resistance ultimately was futile, it was immoral to do nothing. What we decided to do in response was childish and naive. But it served as a dress-rehearsal for my later decision to become an "onderduiker" (i.e., a person in hiding). I think that was the first time when I really considered not sitting by and having myself grabbed by the Germans without doing anything about it. But everything was still vague in my mind.

The Apeldoorn Story

After the razzias, my friends and I on our farms reasoned that it was more important to hide from the Germans than to protest against them. Even though we didn't know what hiding or fighting entailed, we struggled with the dilemma – hide or fight? With everything in turmoil, we came up with the idea that the last place Germans would commit a razzia was at the Jewish Psychiatric Hospital in Apeldoorn, a town 65 kilometers from Almelo. In February 1941, together with a few of my friends in the Zionist movement, I bicycled to the insane asylum that cared for 900 adults and 74 mentally disabled or delinquent children. It was a most foolish thing to do. We had no understanding of underground work. We took no precautionary measures. We just told our farmers, naively, that we were going into hiding for a few days because we were afraid the Germans would pick us up.

When we arrived at the hospital, the Jewish nurses gave us all the help we could ask for. We climbed into the attic of one of the outbuildings and settled down in the narrow space under the roof.[50] *We had a fairly good time. I even went so far as to send an open postcard written in Hebrew to Ilse, telling her that I was safe! This was really the height of frivolity and carelessness. After a few days we heard that the razzias had stopped, and so we returned, each to his farm, as though nothing had ever happened.*

On January 21, 1943, approximately two years after Dad's Apeldoorn adventure, the Germans evacuated the hospital in a particularly cruel way, reflecting their contempt for anyone who was Jewish or had a disability, or worse, was a disabled Jew. "The evacuation from the Jewish mental hospital in Apeldoorn remains one of the most horrible chapters in the dark history of the Holocaust."[51] That is saying a lot. Ironically, the Jewish asylum was also the first institution to be evacuated by the Germans in Appeldoorn.

Most of the nurses stayed with the patients. My heart aches when I think of those lovely young girls whom we met during our first attempt at going into hiding, young Jewish nurses whose professional ethic commanded them not to leave their charges.

Those nurses belong to the thousands of unsung Jewish heroes. They would not desert the patients placed in their charge...all of them welcome "material" for the early experiments of the Germans, intended to serve as tryouts to refine the murder techniques to be employed later in Auschwitz on a mass scale. In the cattle cars with their patients they went, those dear girls. I thought and talked about the Apeldoorn nurses forever.

Another Letter Home

I wrote to my parents: I long to see you more and more with each passing day. I think about you constantly and I want more than anything to be able to help you out and contribute some earnings to everyone's cost of living. But it appears that I won't be able to make that a reality anytime soon. As always, I must report on my endless efforts to leave the Netherlands and the proliferation of bureaucratic hurdles: I now have gathered all the necessary papers. I just received affidavits vouching for my good character, which Oma Betty mailed from Munich and which I immediately sent on. They are from Dr. Schaeker and Mr. Adler. However, by now we have learned that permission to leave the country can no longer be granted from here – or only in very rare circumstances that don't apply to me.

And yet, I have also heard that Jews are still allowed to emigrate directly from Germany! You can rest assured that I am following up on every little requirement and that I intend to do everything it takes to get my application approved (my case is being handled by top people), but I also know very well that I mustn't allow myself to have high hopes, as hard as that is to accept.

What we're all hoping is that peace will come soon, and if it does, that I will finally be able to reunite with you... I am in really good shape financially now – relatively speaking, that is – and just yesterday, my first student came by to tell me that she had passed her Abitur exam. That reflects well on me, of course, and I hope that I will get some more students to tutor. There is even a possibility that I may soon receive some monetary compensation for my translation work, which would be a nice source of extra income. I am doing well here. I have already met lots of nice people in Almelo, some of whom have good books and with whom I can have a serious conversation now and then — I'm sure you'll understand how much that means to me here at the farmer's place.

I am also starting to know some musicians... I was recently invited to a Dutch doctor's feudal villa for a house concert in which a well-known pianist, a compatriot [i.e., a fellow German Jew] played. It was a joy beyond words. Clearly, I am trying to live a normal, even stimulating, life, despite the threatening conditions around me.

As late as March 1941, there was even a functioning synagogue in Almelo that Dad attended occasionally.

This week is the anniversary of our dear Thekla's death, may she rest in peace. My memory of her is slowly fading, I am sad to say. It is good she did not have to experience all of this. I am going to go to services in Almelo and say Kaddish [the memorial prayer], and I will be united with you in my thoughts.

I was in Amsterdam for Pesach [Passover]. I spent the first evening with friends at our youth home and the second with Ilse at the Steins... We are very good friends. But my visit was mostly with Ilse. She is currently in Amsterdam and was quite downcast although it sounds like things have improved for her parents somewhat. Please accept my thanks once again for what you did to help them. I am thinking of you, dear Father, and I just hope that you will soon be met with success in your efforts to earn a living. One must get past all these hurdles. I've been scrounging around to find something for over two years now. I have a great deal of respect for you, mother, and I admire your and Hannah's stamina. Are your jobs difficult? I often hear from Munich. It is always the same thing.

The Gast Family

When Dad returned to Almelo from Amsterdam, the Deventer Zionist Organization gave him a new placement.

I landed on a farm with a slave driver of a boss, a farmer named Gast who was much feared in our group. He received me with a bunch of straw in his hands: he cut the straw off at my height and told me that this was my bed, right next to the horses. The work was brutal. Occasionally, German troops were engaged in field exercises right on our grounds. They never suspected that the begrimed, sullen, and stupid-looking boy who gave them a drink of water was a Jew from Munich... In the long run, I could not take the heavy work anymore, and asked for a transfer to an easier place. This was also near Almelo, but on the other side of town. Meanwhile, we succeeded in finding a place for Ilse nearby, and this new situation helped make everything more bearable. The farmer Gast was a story in and of itself.

Gast was an uneducated but highly opinionated man who did not enjoy the best reputation among his neighbors because of his laziness and the fact that his poor wife, an ugly, but not unkind, creature did most of the work. Gast invented ever new ways to get out of work. He used to bicycle to town on any pretext. There was always a pregnant sow to be looked over for possible purchase or an auction to attend. Gast could have his kind moments towards me, whenever he felt this to be to his advantage, or whenever he was pleased that I did his work for him. The nicest person in that household was the old grandma, who lit the stove every morning and prepared all the meals for the family. Everyone called her Opoe, the Dutch word for granny. She was wise and kind. She was afraid of her son-in-law's temper and saw easily through his lazy tricks. Unlike Gast, she was aware of what went on in the outside world and was not afraid to express her opinions on "politics," which at that time meant the German Occupation. The children of the family were spoiled and obnoxious.

After I had proven myself to Gast as a worker, I got my own clean room with an electric light overhead. It had a reading lamp, a chest, and a few other luxuries that I had only dreamt about before. In addition, the farm was located on a country road not far from Almelo where all our friends were living. This place was less backward than my previous farms, and while it could not be called more sophisticated, at least it was less isolated from the inhabited world.

The boss made no secret of his sympathies. His pro-German arguments were not clever theories, but rather plain stupidities; he swallowed the official Nazi line in toto. He was not an active traitor, but his pro-German feelings added to the dislike in which he was held by his neighbors, all of whom were fiercely nationalistic Dutchmen. I think that Gast was simply too dumb to be an active traitor, and in addition, he was afraid of these neighbors. Perhaps he felt that the Germans would win the war, and so it would be good to be on their side. It was always difficult to contradict his inanities during table conversation, although he usually welcomed "a fight" with words. When I saw pictures of Senator McCarthy later in America, I was reminded of farmer Gast. He had the same facial expressions.

In addition, Gast's wife's sister, a charming, unmarried lady who worked at the Almelo hospital as a nurse, sometimes would come over on Sundays to visit Opoe, her mother. She was a delightful, educated, and entertaining person who never made a secret of her hatred for the Germans, her sympathies for the resistance movement, and her willingness to help the Jews, whose fate she sincerely regretted. Gast's sister was exactly the kind of person that Ilse or I might have turned to for help when we decided to hide.

About a mile or so down the road, closer to town, was the farm of Gast's father and brothers. The old man was still there, as well as the sons with their families. They were less lazy. On the other hand, they could be real slave drivers when it came to poor Gerd, one of our chaverim, who was in training on their farm. Gerd was a fine, simple, decent Jewish boy who worked hard, much harder, I am sure, than I. He had a difficult life. His only solace was another chaver, his closest friend, who worked on a farm several miles away. The two boys were each other's help and comfort. Their families had ceased to exist. Later when the Germans were rounding up Jews in the Almelo region with the deceitful recruitment ploy called "Harvest Help," I tried to convince Gerd to go underground. We could surely have helped him. But he was inflexible, perhaps cowed and influenced by the political views of his farmers: "The authorities must be obeyed!" Gast would say, "If they tell you to register for 'Harvest Help,' you have to go and register; although we hate to see you leave us because we need you so badly on the farm."

Gerd lacked non-Jewish contacts of the kind Ilse and I were able to establish. And yet, he was physically much stronger than I and could carry a much heavier load on the farm. The constant insidious comparison which my boss and his brother, Gerd's boss, used to make quite shamelessly about our respective performances, played one "Jew boy" against the other. I was said to perceive more intelligently how to load a wagon of hay, but G. was much better with the horses and so forth.

Most of the time I worked alone in the fields, although occasionally the farmer's wife joined me. This was not agricultural training – I produced cheap work and I received room and board for it. Towards evening, following an old Dutch proverb, the boss would show up and do a little bit of his own work next to me ("When the sun stands in the West, the lazybones work best."). My hours of spreading manure, or weeding, or pulling beets, or carting around with the horse, were hours of peace and often deep contemplation. In addition, I had some delicious moments of reading at night in my own room, or even during resting time after the noon meal.

Inspiring Writers

One of my spiritual mainstays was Jehuda Halevy, the Spanish, Jewish poet who died in 1141. I was in love with the great medieval Hebraist. I had succeeded in getting the old Insel edition of his poems in the original, as well as philosopher Franz Rosenzweig's German re-creations. I do admit that I had many near mystical feelings when I immersed myself in Jehuda Halevy at that period, lying in my attic at the farmer's house after a hard day's work. I could savor those precious moments before going to sleep, and I could think in a kind of abstract fashion about our troubles and the dangerous future, about the fate of Ilse's parents and of so many of our friends, about our loneliness, and about the fact that we were hopelessly cut off from our loved ones.

There was certainly no dialogue there, no response from Halevy's spirit out of heaven, or anything outside my own ruminations and spells of enthusiasm over a wonderful Hebrew phrase. I am sure that the hopelessness of our situation contributed to the overcharged state of my nerves and my belief that supernatural events were occurring. I did my own translations of a few of Halevy's poems and of modern Hebrew poems with my own commentaries. Those translations into German found their way into the publications of the Hechalutz *and one or two Dutch Zionist journals. This was surely no great literary achievement of the 20-year-old, and all of it has deservedly been lost.*

For some psychological reason that I do not understand, my father typically disparaged his own accomplishments in this way.

Compared with many of my fellow-trainees of whom there were a dozen or two in the vicinity, I enjoyed great advantages that got me through the difficult period preceding my entry into hiding on August 16, 1942. My actual working conditions were among the best, comparatively speaking. But, above all, there was Ilse. We were able to see each other regularly. At first, she was on a farm not far away, owned by cousins of my own boss, deeply religious and decent people who were kind and understanding to both of us. They had little use for cousin Gast and his pro-German opinions.

In 1939, shortly after losing everything on Kristallnacht, *Ilse's parents had been deported from their home in Ludwigshafen, Germany to the Gurs concentration camp near the Pyrenees in France. Some mail contact was still possible through Ilse's cousin Ernst Gern in Switzerland. At one point, Ilse had received word from her mother that Ilse's father had died of starvation in the camp. Distraught by the news, Ilse hurt herself splitting wood on her farm with an axe. She then decided to ask for a transfer to the Kolthoff family as a housemaid where she might earn a few extra guilders to send to her mother and where she would feel safer than working on a farm.*

The transfer was approved by the Deventer Vereeniging, and thus the Jewish Kolthoff family in Almelo became a second home for both of us, despite the somewhat awkward status of Ilse working for them as a domestic. Clearly, the ideal of training for Palestine had gone out the window, replaced by a focus on survival as the Nazi machine grew increasingly threatening. To have one's girlfriend as close by as I had Ilse – that was the most any one of us fellows in training could ask for. It made life bearable. Then there were many new friends. Their number had grown as the months went by, those ever more worrisome months with the Germans tightening the vise. We could spend an occasional evening with friends and thus get a glimpse of "normal" life. Just being able to get away for a few hours from the farm, the manure, the idiocies of the boss – this was bliss.

Music as Resistance

Dick Kolthoff, a man with whom I developed a "warm understanding" was the head of the family for whom Ilse worked. Although he had long since removed himself from the Jewish tradition and had adopted Buddhist philosophy as his way of life, he came from old Dutch Jewish stock. Our common meeting ground was classical music for which he had a deep love. I can still see him handling his phonograph records with something bordering on worship – Beethoven's last string quartets were his favorites. He would just sit there in silence and let that heavenly music fill his heart and ours, oblivious to the Nazis and the farm, the dirt and the misery, and the many frightening rumors around us. Those evenings with music in the Kolthoff home belong to the moments in my life that left a lasting imprint. They reminded me of those study sessions with Martin Buber, years earlier in the Munich congregation, when we heard the Nazis stomp through the street with their jackboots, singing their bloodthirsty songs while Buber calmly explained the meaning of the prophet Jonah to us.

The Kolthoff family's love of music extended beyond listening to recordings. They also arranged live home performances in the spring of 1942. Once or twice, they had house guests, well-noted pianists such as Miss Taussig from Vienna, for whom they sponsored a private concert, combining charity with an exquisite musical experience. Another artist was pianist and composer James Simon. We corresponded with each other for a few months after his appearance in Almelo, and he even dedicated one of his compositions to me. I remember that it bore the inscription "to the Jehuda Halevy lover..."

One of James Simon's postcards covered in tiny letters later appeared in Dad's New Jersey basement.

The concerts were held in private homes of the social and cultural elite in little Almelo, all of whom were friends of the K's. In this fashion, people expressed their interest in the fine arts, so mercilessly suppressed by the Nazis, but also their spirit of resistance to the occupiers. I remember the exact programs of both Miss Taussig's and James Simon's piano recitals. These musical evenings were an example of cultural activities that I experienced as resistance.[52] The clandestine atmosphere, the almost conspiratorial mood, was something of the order of the illegal gatherings of Jewish artists and scientists in the Soviet Union in our own time. Those of us who know something about Jewish history easily see repetitions of these phenomena.

At the time, my new and old friends began to discuss "hiding possibilities" in a vague manner.[53] I cannot say that I was particularly interested, since I still dreamt that the war would be over before Ilse and I would receive the call-up to report for "Harvest Duty" in Germany. I was not at all sure that I would want to go underground so I did not discuss these prospects with Ilse at all. In addition, being removed from such large Jewish centers as Amsterdam reduced our knowledge of the ever-increasing anti-Jewish measures. All we knew was that we had not heard from many friends who had been sent to Mauthausen. Since February 1941, the word "Mauthausen" induced enormous fear and hung over us like a dark cloud. When suddenly, according to the police order of April 28, 1942, we had to wear the Jewish star [German: Judenstern or Hebrew: Magen David] we read that Mauthausen was the threatened penalty for any Jew caught not wearing it, or having it sewn too loosely on their coat.

I was fortunate that many of my newly won Dutch friends – Jews and non-Jews – came to visit me on the farm. But the boss did not like that at all. He thought that I would work more slowly, but instead I worked faster when somebody walked beside me while I raked the ground or plowed with the horse. In retrospect, those visits during working hours were ill-advised. I remember some of these people with a heavy heart. Good people who were victims of their own misguided idealism. The underground Communist Party used them for foolhardy terrorist actions against the German military. In the flower of their youth, they were executed on the spot.

My boss remembered the names of my visitors. Had he wanted, he could have put two and two together, and if not betray those people outright to the Nazi authorities, he could have gossiped about them. I certainly was never careful enough. And I want to stress that we were totally uninformed about the ultimate plans of the Nazis. The BBC, our only source of outside news, used to broadcast downright inanities at that time, in typical British fashion. I distinctly remember listening with some friends in the early summer of 1942 to a clandestine radio-set. At that point mass deportations of Jews from Holland had already begun. One such evening, "Shakespeare in review" was beamed to the Netherlands and listened to by many people at the risk of their lives!

Dad wrote to his parents: *I live quite peacefully on the farm, and if things continue as they are, then I can simply wait things out. The work isn't difficult for me, and I have plenty of free time to read or study. I also go into Almelo itself quite often. Some of my translations have been published, and Prof. Lefkowitz, previously a resident of Breslau, Germany, sent me high praise for them. I was very pleased about that. I am also doing much better financially thanks to my wages, minimal though they are. I may not be able to make big purchases, but I can buy something useful occasionally.*

In a follow-up letter to his parents three weeks later, Dad raised "one last idea" for getting out of Holland.

The man from the Comité's emigration office agreed it was a good idea to apply to the German emigration office, emphasizing the fact that I am a minor who desires to be with his family to help support them. I don't know if that application has any chance of being approved, but one mustn't lose hope. The matter is tied up with things that are beyond my knowledge. I have really done everything that it was in my power to do, and now we just must wait, as hard as that is to accept. It has been almost two years since we last saw each other.

The Horse Story

Dad experienced "miracles" several times during the Hitler years. In the course of being interrogated in Buchenwald in late 1938, for example, he miraculously knew to play dumb, frustrating his interrogators who wanted to be sexually aroused by Dad's stories. The "Horse Story" was another such miracle. This was an event that took place during the final months of Dad's stay at farmer Gast's.

It was a dismal day in late fall or early winter 1941-2. The news of Ilse's poor father who had wasted away in Gurs weighed heavily on me. As usual, my boss sat in his house smoking his cigar by the cozy fire, letting me do the work outside. My task was to haul beets with an old three-wheel wagon, a cart typical for that part of rural Holland. The wagon was drawn by the older and stupider of our two horses, a decrepit, emaciated nag getting more useless by the day.

The boss had warned me to make sure that the horse never took a step backward and thus would bump into the front part of the wagon while I was loading it. I had always tried my best to avoid this. However, on that afternoon, the horse in an unguarded moment made that one step and promptly got one of its hind legs caught. There was no escape. The horse fell, groaning with pain, and with it, the wagon keeled over. No matter what I tried, the horse could not free its leg but only managed to get it wedged in more tightly. It must have suffered agonizing pain. It seemed to me then – as it seems to me today – that there was absolutely no solution to this crisis. Either the horse would have to be destroyed or the wagon would have to be sawed apart, and I don't think the latter would have been possible because of the heavy metal parts. There was no such thing as insurance. I personally would have been held responsible for the loss of the horse and although this might seem somewhat ridiculous today, it loomed as a real, dreadful possibility. It was the end of the world for me.

I was desperate. I could not leave the horse for a moment and run to the farmhouse for help. And even if help were to come, there was little one could do, perhaps anesthetize the horse in some fashion and extract its leg. Whoever reads these lines may think that all of this is blown way out of proportion. It is not. For me – and I can even now, after 40 years, put myself into that situation totally – it was like imminent death. The farmer would yell at me, throw me out – and where would I go? My anxiety could be compared to Sartre's No Exit*. It was that bad! I began to pray, as intensely as I have ever prayed.*

To be sure, there were many desperate reasons for prayer later, but I never prayed as fearfully, as desperately, as at that moment. Even in the most crucial moments during the underground, such as the day Ilse saved my life during the November 1944 razzia in Rotterdam, I did not pray so hard. I was filled with an animal-like instinct to survive. Alone with that agonizing horse in a field on a cold and miserable gray November afternoon, there was nothing left for me but prayer.

I can swear today that these circumstances were as I am describing them, and that from a purely technical or mechanical point of view there was no way to free the horse's leg. But then it happened, lightning-like. I had the feeling of an answer, of a reaching down towards me to offer immediate assistance, unquestioning, quick, effective. For a moment I thought it was Mammiah who had interceded on my behalf for a miracle from heaven, although I did not believe in any of those things.

Just when I was near despair, the horse unexpectedly pulled its leg out of the vise and jumped up on all fours, badly bruised, to be sure, and highly nervous, but otherwise none the worse for the experience. I wept. I could not understand how this happened, and I cannot understand it today. I quickly unharnessed the nag and tied it to a fence to rest up, and then I started running to the farmhouse as fast as I could, vaulting a few barbed-wire fences, tearing my pants, and injuring my bottom in the process, but that mattered little. I yelled to the boss who came quickly, examined the horse's leg, snorted "that's real Jew work," and returned just as quickly to his stove and his cigar. It was an especially biting remark, calculated to sting. His mother offered to fix my pants.

This event with the horse, in all its banality, remains one of the great and decisive mysteries of my life. I think of it frequently. The mystery is the same today as on the day it happened. I cannot explain it. When sometimes I think that a "helping hand" reached down to me, I catch myself for being so presumptuous. I certainly did not deserve being rescued from that agony and there were moments of far greater despair in the lives of people ten times better than me. All of this is true.

The mystery remains and probably will be with me until my dying day. I cannot explain it, nor can I explain the distinct feeling at the time that my prayer was answered on the spot. I did not become religious again because of that experience. That happened much later. I just experienced an event which brought instant relief from overwhelming anxiety and which – this is so important – went against all laws of nature or mechanics. There was simply no way in which the leg of that poor nag could have been extracted from its iron trap. But there it was, and is, and will be. Today I am not ashamed to call that moment, when the horse miraculously freed its leg, a true religious experience, something offered to me, some undeserved display to me of divine grace.

It is unclear how the horse extricated its leg, but it is possible to understand why the story meant so much to my father. He identified with the horse and saw it as a symbol of his predicament – stuck and yearning to be free. He prayed for a miracle that would liberate the horse, and it occurred. That prayer was also for himself.

Shushu

Numerous people, organizations, and what Dad called "miracles" saved his life between the mid-1930s and 1945.

But perhaps foremost among these was my dear friend, Shushu, a charismatic half-Jewish German Zionist, two years older than me. Since meeting at the Zionist training camp in Germany in 1938, Shushu and I shared our lives whenever we could. I adored Shushu, and I believe the feeling was mutual. When we met on the farm in Ellguth, we sang, danced, and burst with joy as we worked in the fields or milked the cows. After Kristallnacht, Shushu and I were thrown into the Buchenwald concentration camp together. There, too, we found bits of time to study Hebrew poetry as we sat side by side on the top bunk in our filthy barrack. When released from Buchenwald, we emigrated separately to Holland and worked on nearby farms in the Almelo region. We stayed in close touch until Shushu killed himself on January 27, 1943, in the Dutch town of Breda.

In January 1940, after Shushu and I had been in the Netherlands for a year, he grew tired of his farming apprenticeship and became a kind of independent agent, traveling throughout the Netherlands, Belgium, France, and Switzerland, trying to find possible evacuation routes for Jews. Shushu was always on the go, gaining him access to knowledge that others, including me, did not have. At that time, his focus for helping Jews was the "fleeing option," but soon it changed to the "hiding option."

Shushu's resistance focused less on fighting the Nazis than on helping the Jews. Most important, when he realized that the situation was dire, he dropped the nearly impossible task of helping Jews flee and urged Jews – in one-on-one secret conversations – to go into hiding. In many cases, he also secured hiding places for them. Shushu was a true leader – both practical and inspirational. He gathered data, drew conclusions, advised people what to do, and then helped them do it. In the Netherlands, France, and Belgium, he identified potential safe houses, working with others to set up an underground railroad.

Hiding

In July 1942, a significant and tragic month in the history of Dutch Jewry, Shushu learned that a mass deportation of Dutch Jews was underway.

On the 14th of the month, in what we now know was the first step, a train bringing 1,132 Jews "to the east" left Amsterdam. The initial leg of the trip was short, a 165-kilometer ride from Amsterdam to the Westerbork transit camp in the center of the country. The next day, this transport's passengers were sent to Auschwitz...the first of 94 trains stuffed with Jews. Shushu found out that the mass deportations would be disguised in a notice that the Nazis would send to every Jewish person in the country, telling recipients they had to report at a particular place and time – usually tomorrow – to serve in the "Harvest Help Program" in Germany.

In this context, Shushu contacted me and then met me in Almelo. On that visit, Shushu gave me a unique gift – information about how to save my life by hiding. He not only persuaded me to hide but encouraged me to act as soon as possible. Little did either of us know that of all the Jews in the Netherlands at that time, those with the greatest chance of being alive at the end of the war were precisely those who had become "onderduikers," the Dutch word for people – especially Jews – who hid.

For me, the decision to become an "onderduiker" emerged directly from my talk with Shushu, the most important conversation of my life.

My decision to hide came on an afternoon in August 1942. It must have been a Sunday, for my farmer would not have given me half a day off otherwise. I had gone to visit Ilse at the K's. Shushu arrived by train early in the afternoon. We started to go for a walk, just the two of us, Shushu and me. Shushu told me that he had come to Almelo to visit the farmer for whom he had worked for a few months immediately after our arrival in Holland. He was going to ask his former boss whether he could hide on the homestead. When Shushu and I entered the woods, I listened carefully. Shushu, my dearest friend, knew what he was talking about.

Shushu had learned that the official deportation order for the Jews in the Netherlands had just been sent, secretly, to various Nazi officers in the country, and somebody, somewhere, had intercepted one of the letters. Although we both had witnessed the growing attack on the Jews by the Nazis, Shushu thought things were coming to a climax. He spoke about deportations to forced labor camps in the Balkans and Poland. There was a false rumor that those who reported as volunteers would get preferential treatment and would be permitted to choose their own camp.

Shushu was quite secretive... When I pressed him for details, he said that he had just listened to the BBC, and for a few days in a row, their official line had been that the war would be over in three to four months at most. For that reason, it would be much wiser not to report for "Harvest Help," but rather to go into hiding right away. He said we should prepare ourselves for the work of rebuilding the Zionist youth movement after the collapse of Germany, which was just around the corner.

Shushu had an additional argument for hiding: Large-scale deportations had already begun from Amsterdam to Westerbork and then to the east into Germany, but not even Shushu was aware that these transports were anything but roundups for help in the harvest. Although he didn't know exactly what the transports were for, he asked me,

"What's the sense of risking our lives in the Allied bombardments of Germany that now occur on a daily basis?" His ideas sounded reasonable. And thus, he convinced me during that afternoon's conversation, our last one. Then and there I made up my mind not to report for the work camp should the call-up arrive. Shushu saved my life.

Immediately I started to contact my non-Jewish Dutch friends, and so did Ilse, whom I told about my talk with Shushu. One of our friends, H. te Riet, the first farmer for whom I worked, promised me that very evening that he would help me when the time came. What an amazing man H. te Riet was![54] *There are others like him. But when Shushu and I returned from our walk, we told our plans only to Ilse and Mr. te Riet. Shushu left on a cheerful note. That was the last time I saw him.*

Those who chose not to hide should not be criticized. Not everyone was able to choose this option. Not everyone was able to save themselves by doing something as strange as hiding. People who suffer from claustrophobia cannot hide. Nor can infants whose crying cannot be controlled. Nor can people with illnesses like asthma or digestive disorders requiring frequent use of bathrooms, or those who are obese and can't fit into tiny crawl spaces, or those who cough regularly, even those who snore loudly or talk in their sleep. And so on.

The Decision-making Process

In a few rare cases, people hid spontaneously. But typically, going into hiding was a five-step planned process leading to someone's near total disappearance. **The first step** was to understand the need to hide and **the second** was to make the decision to hide. For many people, this was the most difficult part.

I had relatives in Amsterdam who just could not bring themselves to do it. Others couldn't figure out how to do it. Yet others, on principle, did not hide. For example, the Dutch Jewish woman, Etty Hillesum, had become a typist for the Judenrat, a job which entitled her to travel back and forth between Amsterdam and Westerbork. She used this opportunity to help the Jews incarcerated in Westerbork, but ultimately, she was swallowed up in the mass forced transportation to Auschwitz. She could have hidden but didn't. Etty's diary records her reasons.

> Many accuse me of indifference and passivity when I refuse to go into hiding; they say that I have given up... [but] I feel safe in God's arms.... People often get worked up when I say it doesn't really matter whether I go on the trains or somebody else does. But I don't think that I would feel happy if I were exempted from what so many others must suffer.[55]

I was not paralyzed by fear. I had made a commitment to Mammiah to survive. Since I was in high school, I had tried to live by the creed of not obeying the Nazis, although I didn't always succeed. I was in love with my girlfriend and wanted to marry her. I ached to see my family again. I had a lot to live for.

The **third step** (after deciding to hide) was to find a person who would shelter the Jewish person or affiliate with a group that would find a hiding place. The crucial point was that a person could not hide without someone's help, and obviously, the people who were hiding others were almost never Jews. Thus, it was crucial for any Jew who wanted to hide to consider which of their non-Jewish acquaintances might agree to help. Many Jews did not have, or no longer had, such acquaintances.

Hiding conditions varied widely. In some horrific cases, Jewish children or women were taken in and sexually abused.[56] There were situations in which the hosts betrayed "their own Jews" as a way of getting a financial reward. Hiding circumstances differed in other ways. Some were rural, with the benefit of food but perhaps limited interaction with like-minded people. In some cases, the resistance organization paid the hosts to care for their "guests," and in others, there was no payment. Sometimes there was tension in the household or limited interaction with the hosts. And in other situations, the shared places were filled with love and understanding.

The **fourth step** was to prepare to hide. The difficulty stemmed from the fact that no one knew how long they would be in hiding and what they would need. How do you pack for an indeterminate period of hiding? Should people bring money? What clothes should they bring? How about books, pens, and paper? The more items people brought, the more difficult it would be to move from place to place, and the more challenging it would be to obliterate signs of their presence should the Germans discover their hiding place. In addition, if one opted to hide, all preparations had to be in place when the call-up letter came because the recipient would be instructed to report the very next day or suffer dire consequences.

The **fifth step** was to hide, to cross the divide between being part of society and disappearing. Upon receiving a deportation order, a Jewish person could either comply or vanish. There was no other option except suicide because it was nearly impossible to leave the country. Although many people disagree, Israeli scholar Chana Benninga Arnon wrote that by August 1942, it was well understood that the "unknown fate awaiting the deportees was indeed extermination and therefore nothing could be lost by trying to evade arrest."[57]

Two leaders of the Dutch "Palestine Pioneers" who chose the hiding option were Dutch-born Menahem Pinkhof and German-born Joachim Simon, or Shushu as everyone called him. Dad didn't get advice from the Deventer Zionist organization, whose leaders undoubtedly were struggling with the same conflicts for themselves. One of the *chalutzot* [Hebrew: female pioneers], Miriam Pinkhof, gave testimony after the war about the need to be prepared to hide. "At first, after the beginning of the deportations many lost their lives because they were unprepared mentally and practically to go underground; they were inexperienced and lacked hiding places and contacts. In addition, many questioned the decision to go underground. The ideology was that one must identify with the suffering of the Jewish people, share its fate, not escape it. People asked themselves if it was practical to go underground and whether they would be able to cope with the hardships of an underground life. They shrank from taking such an irreversible step that would lead to unknown consequences."[58]

The Westerweel Group

Like Shushu, Menahem Pinkhof alerted "Palestine Pioneers" to prepare to hide.[59] His girlfriend, Mirjam, made a connection with Joop (a nickname for Johan) Westerweel (1899-1944), and his wife, Willie (short for Wilhelmina), who had by mid-1942 already been involved in some small-scale illegal action on behalf of Jews. Shushu and Joop Westerweel, a devout Christian, pacifist teacher of young children, and a conscientious objector, created an informal organization that used exclusively non-violent means of resistance. Called "The Westerweel Group," it was the only Dutch resistance force where Jews and non-Jews worked together. In 1942, when Joop saw a deportation order with his own eyes for the first time, he decided the time had come to devote himself to large-scale rescue work.[60] He was not asked to help – he stepped forward.

Through his Jewish friends, Joop Westerweel met young *chalutzim* in Loosdrecht, a small town near Amsterdam, and was impressed with their idealism. When the 50 Loosdrecht youngsters received a tip from the Jewish Council on August 15, 1942, that the children were about to be deported to the Westerbork transit camp, Joop and other group members provided safe hiding places for every one of them. Evacuating these young Jewish residents to safety was the Westerweel Group's first action.

Joop Westerweel was a charismatic figure whose passionate belief in freedom inspired others. At the peak of its activity, the Westerweel Group arranged escapes from internment camps, found hideouts, and managed forgery and printing operations to produce identification papers and ration cards. Dutch historian Dirk de Klein stated, "the Westerweel-Simon group smuggled 200-300 Jews through Belgium and France and then into neutral Switzerland and Spain. Other estimates put the number at 150."[61]

Joop himself was captured in March 1944 while crossing back into the Netherlands at the Dutch/Belgian border. The Germans transferred him to the Vught concentration camp in southern Holland where he was tortured and then executed on August 11, 1944. In late 1944, James MacDonald of *The New York Times* published a description of Joop's torture, parts of which were reprinted two years later in *The Black Book: The Nazi Crime against the Jewish People*.[62] Imprisoned in the same camp, Willie was forced to witness her husband's execution. One of the four Westerweel children, Marta, later settled in Israel. A national hero of the Dutch Resistance, Joop is memorialized by a monument near Vught, into which the names of other Vught victims are also etched.

In 1964, 20 years after his murder, the Jewish National Fund [JNF] planted a small forest in Israel in Joop Westerweel's memory.

An Official Call-up Notice Arrives

I soon completed the initial steps to become an "onderduiker." I made the decision to hide, I found someone to hide me, and I was preparing the money I had saved and the items I would take with me. There was one step left – to hide. Two weeks after that memorable talk with Shushu, I received my official notice in the mail: "You must report for 'Harvest Help' in a labor camp." By that time, I had already made all my preparations. I kept everything secret, even from my closest friends. Today I think this was foolish, and perhaps a bit selfish on my part. I should have influenced others to go into hiding. Of course, Ilse knew all about it and had made her own preparations.

Many Jews, among them some of my friends, believed that we ought to join the "Harvest Help" to support elderly and sick Jews. I don't remember our discussing why the elderly, young children or sick people were recruited for "Harvest Help" in the first place. Yes, that idea to help the weak while we were still young, strong, and well-fed because of our stay at the farm – these thoughts moved quite a few in our group, and many others as well, to obey the German orders! I bow my head even today when I think of those good people, boys and girls who were highly motivated. They were greater heroes than many of us.

My heart aches for them. They were so idealistic. Where, o where, was Allied intelligence then? And where was the Jewish Agency? One word from the BBC, one word from our Zionist leaders who by now were in safe lands, would have sufficed to save those beautiful people. They would all have gone into hiding and most of them would have survived just as we did. Instead, the BBC continued to speak of an early end to the war, and it would intersperse this political wisdom with reports of festivals in August of 1942![63] *As if anyone in Holland could attend.*

Half a year later, the decision to hide or not was moot. The die was cast, and even the most idealistic among us would not of their free will go to a labor camp to help the old and the weak. By that time, word had already gotten out about the true nature of Auschwitz. And surely everybody saw that the war was going to last longer than the BBC predicted. I felt apologetic towards those of our group who had so steadfastly considered it their moral and Zionist duty to help other Jews. I also felt uneasy in the family of farmer Gast, where I still lived, when arguments about obedience to the Germans went back and forth.

The problems with farmer Gast and his family were that they confused the perpetrator and the victim. And they didn't differentiate between just and unjust laws. They thought only of "the law." They didn't recognize that a law not reached by a fair process need not be obeyed. Gast represented a large segment of the Dutch people that was willing to go along with the Nazis because "a law is a law" no matter how it was created. *To my boss Gast, resistance people and those who went into hiding were outlaws who made it bad for all the other Hollanders and who caused the Germans to issue ever stricter regulations, week after week. Perhaps to quell my loneliness, I kept up my discouraging conversations with Gast. When some of the brave guerillas were sentenced to the firing squad, Gast would say that they got what they had coming to them. It was stupid of me, up to the very last moment of leaving the Gast family, to take the opposite view. But I did it anyhow.*

Fortunately, however, there was a different point – on which such people as farmer Gast agreed – i.e., not to snitch on people who broke the law. The commitment of the pro-German farmer not to snitch saved my life. Perhaps for this, he should have been honored in some way by someone after the war.

Looking at the situation in retrospect, my having visitors on the farm seems unforgivable. How easy it would have been for Gast just to tell someone the name of a friend who had come to visit me! Instead of keeping my mouth shut, several times during the family meals I said that if I were to receive the call-up, I would not go. The boss would get annoyed with me and point out that Gerd who was a chalutz on the farm of the boss' father and brothers would of course go, because he was a good, law-abiding fellow. Gerd was indeed a good soul. I prayed many times that he and his friend would be able to give each other support and go to their death in dignity.

In early August 1942, during those last weeks of my stay at farmer Gast's, the reports of razzias and call-ups for labor camps increased daily. I made my preparations. Everything had to be done during daylight, unfortunately, because a curfew was in force after nightfall. In addition, we had to turn in our bicycles. Ilse walked over to my farm a few times from nearby Almelo to be with me. One night she slept in the stable, not far from the pigs! The few clothes I had, as well as my books and other belongings, were packed into my ship trunk and left in Almelo for safe keeping.

By that time, mail had to be sent clandestinely. I tried to get a note to my parents via Dr. K., brother of Mr. Kolthoff, through his home in Sweden, and I think that my folks learned some time later that I had no intention to report for 'Harvest Help.' Rumors, radio messages, all kinds of stories filled the air in that intensely charged period of August 1942. But, in the last analysis, we were terribly alone, alone with our decision to go underground. I do not think that I ever felt as lonesome as during those few days preceding my going into hiding. Although I almost lost my life several times in the remaining nearly three years of the Occupation, the last moments before hiding were some of the most difficult.

It was easy for the Occupying Government to know that I existed and where I lived because from the day I arrived in the Netherlands to the day I left, I had to be registered. On April 30, 1942, four months before the Harvest Help notice arrived, I had gotten an identity card from the Joodsche Raad voor Amsterdam, the Jewish Council that managed the Jews on behalf of the Germans. The photograph in my identity card depicts me as thin but healthy. For some reason, I was listed as living in Aadorp with the profession of teacher. The two leaders of the Joodsche Raad, Mr. Asscher and Professor Cohen, both signed the card.

For about 25,000 of the 140,000 Jews living in the Netherlands, the call-up notice was the figurative straw that broke the camel's back. It was one thing to be discovered during a *razzia*, thrown onto a truck, and driven to a collection center. It was another matter altogether to receive a personalized mailed directive and choose to obey. Not reporting for deportation was a crime vastly different from going to concerts, riding a tram, or not wearing the Jewish star. Jews understood what being barred from swimming pools meant. But "deportation" and "Harvest Help" were undefined and thus particularly frightening.

Although most Jews did comply with the order, a small minority decided to "disappear." *I was part of that small group and "dove" underground on August 16, 1942, a full month after receiving the order that I was supposed to carry out immediately.* A review of Jewish responses to the anti-Jewish decrees since the start of the Occupation shows how out-of-character it was for Jews not to obey the round-up call. Jews probably believed that they were alive precisely because, up to that date, they had followed all the rules. Now they had to switch gears and recognize that only by disobeying could they survive. A Dutch woman three to four years younger than Dad wrote: "It was not until the summer of '42 that it finally dawned on us that if we were going to save ourselves, we had better do something about it – soon."[64]

In Holland, there was at least one town that did things differently.[65] Against the advice of the Jewish Council of Amsterdam, the three leaders of the Jewish community in Enschede – Sig Menko, Gerard Sanders, and Isidoor Van Dam – convinced their Jewish community to go into hiding. These three men had access to funds, power in the community and a well-developed underground movement headed by a prominent Protestant minister, Leendert Overduin. By the end of the war, the community in Enschede had saved 500 Jews out of a population of 1,300 (38.5 percent) whereas the survival rate for Jews in the Netherlands was around 15 percent. The leadership of the town of Almelo, less than half an hour's train ride away, did not consider it a community responsibility to help Jews.

Even though the Jewish Council leaders were loath to compile lists of Jews for deportation, they complied with the government order to do so. The leaders "threatened to resign if [the deportations] continued, but they never summoned the courage to do so."[66] Perhaps to ease their conscience or share the blame, some of them even consulted a rabbi to see which action they should take based on Jewish law [*halacha*].[67]

Relying solely on Shushu's advice, Dad became committed to hiding.

But then, in my foolishness, I told the farmer's family that I had received my slip and had no intention to answer the call-up. In fact, I planned to go into hiding the next day! As expected, they strongly disapproved. "You must obey the law," they said, "and it was no wonder that the Jews were hated by the Germans because they always used tricks to slip out from under the law."

A Brazen Response

The feared notice arrived in the mail. Just a mimeographed slip sent first class, forwarded, if I am not mistaken, by the Dutch police, ordering me to report for the "Harvest Help" at a certain gathering place. I had to appear the day after receipt of the notice. How bizarre – you receive your death notice on a mimeographed slip in the mail. If I remember well, that reporting place, a collection center for our part of Holland, was quite a distance from Almelo, some 30 or 40 miles! It seems that the Germans expected us to walk there. After all, bicycles were requisitioned, and Jews could not use public transportation.

The order to "appear the day after receipt of the notice" was part of the Nazi strategy of terror and confusion. Everything had to be done quickly. "*Schnell! Schnell!* [Quickly! Quickly!]" the Nazi guards always barked at Jews while pushing them into trains or gas chambers or pulling them out of their hiding places or beds. Being forced to move quickly left no time to strategize, to enlist help, or even to organize one's thoughts. If a person had not yet made plans to hide, it would be nearly impossible to do so in the one day between receiving the notice and appearing at the "collection site."

Next came one of my favorite stories of resistance, one of my proudest moments. When I received my notice, I became so furious that I tore it in two or three pieces, put it back in the envelope, sealed it and put the return address on it! I walked to the mailbox half a mile from the farm during the noon meal and sacrificed a few pennies for the stamp to feel some sort of victory. Nothing could have been more stupid! Others had received their slips and either answered them, applied for a postponement, or ignored them and gone into hiding. Again, as I look back upon my attitude at that time, I did not understand in the slightest the true nature of the catastrophe. I approached the situation, so to speak, with an air of normalcy, as though I was arguing with the proper authorities for a bicycle license or some extra food coupons.

After the war, I spoke often with pride about mailing that destroyed call-up notice, and about my defiance and courage. I now believe that ripping up the notice was intended to dispute the authority of the government. Returning the torn sheet of paper was a rebellious insult, which neither the Dutch Nazis nor the Germans could have misunderstood.

Just as Jews debated whether they should hide, so too, Gentiles debated whether they should help Jews hide. As one Dutch Christian wrote: "We talked often... about what we could do if a chance should come to help some of our Jewish friends."[68] They, too, had to act quickly and not just talk.

I asked the Gasts to take my big trunk for safe-keeping and gave them a few of my belongings (my good bike had already been appropriated) as gifts. I took a small suitcase and said goodbye to the Gasts. I walked through the fields on that beautiful August day, but I did so with a heavy heart and close to tears – something I had to try to camouflage by my brashness with the farmer's family. I wore several layers of clothes and sweated profusely. I was sure that my Jewish star protected me. If I were stopped, I could always say that I was en route to the call-up.

Queen Wilhelmina

Ensconced in England with the Dutch government-in-exile since the start of the war, Queen Wilhelmina decided to visit the US for 48 days from June 24 to August 11, 1942, as a guest of the US government. She vacationed in Lee, Massachusetts and visited New

York City, Boston, and Albany. She addressed the US Congress on August 5, 1942, and was the first queen to do so. As could be expected, her address to Congress consisted of platitudes, fantasies, and omissions. She claimed that her people were engaged in "resistance, resistance until the end, resistance in every practicable shape or form." The truth was that many, if not most, of the crimes against the Jews were carried out by Dutch people, especially the Green Police. The special and extraordinary plight of Dutch Jews was not even mentioned in her speech! The period of Queen Wilhelmina's vacation was one of the worst for the Jews of her country. It coincided with the Germans ordering the Jews of the Netherlands to register for "Harvest Help." Nine days after the Queen addressed the US Congress, Dad went into hiding and the Queen continued her vacation.

The Star of David

Three months earlier, all Jews in the Netherlands had been required to affix onto their outerwear "Stars of David" containing the Dutch word *Jood* [Jew] in Hebrew-looking black letters. The stars had to be the size of a palm of the hand and sewn to clothing at chest level so they could easily be seen.[69]

The star was a complicated psychological issue. For some Jews, their previously hidden or sometimes insignificant identity as a Jew was now obvious to everyone. Many Jews were humiliated. Others were defiantly proud. A few non-Jews wore the star as a sign of solidarity. Some memoirists wrote that the streets of their towns looked "ridiculous," with so many people wearing star-adorned clothing. In Holland, an underground newspaper expressed its support of Jews by printing alternative stars, inscribed with the words "Jews and non-Jews are one and the same." Had everyone in the Netherlands worn the star, Jews might have been protected.

I wore the star when it became mandatory to do so. But I took it off or used clothing onto which no star had been sewn when I chose not to be identified as a Jew. This was very risky.

A Matter of Life and Death

Only 21 years old, Dad had been on his own since he left Germany right before his 18th birthday. Now he had a life-or-death decision to make and hardly anyone to turn to for advice. Shushu had left Almelo.

Forty-two years later when remembering the days leading up to hiding, I still feel the pangs of loneliness. Having no family nearby, unsure if I should confide in people, and recognizing that the whole world had turned its back on me – weighed heavily. Here I was, helpless in a country whose government was determined to kill me for the crime of being a Jew. I poured out my heart in an imaginary conversation with Mammiah.

Dear Mammiah, A prime mover in the chain of events... leading to my survival – was the decision I just made (August 1942) when I was influenced by Shushu, and made up my mind not to join my friends at a "labor camp" to help with the harvest, but to say NO; NO to the Nazi authorities that cloaked themselves in a mantle of lawfulness; NO to anybody who wanted to order me around; NO to anybody who wanted to control my life. I did not guess, neither did any of my friends, that total annihilation, brutal torture, and murder would await me if I went to the camps. I only thought of you, Mammiah, and what you said to me that afternoon, long ago, when we sat on the sofa in our living room in Gunzenhausen, when I was a little over 11 years old. Survive!

I imagined my mother heartily approving of my choice to resist the Nazis by hiding. Even though at first, I felt unsure, the more I thought about it, the more I realized that hiding was the only means for possible survival. I owed it to my mother to try. Rabbi Hillel, who lived in the first century B.C.E., wrote in Pirkei Avot *[Ethics of the Fathers], "If I am not for myself, who will be for me? If I am only for myself, what am I? And if not now, when?" More than 2,000 years later, I was struggling with these same questions, especially the first.*

The days passed. I did not report to the collection site. I knew only one thing about what would happen next – that E.V.,[70] the young Jewish woman whom I had met at the Kolthoff house, was my contact, and that she would send someone to pick me up when the time was right. I needed trust and patience, both of which were in short supply.

When I left the Gast farmhouse for the last time, I went to Almelo on foot, straight to the Kolthoffs' house where Ilse was still serving as a domestic. Did the few people who saw me on the way look at me in a curious fashion? Was it possible to tell that I was planning to go underground? As soon as I arrived in the house, I did another silly thing. I wrote two open postcards, one to Shushu and one to my other dear friend, Jacobus Hanneman, telling them I had gone into hiding. I wrote in Hebrew. Any German translator could have deciphered my simple message. And then the German censors would have had no difficulty finding me. Shushu and Hanneman disappeared shortly thereafter: Shushu into his resistance work and Hanneman into hiding, only to be betrayed after a few weeks. Those two boys were our unofficial, but commonly recognized, leaders.

The Process Begins

When I arrived at the Kolthoffs' house, I contacted Hennie te Riet, the first farmer for whom I had worked, the man who had offered to help me. The K. family, Ilse, and I had grown close during the preceding year, despite many differences in background and outlook, and even though the lady of the house sometimes treated Ilse shabbily as a domestic. Mr. K., with whom I had listened in silence to so many Beethoven string quartets, with whom I had savored so many unforgettable talks on Buddhism, Mr. K. my good fatherly friend, took me by the hand and finally told me what I had suspected all along. He and the entire family would do what I was about to do when their notices came.

The Kolthoffs were respected burghers in Almelo, with no lack of helpful contacts among the non-Jewish population. I knew that Ilse was provided for, although she had not yet received her call-up notice. I felt sure that she would be saved. Her contact, Judge Veth, a rare human being, was totally reliable. We had discussed this several times. Both of us were prepared. My call-up letter instructed me to go to a "collection center" where I would board a train to "participate" in the "Harvest Help" program in "the east." This slip of paper made me a slave. There was no labor contract to sign, no wages, no description of the work or housing, no promise of adequate food and medical care, or anything else.

Most disturbing, there had been no communication from friends and relatives who had already left to participate in the Harvest Help. The Jews who were told to appear at an assembly center did not know anything about what was planned for them. All tried to pack sensibly and some hid valuables in their clothing, not suspecting that the Germans would steal their jewels or cash as soon as they arrived at their destination. Construction of a genocidal machine such as that which they were encountering had never appeared before in human history. No one could imagine such a thing except those who created it.

I was targeted together with all the other Jews on Dutch soil, because official German policy was to make the Netherlands Judenrein.

Nazi headquarters instructed the occupation forces to adopt the principles and practices of the "Final Solution" articulated formally at the Wannsee Conference on January 20, 1942. The single surviving transcript of that fateful meeting at Wannsee, visible under glass on the wall of the Wannsee Museum, reports the following: "SS Lieutenant General Heydrich, Chief of Security Police and Security Service, opened the meeting by informing everyone that Reich Marshal Goering had put him in charge of preparations for the Final Solution of the Jewish Question. Heydrich was pleased to announce that the first two stages of the Final Solution had already taken place: a) forcing the Jews out of the various spheres of life of the German people; and b) forcing the Jews out of the German people's living space."[71] "Now the Nazi efforts could concentrate on killing every Jew in the German occupied lands," was a sentence said out loud.

I had made all my preparations. I cannot stress often enough that at that time – August 1942 – nobody, not even the worst pessimist, had an inkling about the true nature of the deportations or the so-called "Harvest Help." This was truly the fault of Allied intelligence, although a little over a month earlier on June 27, 1942, The New York Times *published a small article about the mass killing of Jews in various countries.*

I should have influenced others to go into hiding, as I warned Ilse. The whole idea of Harvest Help had sounded innocuous, and one could even argue that the Germans had the right to call up extra workers. But the thought of falling once again into their hands was so frightful to me that it outweighed all other considerations. In truth, I did not keep my decision a secret but shared it with the Gasts, the Kolthoffs, the te Riets, E.V., as well as Ilse. I also debated hiding with my friends. You must understand that none of us were absolutely convinced that we were doing the right thing.

What grieves me sometimes is the total lack of understanding of the motivations of those of my many friends who, in the early stage of the deportations, resolved to obey the German call. I recall the conversations we had, the arguments back and forth. Where are they now, those dear ones, who tried to convince me and others like me that we, as chalutzim, had a special task towards our people, that we would set an example, that we would impress the Germans with our will to work, our ability to do physical labor, and that we should show them our skill as farmhands. Above all, however, their argument was that we ought to accompany the elderly and the sick.

The BBC was a particularly spineless culprit and did not provide its listeners with pertinent information. On November 18, 1943, when I had hidden for more than a year, the head of the BBC warned his employees not to broadcast anything that might correct the undoubted antisemitic feelings which are held throughout the country...[England].

The BBC downplayed the Holocaust well beyond the end of the war. Despite having a reporter in Bergen-Belsen, it wouldn't air his reports until they were "confirmed" by the printed press.[72]*Even if those authorities in England did not yet know the true meaning of Auschwitz, they could have warned us not to go voluntarily to the German labor camps, not to participate in their "resettlement" programs, not to help with their harvest. All they had to do – as they did later – was to declare it a crime to cooperate with the enemy, and many more would have been convinced that going into hiding was the right thing to do.*

I did not get direction from Jewish leaders, non-Jewish community leaders, rabbis or Zionist groups.[73] *Only one person – Shushu – was sure of what to do. Where were the people and institutions who could have helped us Jews act? When the call-ups arrived, many of those leaders said that the youth should obey the law! The Zionist Youth Federation was* "against illegal action" but had not made a clear-cut decision about the call-up order.

On the other hand, an overseer of our Vereeniging, Mr. R., who had always been a decent, compassionate man, although perhaps not too perceptive, made the rounds of the farms and visited the boys and girls, to see how we were getting along. He passed through my place just a few days before I disappeared. He still had a special permit allowing him to use his bicycle.

After talking to the farmers about the weather, he took me aside and said that he himself would not go when the call-up came. "They would have to carry me to the deportation train rather than seeing me walk there on my own two feet." These were brave words. Later, while I was in hiding, I learned that Mr. R. followed along without protest. He said that he wanted to help others bear up. He, too, did not come back. My intention in writing about Mr. R. is not to ridicule him, but rather to illustrate how frightening it was to disobey and hide.

The Allies and the Rabbis

I have more criticism, this time concerning the Allies. I have always been convinced that one word from the Allies would have brought a change. Perhaps no miracles would have happened, but there certainly would have been an entirely different attitude on the part of those Jews who reported for work camp. All the Allies had to tell us was the true nature of those "harvest camps." Even if the extermination program had not yet been understood in all its monstrosity, the Allies were aware of the mass murders that had already been perpetrated, of Mauthausen where hundreds of young Jews from Holland and elsewhere, as well as Allied prisoners of war, had disappeared half a year earlier. All the Allies had to do was broadcast an appeal not to go under any circumstances, and that even a heroic and self-sacrificing argument such as "support for the people" was the wrong decision, morally, politically, and from the point of view of religious responsibility.

I also have complaints about the rabbis: If one single rabbi, one emissary from Palestine, would have broadcast a serious admonition or reminder that Pikuach Nefesh [Hebrew: saving a life] was the overriding consideration, word would have spread, and many more people would have resisted or looked for a hiding place.

In my view, Dad's charge is too harsh. Although European rabbis could not take to the airwaves, many Jews throughout Nazi-occupied Europe, including the two leaders of the Jewish Council of Amsterdam, did address questions to rabbis steeped in knowledge of the ancient texts, the source of Jewish law. In general, Jews are encouraged to ask a question (called a *sheilah*) of rabbis, who, in turn, offer a written answer (or an oral one, if necessary). This answer is called a *responsum* or *tshuvah*. A famous example from the Holocaust is the case of a man who asked a Lithuanian rabbi, "Was a person guilty according to Jewish law when he put a pillow on the face of a screaming child in a group of Jews in hiding, thereby suffocating the child but saving the group?" The *responsum* was that the man was not guilty. And the rabbi included the text that was the source of this judgement.

The Jewish Council leaders in Amsterdam sought rabbinic advice as to how to handle their Nazi-imposed task of choosing between "who should live and who should die." According to the principle of *Pikuach Nefesh*, you "shall not stand idly by the blood of your neighbor:" Jews must do everything in their power to save the life of another person. But how does one decide whom to save when so many people are at risk?

Dutch Gentiles

From the start of my stay in Holland, I befriended trustworthy non-Jewish Dutch people in the Almelo region. A Jew with no Gentile friends during the Occupation was doomed. But since everything was secret, I had not known that H. te Riet, my first farmer, for example, was himself part of the Dutch underground! H. te Riet would not tell me with whom I would hide, or where or under what circumstances.

My first concern – again a reflection of our shortsightedness and total lack of information – was... money! I had perhaps 50 Dutch guilders saved up, sufficient for about three to four weeks of food supplies, and I had some clothes and books in a big trunk. I started figuring out how much their sale would bring in. If I would eat very little, perhaps if I could also do some clandestine work, I might get through the coming three to four months until liberation time! Perhaps it would be possible to obtain a loan from some organization; my parents in America would always be good for that sum later! Te Riet said not to worry. Money was not the question – and, as it turned out, he was right. The main thing was to disappear right now, and not to answer the call-up.

Whereas Dad did not know with whom he would stay, Ilse had identified a potential helper for herself in Almelo – the lawyer and high school teacher Henriette Geertruida Veth, whom Ilse and Dad called "Judge Veth." Decades later, Ilse told an interviewer the following about Miss Veth:

Ilse: Before we went into hiding, we needed some people to talk to because at the farmer's there was no intellectual stimulation. Occasionally in the evening, Max and I went to Miss Veth, a Gentile woman. I spoke to her in a very naive way. I said, 'I want to hide. I don't know where to go.' She said, 'You come to me.' This was a few months before we went into hiding.

Interviewer: Why was it so naive?

Ilse: Because it would demand so much of this woman. She would be endangering her life. At that time no one knew much about hiding, but it meant not to accommodate the Germans. Miss Veth had a somewhat mentally disabled child. And although Miss Veth was not married, she took care of the child.

Dad also wrote about Miss Veth.

She gave herself totally to social work... Her work in juvenile justice endeared her to everybody. She was one of the most esteemed citizens of Almelo and a respected member of the bench and bar. This good woman took Ilse into her house right away, without much ado. At first, I had no idea that this was the place where Ilse would go into hiding, because we had to keep these things secret even from each other.

Despite the warm connection between them, Miss Veth asked Ilse to leave when "it became too dangerous." The problem was that her nosy neighbors had realized that suddenly Miss Veth had more food stamps than before, and that these extra stamps were probably being used to buy food for a hidden Jew. They suspected that Miss Veth was involved with an organization that stole and distributed food stamps. The neighbors were right!

When Ilse left Miss Veth's home, an underground organization sent her to "a gardener in Almelo, a great hero whose name was Mondriaan," with whom my parents remained friendly beyond the end of the war. After a year or so Ilse became restless at the Mondriaan home. The underground organization then found her a new place to hide – in Wieringen, a small northern town. In addition, Mom obtained a false *Kennkarte*, or German mandatory identity booklet, most likely stolen. The name on the card was Tina Ressen. "All they did was take out Tina's photo and put in mine," Ilse said. The card indicated that Ilse's occupation was "servant." Once she got this *Kennkarte*, she was Tina Ressen until the end of the war.

Starting the Underground Life

Many terms were used to describe what I was about to do. "Go into hiding," "go underground," "become an onderduiker," "live illegally" were some of them. Whatever it was called, I was ready. When Mr. Kolthoff said goodbye, he mumbled that he felt like a father to me. We even kissed each other, as did all the others. I was embarrassed, and I put on a stupid smile to hide my feelings of sorrow and anguish.

After those emotional moments, I got away quickly on an old bike provided by Hennie te R. who rode ahead of me. I followed, wearing my Jewish star openly, just in case. But after a few miles, I took it off. Ilse rode by my side. We said only a few words to each other, not knowing whether we would see each other ever again. I was so conceited, I must confess, that I did not even tell her where I was going, as though Ilse, of all people, would gossip and give my hiding place away!

And so when Ilse and I said goodbye on that memorable afternoon of August 16, 1942, we could only hope that each of us would find a safe place, and that sometime in the future we would see each other again. We did briefly discuss the possibilities of staying in touch. The most ill-considered part of that episode was that I took off my Jewish star. Luckily again, nobody paid any attention that afternoon. There were no German police or soldiers around as we bicycled along some back paths by the side of a canal, northward. Halfway up the road, Ilse waved goodbye and turned around on her bike.

I still remember my total immaturity. I am ashamed that I put on that macho smile when Ilse had tears in her eyes. And even worse, as soon as Ilse left, I spoke to Hennie te Riet with contempt about the sentimentality of "those girls." "How much of a burden those little sentimental girls were for us great men..."

I did not know that section of eastern Holland. After an hour or so of steady bicycling, we were close to the German border. A young fellow waited at a crossroads. Hennie said goodbye to me and repeated last-minute instructions.

Ha. B. [another Gentile Dutchman], my new host and protector, took everything very naturally. For him, there was nothing unusual in hiding out somewhere, or in taking some fugitive with him. Because Ha. B. had known Hennie te Riet from their school days, Hennie felt he could approach him with the idea of taking in a Jewish boy and giving him shelter from the Germans... But, to my mind, there was a problem. Ha. B. did not have a fixed address! An outcast of sorts, he made a living smuggling goods between Germany and Holland, in both directions. He lived in haystacks, going back and forth between farms whose bosses had tolerated him for years. Ha. B. may even have given them a little cut of his profits. All this was new to me.

At first, I was scared about Ha. B.'s being a criminal, not realizing that what I was doing was not exactly in total obedience to the "law." At that time, we still were quite law oriented. All of us still tried to perceive some kind of order, albeit a cruel one, in the German governmental ordinances concerning us Jews. I somehow looked down on Ha., his poor clothes, the fact that he looked like a real bum, his total lack of interest in anything like books, girls, and such things. But he was a good soul, totally unafraid of anything, not in the least nervous or bragging, and always willing to share with a buddy... Ha. was the only homeless person to shelter me. Others who provided shelter were lower to middle-class, not wealthy, but all had homes.

We came to a farm, climbed into the hayloft in one of the barns away from the main house, and settled down for the night. Ha. provided some simple but tasty food. Nobody bothered us. The next morning, he went away "on business," he said. I was not allowed out of the hayloft, and when I had to respond to a call of nature, it had to be done somewhere inside the barn and with great care. All this did not matter too much to me, because the war would be over at the most within a few weeks, even Ha. B. said so and for that span of time I could certainly stand this new kind of life.

In the evening, Ha. returned and took me for a walk around the barn. He was not very talkative. I felt embarrassed that I had read some books during the day as I was lying in the hay. Thus ended my first day of nearly three years of hiding.

I always had a book on me, and I liked to record my thoughts about what I was reading. Throughout my years in Holland, I filled countless notebooks with comments, summaries, and questions. In addition to reading for pleasure or to pass the time, I was trying to educate myself.

One notebook dated July 1941-1943, which included the time I began to hide, opens with a phrase from the Roman philosopher, Seneca. "Singulas Dies Singulas Vitas Puta," or "Make haste to live, and consider each day a life." But I had little time to contemplate Seneca's ideas because after another day or two, Ha. came back and told me that I would have to move. The farmer had seen me from the distance and had said to Ha. that I looked too Jewish for him to have on his homestead.

That night things began to dawn on me in all their seriousness. Ha. and I bicycled back to Almelo. First, I had to try and rid myself of the traces of hay in my hair and on my clothes. I could not wear a Jewish star on that trip, because I had no identity papers.[74] I had ceased to exist as a legal person. All I could do was trust my luck that we would not be stopped for some trivial offense such as one of the bike lights being defective. Ha. led the way very skillfully, weaving in and out of alleys and always avoiding the main route. Because we rode at night without proper lights on our bikes, this was quite a feat. I was very nervous. Had we been stopped, it would have cost me my life. Ha. was quiet and almost jolly. He said he was taking me to a friend who would be happy to have me. This move was my first relocation in hiding.

Moving from place to place soon became a pattern for Dad and for *"onderduikers"* in general. For this reason, it was essential that whenever a hiding place was jeopardized, someone was ready to take the person to a more secure spot. This meant that a flexible network of rescuers and hiding places had to be available at all times. Clearly, it took a village to save a Jew in hiding. Irena Sendler, a Polish Gentile rescuer of Jewish babies and children in the Warsaw Ghetto, quantified the relationship: "To save one child, ten Poles and two Jews had to risk death."[75]

The house where Ha. deposited me that night stood in a seedy section of Almelo that I had not known. My new host was a middle-aged, single man, somewhat evasive about his occupation, but fiercely anti-German. He put me up in the attic. There were a few small cubicles there, each with a bed. My own bed was full of stains, about whose origins there could be little doubt. Clearly, the attic was a former and perhaps current brothel!

The main danger in this hiding place was noise, extra noise made by me and another resident-in-hiding, because the house was attached on both sides to dwellings of the same build, with very thin dividing walls separating them. Even flushing the toilet was a problem. Mr. F., my new host, taught me to cook vegetables. He went out a great deal, including one long weekend. That, I remember, was a particularly difficult time, not only because of my loneliness, but because I had to keep completely quiet since the neighbors had seen F. go out. They might have suspected a burglar, had they heard anything unusual, and of course, if the police had come to investigate, it would have been the end.

By now, Dad's network of helpers included a Jewish man and woman – Kolthoff and E.V. (the coordinator of the hiding network) – and three non-Jewish men – Hennie te Ret, Ha. B., and Mr. F. – as well as others behind the scenes. What was it like to be part of a network helping "*onderduikers*"? The following is an unlabeled list of "Rules for People Working in the Underground" that I found in the Utrecht city archives. These rules varied among groups and locales, but the spirit among the groups was likely the same.

<u>Guidelines that should not be forgotten when one works for O</u> [a resistance group]

1. Speak with no one, even if you risk getting into uncomfortable circumstances with people you know.
2. Always work quickly; be brief and to the point.
3. Visit female couriers only in times of need or extreme circumstances.
4. Couriers are the only ones who deliver mail. If there are difficulties, inform someone as quickly as possible.
5. Every worker is on his own and is completely responsible for the work he carries out as to the safety of himself and others.
6. Pay attention to everything you see and hear around you and process as much as possible in writing.
7. Strive always to raise funds.

Soon, F. told me that I could not stay in the attic and that I had to find a new hiding place. F. took a note to E.V., the coordinator, with her husband, of the Almelo organization hiding Jews. F. explained that I had to leave. E.V. wrote back to me that friends would soon come and pick me up, but first they would have to find me a more permanent hiding place. E.V. also wrote that it did not look as though the war would be over so soon.

E.V. had married a non-Jew, the young and brilliant lawyer, H.V., who shared her convictions. They were a very special couple, highly ethical, non-religious, humanistic, a type I was to meet several more times during the long underground period – men and women whose likes I had not encountered before, and whom I rarely met afterwards.

All of this, however, took place at a time when nobody had yet been arrested, at least nobody we knew, and certainly no mass deportations had begun. But shortly afterwards, the first death notices appeared of a few individuals who had been picked up on some pretense or another. My friend, van W., had died from diabetes, somebody else from influenza. At that early stage, the Germans took the trouble to inform next of kin and to think up all kinds of imaginary diseases for those who had been taken away.

Cultural Resistance

I had come to know E.V. and H.V. through the Kolthoff family one year earlier. They were newlyweds. H.V. had just started his law practice and had already succeeded in creating a name for himself by defending the underdog. He was an outspoken pacifist who had spent a few months in prison before the war, because as a conscientious objector, he refused to serve in the Dutch colonial army.

Before people began to go into hiding, there were occasional gatherings of friends in E.V.'s apartment for discussion of cultural topics. This was the nucleus of something that could be called "cultural resistance" to the Germans. Speakers were invited, or musicians, and the atmosphere during those evenings was on the highest intellectual and artistic level. As participants, we felt something extremely precious: a measure of freedom or normalcy for two or three hours, even a hint of inspired living, the possibility of free creativity amid the daily misery, something unheard of, away from the daily worries about call-ups, razzias, food rations and the ever-increasing, anti-Jewish measures. Cultural resistance strengthened us immeasurably.

What a privilege it was for Ilse and me to be invited, rushing there from our farms after a hard day's work, sometimes unable to rid ourselves of the cow stench which stuck to our clothes. But to sit in a circle of men and women over a glass of tea and hear a lecture about Nietzsche or Kant, or a critical analysis of an opera, and to be able to forget, just forget everything that happened outside... Politics were never discussed; talk about the war was taboo. Professor v. Pr., E.V.'s brother, reported...on major trends in European philosophy!

The musical evenings at the Kolthoffs' were similarly a kind of "musical resistance." I would not be surprised if the evening's program even included a Jewish composer. I think it is no exaggeration to say that here was to be found Jewish resistance to Nazism, real resistance, positive, morale-building resistance.

But now I was in a different situation. It was approaching late August 1942, and I had no permanent hiding place. I had left my girlfriend behind and given my life over to strangers. Not only were these kind people natives of a different country, but they were also natives of a different social class. I trusted them but never knew if I was walking into a trap where someone, particularly a neighbor, might denounce me.

Denouncing Others

Why would someone betray a Jew during this period? On May 5, 1943, Dr. Harster, SS Brigade-Führer and Major General of Police, revealed an answer to this question in a letter he wrote to various German authorities. "People," he declared, "would receive a 'premium for denouncement' of a Jew." In other words, denouncing would be a way of making money. The details of this premium had not been decided, but the German authorities stated that Dutch soldiers who had escaped from German prisoner-of-war camps and now were denouncing Jews would be immune from being returned to the prisoner-of-war camp. This was quite a reward!

Some Dutch people made a career of "bounty hunting," a topic that Dutch investigative journalist Ad van Liempt examined.[76] He asked some basic questions: Why were the Nazis so successful in deporting Jews? Why did families such as Anne Frank's get turned in? Van Liempt discovered that Dutch bounty hunters were so numerous that their actions must be considered part of the Nazi "success" in killing such a high percentage of Jewish people in the Netherlands. This speaks poorly of the Dutch, of course. Van Liempt showed that ordinary citizens had no concern for the age of the Jew they denounced, including young children.

How many Dutch non-Jews betrayed Jews, what were their names, and why did they do it? Because the Germans destroyed their archival records as the war came to an end, these questions are difficult to study. A bureaucratic form on display in the Jewish Historical Museum of Amsterdam, however, shows that financial reward motivated many denouncers. The form below had to be filled out for each denounced Jew.

Date
 Chief of Secret Police and SD [Sicherheitsdienst or Security

Organization, declared a criminal organization after the war] for occupied Netherlands:

Receipt

The Dutch subject...(name)

Born (date); (place of birth)

Is to receive a reward in the amount of ...D. Fl [Dutch guilders], the reason being that a fugitive Jew (Strafjuden)

Born (date): (place of birth)

Whose last address was...

Has been disclosed/delivered to the German Security Police so that an arrest could be made.

(name and rank)[77]

Another document makes it clear that the Germans wanted to make as many arrests as possible. In a September 24, 1942 letter to Himmler one month after Dad went into hiding, Rauter wrote: "The new units of the Dutch police are doing good work with regard to the Jewish question, arresting hundreds of Jews by day and at night." And then, with an unbelievable sentence, Rauter continued: "The only danger is that now and then a policeman exceeds himself and steals Jewish property. I have ordered that these offences be judged in front of the assembled units."[78] Clearly, stealing Jewish property was a crime worse than sending Jews to their death, which was not a crime at all.

In 2006, Marnix Croes of the Research and Documentation Center of the Netherlands Ministry of Justice summarized research on betrayal. "While it is clear that betrayal was common, its scale and the extent of its role remain unknown... Betrayals reflected various motives, the most important of which may have been to hurt the people who were hiding the Jews." Croes' statistical research led him to believe that antisemitism was not the primary motive.[79]

Between March and October 1943, a group of Dutch Nazi collaborators created an organization called the Henneicke Column (named for the group's founder) that arrested 8,00-9,000 Jews and delivered them to the occupation forces. The bounty hunters received 7.50 guilders or $4.75 per Jew.[80] Croes' work reveals that, contrary to earlier beliefs, it was largely the Dutch themselves and not the Germans who turned in the Jews.[81]

On February 28, 1944, Seyss-Inquart reported to Party Chancellery Chief Bormann back in Germany that "We have cleaned up the Jewish question in the Netherlands... The Jews have been eliminated from the body of the Dutch people, and insofar as they have not been transported to the East for labor, they are enclosed in a camp."[82]

He then reviewed the categories of Jews who were still alive in the Netherlands: "About 8-9,000 Jews have avoided transport by submerging [going in hiding]. They are being seized and sent to the East. The rate of seizures is 500-600 a week. Jewish property has been confiscated and is undergoing liquidation...when the liquidation is finished, the property is converted into Reich financial papers." It is horrifying to read this letter in contrast to the one Seyss-Inquart issued to the entire Dutch population on May 29, 1940, promising to be fair.

Waiting

Once I had committed to disappearing, I spent a lot of time simply waiting. Waiting for E.V. to send me to my next hiding place; waiting for my "hosts" to come home; waiting for the time when I could flush the toilet; waiting for the war and the Occupation to end. I sustained myself with memories, pleasant and unpleasant. I remembered how much I wanted to be alone with Ilse when I was working at the farms. The young V.s had been kind to Ilse and me even before we went into hiding. They knew, for instance, that the two of us had no place to be alone for an evening; we had no place to sit, to read a book, listen to music, or make love during the few hours the farmers would give us each week. Occasionally, the V.s gave us the key to their apartment, whenever they had a chance to go out themselves. I thanked them in the only way I could: I brought them a sack of potatoes that I had begged off my farmer and smuggled into Almelo on my battered bike.

One day, E.V. asked me if I could spare my rucksack to give to her parents in Amsterdam who had been called up and needed it for the few weeks they would be in a labor camp... A few weeks earlier, I discussed with H.V., the young attorney, in an almost academic and legalistic fashion, the wisdom and desirability of going into hiding should I ever receive a call-up. H. actively encouraged me to hide. Here was, seen in retrospect, one of the many bizarre situations created by the German invasion: the lawyer advising me to do something illegal.

H.V., of course, favored this type of resistance; in fact, it was the only type of resistance he would countenance within the framework of his philosophical outlook. He told me that he had already been looking around for a suitable hiding place for some of his and his wife's Jewish friends, and he offered his help to me as well. When the call-ups started, and E.V. asked if she could buy my rucksack for her parents, she also asked to buy the camping equipment I had brought from Munich. Her parents had nothing with which to carry the permitted items. When I refused to take money, we agreed that I would lend her parents those things and they would give them back to me when they returned after a few weeks. Such was our thinking at the eve of the deportations in the summer of 1942. I believe it was shared by most Jews as well as by non-Jews ready to help.

Behind the Scenes

In helping Jews survive, organizations were as important as individuals. A key example is Mrs. Helena Theodora Kuipers-Rietberg, a non-Jewish Dutch mother of five, who, in partnership with Calvinist minister Frederik Slomp, founded the clandestine National Organization for Assistance to "Divers" (LO) in 1942. Kuipers-Rietberg, known as Tante (aunt) Riek, was "one of the great women of Dutch history. She was the silent force behind the national organization for helping people in hiding." Kuipers-Rietberg was caught and died in the Ravensbrück concentration camp in Germany. On May 4, 1955, a monument in her honor was unveiled in the town of Winterswijk, her birthplace. The statue on the public square named for her depicts a woman protecting a young deer, a symbol of those who were persecuted during the war.

Minister Slomp was one of the few LO leaders who survived the German occupation. Slomp personified the resistance after the liberation when he warned youth about the dangers of ideologies such as communism and South African apartheid politics.

To date, Yad Vashem has recognized approximately 4,000 Dutch people as Righteous Gentiles. The opening section of volume 1 of the two-volume *Encyclopedia of the Righteous Among the Nations: Rescuers of Jews during the Holocaust – The Netherlands* identifies five Dutch rescuing networks: the Amsterdam Student Group, NV Group, Trouw Group, Utrecht Children's Committee, and the Westerweel Group. The glossary at the end of the entry on the rescue groups includes LO, the "Largest Resistance organization and provider of assistance (e.g., hiding addresses, ID cards, ration coupons and other documents) to 300,000 people in hiding, of whom only a small percentage were Jewish."[83]

Although I refer regularly to non-Jewish helpers, it should be noted that Jews, too, were part of the resistance network that hid Jews.[84] "More than 27,000 Jews actively resisted the German measures,"[85] including hiding other Jews. I already mentioned E.V. in this regard. Another noteworthy person was Leesha Bos, a Jewish girl just out of high school with false Aryan papers, who was one of the 1,500 members of a unit of LO called the LKP or National Action Group. Its task was to procure and distribute false identification papers and ration coupons for "divers." These Resistance members often had to raid government offices for the blanks or make up their own with falsified seals, stamps, and forms.[86] When her LKP supervisor, Fritz van Dongen, was arrested and later tortured to death in prison, Leesha Bos took on his dangerous job.

Hiding people was not a "one size fits all" operation. People hid as individuals, as a couple, as families, as groups of families, as strangers, as young children alone, in the cities and in the countryside. Each individual or group had its own needs. And each person required a series of hiding places because a good site could be compromised at a moment's notice or gradually over time.

E.V. and her husband were the ones I notified from my temporary stay at the house of Mr. F., telling them of my difficulties since going underground. They were always in touch with Hennie te Riet, and together they arranged for me to have a more permanent hiding place with the family B. in Almelo. Hennie came one evening and picked me up from Mr. F.'s house. F. was a good host who would never have let a German inside. The brothel keepers and prostitutes in Holland, or at least some of them, had more decency than the German invaders and many Dutch Christians themselves.

Free at Last!

After a few short-lived tries with other "hosts," I settled into long-term disappearance in a working-class neighborhood of Almelo. Carefully, a whole network of hiders and hiding places had been assembled without anyone knowing details lest they divulge information while being tortured. It is not surprising, therefore, that I did not know what I was getting into. My new hide-out after the problems at the brothel was at the B. [Bysterbosch] home. When Hennie te Riet and I arrived, I found a fellow chalutz there! G.S. [Gerhard or Gert Schönebaum, later named Gad Ilan], born in Germany was one of my buddies! I had no idea that he had gone into hiding and certainly not that we would hide together.

According to oral testimony Gert gave to Yad Vashem after the war, he was born on May 26, 1919, in Dortmund, Germany. Gert finished high school in Germany, became a member of *Habonim* and *Hechalutz*, joined the Ellguth *Hachsharah* in Germany in 1939, and had a Dutch girlfriend, Toos, whom he married in 1945. In January 1939, just like Dad, Gert moved to Deventer, became an "Einzel Hachsharah" in Almelo, and worked for a farmer who was a member of the NSB, the Dutch Nazi group, but, nevertheless, treated Gert well. In June 1942, two months before Dad, Gert began to hide. He, too, had received a call-up notice to participate in the "Harvest Help." Toos began hiding in November 1942. Gert hid quite early because he had a "Jewish appearance" and spoke Dutch poorly and with a German accent.

Given the large number of overlaps with my situation, my surprise at finding Gert ensconced in my next hiding place was a testament to the discipline of secrecy even among the tight-knit group of German Jewish Zionist refugees. G.S. had just arrived at the B.s' through his own contacts, and neither of us had known the B. family. How could we, anyway? They lived in one of a hundred little semi-detached houses, which a former progressive Dutch government had built for working people before the war. G.S. and I lived together in the attic room of the B.s' house for close to two years.

Then, I had another surprise. Suddenly, I felt free, free at last! We both began to feel free. I remember that this was my first notation in a diary – which stupidly and without regard to safety considerations – I began at the time. For the first time since the invasion, I feel free! Free from the farmer, free from the constant fear of a call-up, free from all the small and large pressures and uncertainties of my everyday life as a farmhand or Palestine trainee.

I know that this sounds paradoxical, but I also know that these were my true feelings. Finally, at long last, having made my decision to go into hiding, I was not being pushed around any longer. This, no Nazis could take away from me. I had made my choice. It was my decision not to go to a work camp to help with the harvest. Even when it dawned on me the next day that my troubles had only begun, that there was always the chance of being betrayed, always the threat of sweeping razzias, I felt free. Even in the cramped attic that was our hiding place.

Why was the underground life – at least during the first year, while we still had enough to eat – a great improvement over my previous life with the farmer? It may sound strange, but I felt I was a totally different person the moment I left the Gast farm and became an outcast, a non-person sought by the German police. Surely the danger was there, but it seemed no greater than before with all the unexpected razzias and call-ups. At the farmer's I had to work hard, with little spare time for anything. To be sure, there was plenty of fresh air and physical exercise. In hiding, the opposite conditions existed: and yet, I felt spiritually free. At long last I could read, write, think. The main thing was this: the die had been cast. No longer was I subject to the Nazi idiocy, as long as they didn't catch me. Now I could live a different kind of life, even though physically it was as unhealthy as my former life had been healthy.

Nevertheless, those first few days until we settled down to a routine were difficult. There can always be a routine, as we were to find out in our almost two years together, a routine even in constant danger, just as there was a routine during my time in Buchenwald. At first, I helped G.S. deal with his concerns. G.S. did not know the whereabouts of his girlfriend. Was she still safe? That question bothered him, of course. And then he heard that his parents had been sent to a place called Auschwitz, also to help with the harvest. We got ourselves a map from old Mr. B., and when we found the place, we argued whether the proximity of Auschwitz to Germany proper was favorable for the people in the work camp, and what would happen to G.'s parents once the harvest was in.

Sadly, things quickly deteriorated between the two of us who had to live together. Imagine living in an attic room for nearly two years with another person you have not chosen as an attic-mate and who turns out to get on your nerves. I did not write about feeling claustrophobic, but I did write about being unable to live with G.

Two Men, One Bed

G. and I slept in one bed. That was perhaps the most difficult of the many problems inherent in hiding together in a small, cramped place. Either he or I would have a dream during which we would try to embrace each other, only to be rudely rebuffed. We wound up arranging our bed in such a way that there was some sort of elevation in the middle, a little mound, preventing us, at least, from rolling towards each other during our sleep. The nights were sometimes more difficult than the days. Sleeping together with G.S. in one bed was torture for both of us.

I gradually grew to dislike G.S., and apparently, the feeling was mutual. The stress of hiding together began to show early on. G. and I became irritable and quick to insult each other. Sometimes we would not speak – or even whisper – to each other for days on end and just go through our daily routine in silence. We became jealous of each other. Who had the more important share in the underground network? Who had the more important contacts? Often, we would lose sight of the sacrifice, just in terms of food alone, that our hosts and helpers had to make every day. We were yearning for friends. We were anxious for news of our families. We wanted to hear what had become of the other *chaverim* of our group. We had a sexual problem.

Each configuration – hiding alone, hiding with one other person, hiding with one's spouse or lover, hiding with one's family – had its own challenges and advantages. When a group hid together, the *"onderduikers"* could share the essential tasks and participate in joint leisure activities.

But in my case, the solitary acts of reading, thinking, and writing were the only activities available after the chores and nightly card games with our host ended. And always, we had to go about barefoot or in socks to prevent any noise.

I learned to peel potatoes and apples and to wind up wool from mixed-up balls. I learned to play the simple card game which we had to suffer through almost every evening with the old boss. I did not pray at that time. Being Jewish was no longer a religious question for me, and Zionism had not much meaning for me either in my new existence underground. Survival was everything. Our room could not be heated during the winter for reasons of safety. It could not be aired much in the summer either. But besides the quarrels and the times when we got on each other's nerves, beside the occasional moments of despair, there were also times of joy or at least good humor.

Both of us tried desperately to bring a sense of normalcy into our relationship with each other and with our hosts. There were shared fears and hopes, dreams about a future of freedom as well as a constant looking backwards into a rosy past that never was. There was lots of talk about food, about all the good things our mothers used to make for us, and about girlfriends, love affairs and such.

Two things gave us strength. The first was encouraging war news, by rumor or from an actual BBC broadcast caught clandestinely, especially news of German losses and retreats. And the second, visits from our helpers. Just talking to them, and not about current problems either, getting books from them, together with a little present now and then, as well as an occasional letter or news from people we knew. Books were our vitamins, or if you will, our adrenaline shots. I read everything: French novels and German history books, philosophy, and travelogues, as well as language books and readers, and health instructions.

In the attic, I kept a diary in Dutch titled From the Hidden: A War Diary, 1942-44. *Most of its 60 pages are devoted to political or psychological philosophy, i.e., Socialism, Capitalism, Humanism, Judaism, Optimism, Nature and more. But occasionally I recorded flashbacks such as vignettes from my school years. I understood that if esteemed teachers indoctrinated the children in schools, and this material was repeated year after year, it is no wonder that as adults, the Christian youngsters would become willing Nazi ideologues and murderers. They knew no opposition to this ideology. Moreover, the churches preached the same hatred of the Jews as did the school.*

Ah, one could write books about the abominable roles that the German teachers played. One could call it a crime, raising a whole generation of youths as criminals. Among teachers one found the most malignant dispositions. How they had turned from one day to the next in their political allegiance, how little they had been a role model for decency. Their cowardice and lack of character, their delight in militarism, are all to blame for the misfortune of our nation.

True education was missing for German youth — is there a bigger crime? The teachers felt no obligation to instill positive character in a young person...and to make him/her into a valuable member of society. They betrayed the trust which society had placed in their hands. Even Jewish children — or maybe especially Jewish children — were taught to hate Jews and to compete with other Jewish and Christian children in vehement denunciations of Jews.

An unforgettable image: our German teacher entered the classroom half drunk, wringing his hands and snickering. He growled in a voice that even we 13-year-olds knew was beer-induced: "Hurrah, Clara Zetkin is dead!" What did he mean by that? We didn't understand... We didn't know that Clara Zetkin (née Eissner; 1857–1933) was a German Marxist theorist, activist, and women's rights advocate. My teacher probably assumed she was a Jew. In fact, she was born into a Protestant family but took a Jewish lover (Zetkin) with whom she had two children. For my teacher, this was enough to joyfully announce her death to his baffled students.

Under the new Nazi regime our teachers apparently considered it necessary to diminish our already poor education... No one doubted our teacher's 100 percent commitment to Nazism. But this man had already been violent before Hitler... The boys wanted to hear stories about our teacher's war experiences... So he regularly reverted to talking about his own heroic acts during the [First World] war, as did most of his colleagues.

There were riveting stories like those of Karl May: for instance, how he, a proud German teacher and author of American Wild West stories, knew the French soldiers pretended to be dead, and how he stabbed them with his white bayonet as if it was nothing. This story appeared a hundred times, if not more, and every time in a different form. Or how he cut off their skulls with a shovel. This was a popular variation. For descriptive purposes, he would make the respective gestures. I still remember him standing there... The teachers also lied. It later inadvertently came out that he never was on active duty, but from the hinterland of the pulpit, in unity with his brave colleagues, he idealized a heroic death for the homeland among German youth.

Hypocrisy

I was as interested in the future of the German people as in their current and previous inhuman behavior. The question that obsessed me was whether the German character, as revealed during the Holocaust, was permanent and immutable, or if it was possible for Germans to change. I devoted a lot of space to this topic in my "War Diary:"[87] *Was Germany salvageable? Could German schools teach students to think independently and creatively? Why had teachers become such hearty Nazis in the first place?*

Am I being too snide? Certainly, I can remember some exceptions. The teachers didn't betray the trust of society; they were part and parcel of the society whose values they endorsed. About the question of reforming education in schools: It is strange that the youth never took the initiative on this issue. The youth movement of the future has the task to make its voices heard by demanding better education. For instance, regarding history instruction! We've got to get to the point that politically enlightened youth does not simply accept the capitalist, male chauvinist and militaristic fairy tales told at school any longer. Resistance must come from the youth themselves. They will make reactionary education impossible by their own active and passive opposition.[88]

We are responsible for the future of Germany. It will be necessary, with continual mental effort, to replace hate against Germany by an attitude guided by the spirit of reconstructing the world's future... We will not fight blind destructive rage by resorting to hatred. We will try to overcome all of this. Nowadays the psyche of the typical German person is filled with all the despicable characteristics of Nazism that have developed since Hitler came to power. We have all been under its Nazi influence and it continues.

In the attic we had to be careful not to write anything down (although I did keep a diary), not to leave too many books strewn around our room in case the house was raided, forcing us to disappear quickly into our special shelter. It was probably more a question of luck, as well as tight safety arrangements that helped us. Had the Germans come into the house, I have no doubt that they would have discovered traces of our stay and would eventually have caught us, as happened often.

Creating no trace of living in a shared attic hiding place was quite different from hiding in Anne Frank's "Secret Annex," arranged and furnished in the style of many a middle-class Dutch-German home. Anne sat at her desk, writing. Dad spent most of his time lying on the floor, reading.

We read and read. Our friends brought us armloads of books, together with ration cards for the B. family and for ourselves. Those visits, even if they lasted only a few minutes, kept us going, probably as a visit helps a prisoner in his cell.

By the time G. and I were down to our routine in the hiding place, toward the end of September 1942, about a month after arriving, the deportations and call-ups were in full swing. Going into hiding was no longer something extraordinary, as we heard from our visitors who told us who had "disappeared." Unfortunately, for some, the decision had been made too late. For that, I place much blame on the Allied information program. We were lucky – and this is a very important point to consider – that we were young in the first place, and that we lived in the countryside and not in Amsterdam where chances to hide were much more limited.

Of course, by not staying in or moving back to Amsterdam, Dad was breaking the law. As P. Romijn wrote, "At the beginning of 1942, Jewish habitants in Zaandam and various coastal towns in Zeeland were ordered to move to Amsterdam and to settle in one of three areas designated as Jewish quarters... At the same time, up to April 1943, more and more areas in the country were declared closed to Jews as residential areas."[89]

Years later, I wrote that the war would not be over so quickly, and that the "Harvest Help" was something much more serious, although nobody had an inkling about the true nature of those camps. In our thoughts we would compare it to earlier difficult experiences, such as Buchenwald in 1938 and the individual razzias later.

So our life began to be routine. We had to be silent, of course, in the little worker's house that looked like all the others, attached so closely on both sides that you could hear the neighbors snoring. At first, the B.s were unsure whether those neighbors could be trusted, and so we took great pains not to raise our voices above a whisper. Our friends would visit us mostly after dark. Going outside was out of the question for us. When we wanted to air our room, we would lie on the floor with the windows open, so that we could not be seen from across the street.

One day I stared into the street and saw an old Jew, a gentleman I had known before, wandering about aimlessly, his big yellow star on his overcoat. He wept as he crossed in front of our house. Our hosts told us that all his children and grandchildren had followed the call-up, their house had been confiscated. Now he had no place to go and was waiting to be picked up by the Germans. Nobody would take that old man into his home as a hideaway. It was bitter for G. and me to see this fellow Jew so totally lost, and – once again – to be unable to do anything for him.

Our hosts brought our food upstairs to us at set times. In between reading we did light chores, while constantly on the lookout for German soldiers and police. We listened for unfamiliar noises. I suffered from the frequent air raid alerts which made me terribly nervous. As the war progressed, the Allied planes flew over our house during daylight, just as the Germans flew in the other direction at the beginning of the war. Now and then, after a big explosion, we could see an Allied airman slowly drifting down, hanging in his parachute. Those overflights were scary.

On the other hand, they gave us a great morale boost, notwithstanding the fact that now and then a target would be missed. Almelo was so close to the German border that an occasional bomb released a few seconds too soon would hit a Dutch dwelling. This we dreaded as much as the German roundups and searches.

Rumors and Truth

We lived on rumors, we cultivated them, they were food for our soul. A few people still had access to radios and could listen to the BBC on a clandestine set. This was a capital offense, and those who were caught were usually shot, at least that's what the Germans threatened. What concerned us was learning about the fate of Jewish deportees and all those who had responded to the call-ups. Reports about the camps in the east became more and more frightening. After several months of hiding in our shelter, we finally knew the truth. But it took at least a full year for this truth to be disseminated over the BBC.

We had no illusions left. Now and then, during a moment of utter misery, we would ask ourselves whether it was fair to impose upon good people such as our various helpers, when all that was involved for us was a few months of hard labor in a work camp. But I also knew that I had done the right thing in every respect by going underground. Only when the Warsaw Ghetto uprising took place in the spring of 1943 did we become fully aware of the life-and-death struggle of our Jewish people. I cannot stress this point often enough. To blame us for not having resisted is not only factually wrong, but it shows a lack of understanding. I would go so far as to call it cowardly and obscene.

We were alone. In fact, alongside my feeling of being free, I felt utterly alone during the first days and weeks of my underground life. For those of us in hiding, there was never an expression of friendship, sympathy, nor brotherly encouragement from the Allied broadcasts. Our help, and I refer here not only to practical help, but to psychological support, came only and exclusively from our Dutch friends in the Dutch resistance. Here we made new friends, and many of them. These friendships, tested in periods of the greatest adversity and danger, have outlasted the long war, and they will endure as long as we live.

In Hiding or a Voluntary Prison: A War Diary, 1942-44

I wrote In Hiding or a Voluntary Prison: A War Diary, 1942-44 *during my two years with G.S. When the war finally ended, I added a dedication: "To all who have helped me survive the war, the living and the dead." I wrote the diary in Dutch, perhaps because that language had become most comfortable for me and because I hoped to publish the manuscript in Holland "after the war." Shortly after liberation, I typed what I had written by hand and had it translated into English. The* Diary *documented my private thoughts when I did not know if I would survive. It is a paean to socialism, a topic I discussed on nearly every page.*[90]

I recorded my views about the crisis of a doomed-to-fail capitalism. I asked the questions that were my daily companions: "what is easy and what is difficult about hiding? What does it mean to be hunted prey?" I wrote that I did not dare have Jewish books on hand lest they be discovered. For this reason, I refrained from writing about Jewish topics. The Diary *discussed philosophy and many other topics found in the "hundreds" of books I read.*

The Diary *does not open with an overview of my experiences of hiding. If you want to satisfy your curiosity in that area, better not read my diary. You'll be disappointed. Rather, I started with a flashback of witnessing the horrific Bok punishment upon my arrival at Buchenwald because that is what I could not stop thinking about. This is the incident where I stood by helplessly while a fellow prisoner was tortured in front of hundreds of other prisoners. My "enforced passivity in hiding" reminded me of what I considered to be my "chosen passivity in Buchenwald," for which I still felt so guilty.*

Today after five years [since the event occurred in Buchenwald] in the gnawing loneliness of a self-made prison, these images of the past continuously replay in my mind. I am overcome with a feeling of shame. I am ashamed of myself... From such an experience one learns who one is. It was my duty to do something, and I did nothing!!

Letters to or from "onderduikers" obviously did not go through the Dutch postal service. Instead, a network of people supporting the divers brought the mail. Delivering underground mail was particularly dangerous because if caught, the letter-carrier, the rescuer, the diver, plus other divers on site were vulnerable. Nevertheless, organizations understood how important mail was for mental health.

A friend wrote, asking me how I am doing and what the most difficult aspect of my immediate situation is. I have done some long introspection and believe that external conditions are still bearable. We get accustomed to the endless sitting in the small room. If one is young, nothing is as bad as older people might imagine... And above all, the thought of a future helps, a future for which we were saved.

What is the hardest? To sit idly by while other comrades do something. We read and read; we imagine that we are preparing ourselves, but we are merely preserving ourselves. People on the outside, on the other hand, sacrifice themselves day and night in the battle against the Nazis and in helping the victims. Yes, the feeling that one is sentenced to idleness remains, and it represents, I believe, the worst.

Given Dad's idea that enforced idleness is the most difficult aspect of hiding, it is not surprising that imagining the opposite is marvelous: *The wonderful feeling that there will be work when the war is over! An entire world needs to be built. This time we can construct a better one! We no longer have any reason to stay idle with empty hands. They need us! I long for the infinite work ahead of us. The simple thought of the coming work frees us of bitterness. Personal suffering will be drowned in an unfathomably deep lake of the great work!*

Nevertheless, our nerves can't stand this unnatural life, which is less living than vegetating, waiting to live, waiting to act, waiting, waiting, waiting... I wait in constant stress. When you observe this process slowly within oneself, one tries to do something, yet we must recognize again and again that one is basically powerless! And related to it are the smaller and larger daily problems with their human intricacies and occasional unpleasant disagreements... Finally, there is the ever-present feeling that one has burdened other people now for two years already; that one lives on other people's dime, always the taker. Certainly, we will not be defeated, but sometimes a sigh struggles out of our chests – if only the war would come to an end!

Happy to Be Alive

Amidst all the suffering, we are happy to be alive. We have every reason to be grateful for the beautiful... It is the small, the unnoticed, which adorns our lives, which makes it worthwhile to live, a conversation, a letter, an instance of mutual understanding. And above all, the shared experience of nature, of music... They represent the actual value of our personal life... It is so little and yet so much.

Just as is true of all "onderduikers," I have had to tolerate all the difficulties of this voluntary prison, which is so much harder, so much more dangerous and mentally oppressive than any prison can be. This has been described in detail. Why should I repeat and provide additional descriptions of being an "onderduiker" that others have described so much better? Why rehash the almost constant fear of the raids, house searches, betrayal and bombs that seeped into the smallest corners of daily life, which no longer is a life? And why dwell on the mental needs and difficulties of young people, who must sit behind closed curtains for two springs and summers without seeing any blue sky, without taking a breath of fresh air, always speaking in whispers, and hardly moving?

Despite all the difficulties, I was unspeakably fortunate that I was not caught. It is possible that even though neighbors realized B. was hiding a Jew, they did not betray me. Had I been dragged down from the attic or pulled up from my emergency basement hiding place, I might have been shot or, more likely, sent to Dutch concentration camp Vught, Westerbork, or other places whose names are unfamiliar to people who don't know that the Dutch created such camps.[91]

Some of these are Barneveld (a castle in which so-called "Prominent Jews" were incarcerated but ultimately survived); Ellekom (sarcastically labelled "Palestine," which served as a training school for the Dutch SS to learn how to torture Jews); a camp at Schoorl and one at Amersfoort, among others.[92] In addition, a large seminary in Haaren, Noord Brabant was used as a "prevention hostage" camp, created for the following purpose: "If the resistance carried out an attack, a number of these hostages would be placed in front of the firing squad."[93] A variety of camps in Holland used Jews for slave labor. They were a punishment, a waystation for those being shipped to the east for extermination, places of training, or, in one case, some sort of protection. It should be repeated that these camps were run by German and Dutch people.

Thank God for Shushu who convinced me to hide. Thank God for each person who hid me. Thank God for the neighbors who did not betray me. Thank God for my ability to endure the prison of idleness. But on the second anniversary of hiding, I simply could not take it any longer. Against all reason, I sought a way to leave Almelo and return to Amsterdam, the place from which all the Dutch Jews and German Jewish refugees were funneled to Westerbork. What drove me to take this risk? Longing for my girlfriend – Ilse Hertha Strauss.

Admiration and Resentment

While in hiding, I did not write much about fear. Instead, I focused on feelings about two types of people – admiration for those who hid me, people whom I called "outstanding human beings." And resentment toward those who seem to have abandoned me. I admired those who had acted immediately and spontaneously, i.e., even before the temporary underground organizations crystallized into well-run groups. People like H. te Reit and Miss V., whom I would look up to as one of God's rare creations.

Then there were lots of labor union people, church members, men and women who acted out of conviction. In our group, several had been active as conscientious objectors before the war. Others had been active union organizers, political workers, and social workers. There were outstanding human beings among them, such as the unforgettable H.V., the brilliant young lawyer, married only a few years earlier to Esther V., and shot by the Germans in early fall 1942. His personality influenced me even before our underground period. There was an entire family of pacifists, some vegetarians among them, small people if you will, uncomplicated, decent to the bone, upright and honest in everything they did, focused on resisting the German invaders. The idea of helping us was consistent with their philosophy of life. It seemed that helping us was, for them, the most natural thing to do. They could not and would not fight the Germans with weapons, and thus saving Jewish lives, or better, saving human lives, was their form of resistance.

H. te R., who later became mayor of a town in eastern Holland, was a student of political and social sciences. He told me that as a soldier in the Dutch army in May 1940, he had every opportunity to kill some Germans when the two armies faced each other over one of the bridges. But he preferred to shoot over their heads.

All these people had been strangers to us, the "Palestine Pioneers" in training who had come as refugees to Holland, from Buchenwald and other concentration camps. Holland was a different world for us. Our background, our lifestyle, our orientation, our goals were worlds apart. And yet the overriding task and desperate need combined to make us feel very close in a short time. The constant fear of detection, the growing food shortage, and the common resistance to the Germans forged us into a group whose ties were as strong as a family. Everyone involved in hiding others or being hidden was in danger, and everyone had to develop ways of interacting that combined deep trust and respect with caution and suspicion.

Shortly after I arrived in the B. home, after my first weeks in different hiding places, I learned that the German police – irritated needlessly by my having returned the torn slip with the call-up notice for "Harvest Help" – had issued a warrant for my arrest. The warrant came complete with my picture and personal description. I was a fugitive from the law, refusing a government order. I could just see my old boss Gast staring at that mugshot on a bulletin board, as he says to his family: "See, I told you so!" Why did the Germans bother to hunt me down? There were still tens of thousands of Jews to be deported. Many were trying to go into hiding, and it seems ludicrous that the authorities would want to issue a warrant every time somebody would fail to show up.

One possible reason was the Nazis' desire to coat their illegal, immoral, and unjust practices with a veneer of legality. In my case, it must have been the fact that I had the nerve to tear the order in three pieces and mail it back to them. That must have gotten under the skin of some Stürmführer. What chutzpah! But also – what needless stupidity on my part. I did not feel particularly heroic when I heard of the warrant. My helpers didn't like it at all. It might have endangered them needlessly.

My hosts were a family of three. The boss, a typical old Frieslander was a retired carpenter, obstinately anti-German, social democrat, anti-cleric, from the old Marxist trade union school, with a zealous dedication to the memory and the glory of the first days of the Dutch labor union movement in the early 1900s. His wife shared her husband's opinions, and the spinster daughter had little to say. Evenings had to be spent playing cards with the old man. We were, one could say, two young boarders, temporarily out of work, with a little danger thrown in. Gerd and I "had some fun" with Mr. B. when the hiding experience was new. My partner-in-hiding and I had not yet lived through the intense claustrophobia and tedious boredom that were to follow.

Old Mr. B. smoked his ersatz tobacco which made us nauseous, and he told us hundreds of times about his exploits during the first strikes and lockouts at the beginning of the century, and those damn papists and their like. He hated the Church. He was an unbending soul, made of the stuff that irritated the Nazis most.[94] *He was fearless and uncompromising when it came to the "moffen," [the Dutch equivalent of the "boches" or "Huns" or "Krauts"]. There aren't so many characters of Mr. B.'s type around any longer.*

Our hosts, the B. family, were quiet old people whose every movement the neighbors had known for years. Now their toilets were flushed more frequently, the garbage cans would fill up faster, water would run longer – a hundred little things, each quite insignificant in and of itself, but potentially dangerous when taken all together by a nosy blabbermouth. On rare occasions, Gerd and I would be taken for a brief walk in the dark of night, one at a time. This helped us physically and mentally. During the rare visits to our friends, we could talk, listen to a record, get our minds away from the troubles of the day and enjoy some modicum of normalcy. Of course, these visits were accompanied by the most elaborate safety measures. Quick escape routes were always arranged before anything else.

But then, we took up a project – G.S. and I built an extra shelter in the house. This was not so unusual. Many "onderduikers" and their hosts built or dug hiding places within hiding places. These multiple hide-outs within a home increased the possibility of getting to one of the hide-outs in time to avoid capture. There were quite a few occasions when we had to disappear in a hurry within the house itself, at the time of a razzia or when we got a sudden warning that something was brewing. The disappearance operation had to be carefully laid out and practiced. Old B. was in charge. G. and I entered through the pantry on the ground floor where the potatoes were kept. There, behind the pile of loose potatoes, we opened a plank leading to the crawl space directly underneath the living room floor. Old B. would then push the plank back into place and kick the potatoes into a heap, and G. and I would push ourselves forward on our bellies through the mud. We just hoped that neither of us would have to cough or sneeze or, if the Germans came, that they wouldn't have dogs that could sniff us through the floor."[95]

It was a good hide-out, and we were able to get there fast when we trained. Fortunately, we never needed it against the Germans. It always served its purpose when a neighbor came in unexpectedly during the evening and wanted to chat with the folks while we were at our card game. We couldn't take any chances on those occasions and just disappeared.

Neighbors were always a potential problem. One never knew whether they were aware that two Jewish fellows were hiding a few houses down the street or right next-door. Even when the neighbors were considered reliable – a word, a hint dropped inadvertently, just plain carelessness, or perhaps boasting of what so-and-so was doing to resist the hated occupiers, all of this could lead to catastrophe. It happened much too frequently, and in all parts of Holland, quite aside from outright acts of betrayal for money or favors.

It is important to remember that the Nazis – both German and Dutch – knew that many Jews had disappeared into hiding, although they did not know how many or where they were. Eichmann, head of the Jewish Department within the Nazi SS, visited Holland frequently during the Occupation and repeatedly pressed the authorities to increase the prize for informers to increase the number of monthly arrests.[96] As the war dragged on, the hunt became frantic. Eichmann was determined to make Holland *"Judenrein"* and rejected all special pleas to allow some Jews to remain even if they had skills or other advantages useful to the occupying forces. Every Jewish man, woman and child had to be deported and killed. Eichmann seemed fearful that even one remaining Jew might become the source of a possible resurgence of Jews.

Israel's Attorney General Gideon Hausner, Eichmann's prosecutor in Jerusalem in 1961, concluded his summary of Eichmann's activities in the Netherlands by quoting from the Nazi leader's July 1944 chilling final report:

> The Jewish problem in the Netherlands can be considered solved: 119,500 Jews had been deported and a further 2,591 were awaiting deportation in transit camps...

Years later, he told his good friend and Dutch collaborator, Wilhelmus Antonius Sassen (1918–2002),

> "In Holland the deportations started magnificently. Then difficulties cropped up one on top of the other. It is indescribable how many difficulties were made on all sides. We had to fight to get more Jews to deport. Then again, a group would arrive with 10 or 15,000..."[97]

While I was reading and writing about the ideal world I would like to help create after the war, journalists in the US were writing about what was going on in Europe. Under the headline, "1,000,000 Jews slain by Nazis," in June 1942, two months before I went into hiding, The New York Times *reported that the "Nazis had established a vast slaughterhouse for Jews in Eastern Europe," that so far, one-sixth of European Jews were "wiped out," mostly those from Germany, Austria, Poland, Czechoslovakia, the Netherlands, Rumania, Lithuania and German-occupied Russia, in line with Hitler's policy of "extermination."*

A few days later the same newspaper offered details on the extermination of Jews since the summer of 1941, such as Jews being forced to dig their own graves before they were machine-gunned stark naked into the holes.

It is fortunate, I believe, that I did not have access to The New York

Times *or to the information in these articles. It would have terrified me, especially since I had to remain idle.*

Who Gets Credit for Saving Jews in Holland?

Our resistance movement grew entirely from within. It was our little group in Holland that saved Jewish honor, showed Jewish consciousness, and had a Jewish national ideal. In that respect, the Zionism of "Palestine Pioneers" stood at the forefront of Jewish resistance to the Nazis in the Netherlands. For some Zionist spokesmen after the Holocaust to claim this effort of saving Jewish lives – the only active form of resistance possible – as their own achievement, as we heard and still hear so frequently, is untrue and dishonest.

For writers like Hannah Arendt, to look with critical contempt on the behavior of Western European Jewish communities whom she characterized as going like sheep to the slaughter, and not to discuss our chalutzic struggle and our achievements – is a despicable mistake. I remain a Zionist, although I did not settle in Israel – yet. In our own group, it was only because of the foresight and initiative of a handful of people such as Shushu and our non-Jewish helpers that the need to resist through going into hiding was recognized. Our instincts, our fears, pulled each of us one way or the other. This is precisely why we felt the lack of leadership so deeply.

But as the result of our spontaneous activities, there was a larger percentage of Jewish lives saved from our circles than from among the Jewish community in Holland as a whole... What was important was the initial help, the intelligence, the guidance... to go into hiding because there was no other way to survive the onslaught.

I have no apologies for the bitterness in my tone whenever this subject comes up. Mistakes were made that could have been avoided. I was involved in efforts to persuade Greek ship owners to take on illegal immigrants to Palestine shortly before the Germans invaded Holland – only because I knew a little English and there was need for an interpreter. I know what could be done had there been a broader outlook, not the blind attitude of "Palestine or nothing."

Many human lives could have been spared... But our leaders – those that came into prominence later in Zionist politics – had left in time, and from what I could observe after the war, had been able to save their families as well. All this is understandable. But what I felt then, I feel now. We were so steeped in the old Zionist ideology with its incessant debates, we were so filled with slogans, that we lost all sense of the world around us.

After Kristallnacht and the outbreak of the war in September 1939, anybody could sense the fate of European Jewry. But we participated in the terribly important debates over the most ideal form of Jewish life in Palestine. After we had been through Buchenwald, we continued to debate, as instructed, the merits of one form of kibbutz over another. Our leaders did not realize, or did not want to realize, that we were refugees in Holland, living with temporary residence permits tied to our working as unpaid farmhands. The moral pressure, and that is an essential point, of going to Palestine and nowhere else, was as powerful as ever.

During the few intervening months, from our arrival in the Netherlands in January and February 1939 until the invasion of May 1940, before our emissaries from Palestine were interned by the Germans as British nationals, the attitude of our leaders had not changed. That I acted as interpreter during the negotiations gave me a little insight into the problems. Of course, there was only limited space on these ships, and the criterion for selections was strictly based on training in agriculture. But... there were quite a few, including myself, who had a chance to emigrate to such places as the USA and Santo Domingo. I delayed and delayed because of moral pressures. I saw what happened, what we did to one chaver who had secured an entry permit to Santo Domingo and who left Holland a few days before the Germans invaded in May 1940. We ostracized the poor fellow and treated him as a social outcast from the moment his plans became known.

Those with emigration possibilities other than Palestine should have been encouraged to leave. If they pursued those options, they could make room for those of us whose only chance was to go on one of the illegal Aliyah ships. That precious breathing space in Holland between January 1939 and May 1940 should have been utilized to save young and old. Yet our leaders were blind to the situation. Buchenwald apparently had not been enough of a shock. Their own political prestige of bringing Jews to Palestine was more important to them.

These people knew what was going on in the world. We did not. They had helped in the emergency transit of small groups of Polish chalutzim who had been able to flee that country ahead of the invading German troops in 1939, and who had escaped in the nick of time to Holland with the help of the Zionist organization. Those chaverim came through Amsterdam and some of them stayed with us for a night or two. We were proud that we Zionists had saved them. We felt we could rely on our leadership abroad just as we ourselves had been freed from Buchenwald due to their splendid efforts a year earlier.

But for us, living under the total indoctrination of exclusive Zionist loyalty, it was unthinkable to plan an escape route other than Aliyah to Palestine. Even today, 40 years later, I can still feel that moral pressure. There wasn't even a debate! I would never have permitted myself any criticism of our leadership if a debate had been encouraged, but such a debate, contemplating the possibility of emigrating to America, would never have been tolerated.

My judgements about the people I admired and the self-centered people I resented obsessed me. My experiences had polarized into good and bad; trustworthy and untrustworthy; courageous and cowardly; smart and stupid. There was not much gray. Ilse was one of several people I considered good although she was a 100 percent committed Zionist. As I sat in the attic day after day, I realized I would sacrifice anything to be with her. But to do this, I had to leave my hiding place and travel from Almelo in the east, to Amsterdam or Rotterdam in the west. The trip was illegal, but love was greater than fear.

Shushu, Again

For me and everyone like me in hiding, the calendar had been inching forward at a painfully slow pace. No one knew if the passage of time would culminate in death or liberation. The summer day of August 16, 1942, when I became an "onderduiker," had turned into fall, then winter, then the start of 1943 with its hope-inducing spring. Although a complete year of hiding had not passed, I wondered how long I could last. How long could I take it? When I became an actual "onderduiker," I didn't see the situation as hopeless. But then, several of the people I admired, "good" people I might have believed unconsciously would be able to live forever, were killed. Being a good person turned out not to be an effective means of protection.

When Lore Zilly Durlacher [later Goren], my friend and fellow Hachsharah member, learned that Shushu had killed himself, she came to Almelo to tell me.

"It cannot be," I responded. "Shushu really died? How can such a life force be extinguished?" I had not yet discovered the details – that Shushu had slit his wrists right before he was to be interrogated about his resistance activities. Shushu feared he would not be able to keep silent during torture. I do not think that the seriousness of our situation penetrated our minds until the news of Shushu's death, H.V.'s execution, and the first reports of mass deportations reached us. When we heard about the mass killings for the first time in the spring of 1943, nearly a year since we had gone into hiding, we no longer had any illusions. The war would not be over in the time the BBC had told us, and the few guilders we had saved were long gone.

As the heart-wrenching tragedy began to sink in, I became even more committed to survive and be with Ilse. I needed her love, but how could I be with her if we lived so far apart?

The Tragedy of German Youth

August 1943 arrived – one year in hiding had passed – and then four months later, the winter holiday season returned. My diary describes scenes of disturbing Nazi behavior I witnessed through the window curtain on Christmas Eve.

When we went to bed, we heard sounds of the German soldiers who had been drinking in the barracks. They had secured permission to be in the street for hours. And they capitalized on it. Half drunk, they passed the sleeping homes in small groups, laughing and yelling. And they dragged along a couple of "noble Germanic ladies" who appeared to be a gift from the highest command post as a Christmas surprise. They screamed and shouted and made noise as if they were animals. It sent chills down our spines and must have also kept some neighbors up... Who knows whether at the same time the relatives of these soldiers were hiding in bomb shelters in Germany. Perhaps on that same night, their father or mother would be found dead or wounded under the rubble.

I was disgusted by these men's attitudes toward women, their drunkenness, and even their defilement of the German language. They thought only of schnapps (alcohol) and sex. Despite my disgust, however, I strangely began to see the German soldiers as victims. What has Hitler done to these people, to these youth of the nation that he claims to love? For years, they wore no other suit than their uniform.

I disliked uniforms – on other people. As for myself, after the liberation, I proudly wore the uniform of the Jewish Brigade. But while in hiding, I wrote: We will not be put in uniforms. And even if there is nothing else for us to do but die, we want to be ourselves in death, not artificially made the same as everyone else. The uniform horrifies us. It covers the inner self, the spirit and soul. The German soldiers around us don't have a healthy family life. They are not trained for useful work... They know only their barbaric commando tone – oh the foul language they make out of the beautiful German language!

Will they ever be incorporated into the labor force? Will they ever be capable of taking off their uniforms to live and think like normal people? How do these humans expect to ever have decent relations with the other sex; how can they create a family and educate children? This is such a tragedy. What are these beings capable of? At the most to kill or wound themselves on instruction and to do the same to others.

Human beings trained by the Nazi system are the products of Nazi education. Our soul cries out against the worthlessness of such a life. What will happen to German youth? Will it be possible to save them from further deterioration? This is the most difficult problem for the future. German leaders have destroyed their own people's language, culture, and self-respect. German youth know nothing but war. With German youth in such a sorry state, there is no hope for Germany's future. Writing in my diary, I wondered if Nazi education might also account for the lack of rebellion in the German military. Today one wonders why the German generals do not revolt against Hitler and make a peace offer to the Allied forces... The irresponsible persistence of the *generals can be explained by their fear of a revolution in their own country.*

1944 Begins

Soon, Christmas Eve 1943 came to an end. Another calendar year had passed, and I continued to hide with G.S. Tedious months dragged on. Even the weather was miserable. All I could do was read, take notes, and think. I preferred cultural critiques and philosophy to other subjects. Most disappointing were books that purported to explain how the intellectual development of Germany in the 20th century led to the Nazi catastrophe.

Then spring warmed the outside world. May 1944. It was now four years since the invasion and the start of the Occupation. Almost two years in hiding. Little did I know that the coming year would be my last as an "onderduiker" and that in exactly one year I would be free. In retrospect, I wrote that the year ahead of me was to be the worst of my time in hiding. Trying to cheer myself up, I declared that no one could take spring rejoicing from our hearts... We must understand how to be happy... We must create something beautiful. We have a right to joy. There will always be one small blade of grass. I fantasized about singing in a Mozart choir, of seeing the sun shining gloriously. I reminded myself that wonderful human values still exist in the world. But looking around, all I saw was "war-spring," as I called it, the second spring in my self-chosen prison.

Tuesday night. Pacifist fundamental thought: the people must work. He who holds a shovel cannot hold a gun at the same time... The basic pacifist slogan must read: Work! Productive work!

May 21, 1944. One can never completely overcome the unique situation of hiding. This experience will always remain a part of us... How often did we think that our last hour had come, when from our hiding place we saw how the police conducted raids outside, as "Grünen" [i.e., Greens] dragged our betrayed comrades past our house and we thought that next they would come for us.[98] *After a while, we become accustomed to the fear; even deathly fear can become a habit!*

Through heavily curtained windows I watched the Greens or Dutch

Nazi police dragging my friends who had been betrayed. And, once again, I was not able to do anything.

Summer 1944 arrived and with it the two-year anniversary of becoming an "onderduiker." I missed my girlfriend but still lived with G.S. I was not aware that the Allies had landed in Normandy.

August 16, 1944. Today I can "celebrate" my two-year anniversary as an "onderduiker." I look back on the two years that have flown by. It seems only yesterday that I voluntarily disappeared from society. My diary has swelled into a thick pack of notebooks. Shall I publish it? Can the publication of a diary be justified nowadays when actions with which we demonstrate our convictions are more important than words?

After weighing the question of publication, as Anne Frank did, I decided to try to publish for the sake of German youth, because I, myself, had been a student in German schools and knew how damaging that education was. In those schools I was under the influence of Nazi teachings. Because of what I had witnessed among the teachers, I developed the conviction that German youth should be held much less responsible for its negative acts, than the rest of the world thinks. We want to overcome what Hitler has wrought in the psyche. We want to overcome the atrocities of our time by the creation of a new, socialist world. We want to approach German youth as socialists; we want to preach the socialist order to them, supported by genuine socialist conviction, a conviction suitable to confronting hate. We want to eradicate, at its root, German youth's resentment over a lost war and the covert desire for a repetition.

And yet, I do have some things to be grateful for. Under the most demanding sacrifices and dangers, people have kept me hidden and have been caring for me for two years. This hiding place has a toilet, so I don't have to run outdoors to an outhouse. Although I was very nervous, I remained healthy. As I later recounted with pride, 'In the two years underground in Almelo, I almost never left the house. I never was sick and never had to see a doctor. And I did not starve. Nevertheless, after two years, I could no longer tolerate hiding, especially hiding with Gerd. I had to get out of this prison and find a way to be with Ilse.'

Risking It All for Love

Ironically, just when Ilse and I decided to marry, we had to hide. During the first two years of hiding, we were in touch through occasional letters delivered by clandestine couriers after checking their contents for safety violations. It was embarrassing to have others read our love letters, but it was necessary. Letter-writing during the Holocaust was also essential in determining that people were still alive. Couriers delivered information, news, books, false papers, and love letters, among other items.[99] Most of the couriers were women, because they could more easily pass as non-Jews than could [circumcised] Jewish men. Later in the war, Ilse, herself, became a courier. Ironically, she quit in disgust when she discovered she was taking risks to deliver the communist organization's leaders' love letters.

Lore Zilly Durlacher, one of the Jewish women leaders in the courier group, was our good friend and age-mate. A German Jewish Zionist refugee and member of the "Palestine Pioneers," Lore, like Shushu, was fearless and restless. She had no Jewish facial features whatsoever and was thus able to travel freely, under the guise of being a German nurse. Lore devised a complicated plan to free Jews from the transit to Westerbork before they were deported east. Somehow, she supplied the escapees with bicycles, train tickets and other documents, and then accompanied them to a nearby railway station...

As a member of the Westerweel group, she recruited hiding places and stole or helped create false personal documents. Her identity card named her Els Rijsdijk, and her bleached hair gave the impression she was a Dutch non-Jew or a German nurse.[100] With this "disguise," Lore became a roving contact among many chalutzim in hiding. Meanwhile Ilse also became restless and moved to a hiding place in the northwestern corner of the Netherlands.

I assumed that Ilse would be allowed to move again and requested a transfer to be with her in Rotterdam. The organization's leaders discussed the costs and dangers, ultimately authorizing the request. They then turned to Lore to create and implement a plan to bring me from Almelo to Rotterdam. My transfer meant that I would have to leave the protection of the group who helped me in Almelo and enter a new circle in

Rotterdam Zuid (i.e. Rotterdam South). the section of the city that had survived the bombardment during the German invasion. Our Almelo friends did not like the idea too much. But they understood the benefits.

Joining one's lover was not a trivial matter. Having a lover gave people a reason to live when they were desperate. It also convinced them to take chances. To be alone without love could fill people with despair and make their survival seem less compelling.[101]

Dad's transfer across the country from Almelo to Rotterdam was a dangerous enterprise in many ways. For instance, the German occupying government had decreed that Jews were forbidden to visit non-Jewish homes. Simply having the non-Jewish Schouten home as a destination was a crime, as was living there. In addition, Jews could travel only with a special permit that he did not have.

On August 7, 1942, the 45th and last decree concerning Dutch Jews, the German Security Police made three pronouncements: any Jew ordered to a labor camp in the east who does not report, any Jew not wearing the yellow star, and any Jew changing address without permission will be sent to the Mauthausen concentration camp.[102]

I was guilty of all these "crimes." And yet I made the trip. I was informed that our Rotterdam destination would be the home of the non-Jewish couple, Niek and Aag Schouten, whom we did not know. Their full names were Nicholaas Schouten and Agatha Schouten-van Diepen.

My move occurred in mid-spring 1944 when deportations of Jews had nearly ended because there simply weren't Jews left to kill. Perhaps, having survived underground for so long, I felt invincible. Lore provided me with false papers as a Jewish carpenter temporarily needed for the German war effort and thus freed from deportation. Taking on this identity was foolhardy. If challenged by anyone, I could not have displayed any carpentry skills. All along, the Nazis had given passes to a few Jews, protecting them under the category "temporarily freed." For any other Jew to be in public with a yellow star, when everybody was supposed to have been deported, was preposterous and suicidal. Perhaps the sheer brazenness of my action guaranteed its success.

The most common forms of travel in the Netherlands at the

time were trains, bicycles, or canal boats. Automobiles were not numerous, the highway system was not extensive, and gasoline was not cheap. As of March 20, 1942, Jews were forbidden to own or drive private cars. After the Nazis confiscated bicycle tires, trains became even more essential.

The German police, seeing this lonely "Jew boy" in public, must have assumed that I had "special permission," and therefore did not take the trouble to stop me.

My itinerary was as follows: First, Hennie te R. picked me up after dark at the B. home where I had been hiding with G.S. Train schedules had been carefully worked out. Lore and I took a little milk train to a town in northeastern Holland where we spent the night and the entire next day in the home of Hennie's friends. It was a strange experience for me to walk outside. I had to observe all the strict rules that Hennie had impressed upon me. "Don't ever look people in the face, don't talk, act dumb, mind your own business, and above all, never make it appear as though you have any connection with me. In case I was arrested, there was no need for Hennie to suffer along with me. I did most of what H. required. After all, I had acted dumb in Buchenwald.

As I look back, that trip was frivolous. Wanting to be with Ilse and wanting to be free of G.S. in a tiny hiding place – those feelings should have taken second place to the overriding concern for saving our lives, spared thus far. We also should have been concerned for the safety of our Dutch helpers. But the people in the organization were willing to take the risk for my emotional well-being. Still, I had the feeling when I said goodbye to Hennie as he "transferred" me into Lore's hands that I had hurt him and his pride. I was one of his charges and he wanted to see me safely through the war. Now I joined a different underground organization where Lore Durlacher would take care of me, and all this to be with my girlfriend.

The fact that Hennie and his wife remained my parents' friends for decades after the war and visited them in the US in 1997 makes it unlikely that H. had hard feelings toward them. After the visit, Hennie wrote:

We had a wonderful time in America. Talked too much about the war. That will not change. The war has disturbed our lives, and even though we have a good life, it is always present in the background. We enjoyed our trip to see you again and to see how you are living together, and what you made from your life after the terrible time you had in our country.[103]

Hennie was much too decent a fellow to show any kind of resentment, of course, but I suffered for years after the war from that broken relationship.

Lore called for me at the home of Hennie's friend in a small town whose name I have forgotten. From there, we took the express train to Rotterdam. When we changed trains in Utrecht, I abided by all the rules Hennie had laid down for me, but now I had to make a special effort because this last leg happened in broad daylight. There were Germans everywhere. I kept staring straight ahead, the Jewish star securely fastened on my jacket. I never looked anybody in the eye. And thank God, our strategy worked. Nobody bothered me. A few sympathetic Dutch people sitting in our compartment must have thought that when this poor Jewish fellow finishes his mission, he will be deported and gassed. Our fate was well known by that point. Lore sat in a corner of the compartment in her nurse's uniform, and we acted like complete strangers. This trip required nerves of steel, which I did not have. But Lore's presence quieted my jitters as did the promise of reuniting with Ilse.

We arrived safely in Rotterdam, took a streetcar to the south part of town, and then walked to my new shelter after removing my Jewish star. That, in fact, was the riskiest portion of the entire operation. I had become a Dutch workman returning home with his empty lunch box. Again, we were lucky and nothing untoward happened. Having made it safely to Rotterdam, I entered a new hiding place. But this situation was utterly different from being with G.S. Soon I would be living with Ilse! And together we would be hosted by a Dutch couple our age. The relationship with these two people became the strongest of this entire ordeal, except, of course, my friendship with Shushu and my love of Ilse.

The Schoutens

When I arrived in Rotterdam, I moved into the apartment of our wonderful new hosts, Niek and Aag Schouten, who hid us for the next six months. The Schoutens were only a bit older than my 23 years. Because we quickly developed a warm bond, I felt comfortable asking them if Ilse could join me. When the Schoutens agreed, I beseeched the Westerweel Group to send Lore to Friesland to bring Ilse to Rotterdam. Lore already knew the Schoutens through Jan Smit,[104] a non-Jewish unemployed bricklayer and important member of the Westerweel Group.

Furthermore, Lore admired Niek for having rescued several Jewish children in Rotterdam by wearing a stolen Gestapo uniform, barging into the houses where the children lived, and taking them to safety, using the ploy that they had orders to deport the children. Lore agreed to carry out Ilse's transfer. When Ilse learned of the plan, she wrote to me, "I will come to you. Wherever you go, I will go," quoting the famous lines of the Biblical Ruth to her mother-in-law, Naomi (Book of Ruth 1:16). Ilse moved in, two years after we had last seen each other, and felt at home with the Schoutens right away. Being with this Dutch couple signaled the possibility of living, not just surviving.

The Volkshuis Movement

When I arrived at the Schoutens' small apartment, a new chapter began in my life. True, we were rather cramped on the ground floor of this typical workers' house in a typical workers' street in Rotterdam South, where you can find hundreds and maybe thousands of such dwellings, all alike, all attached to each other, all nice and neat, built under labor union auspices before the war, providing reasonable and affordable housing for workers, and...ideal for hiding, precisely because they all looked alike.

Food was in somewhat shorter supply than in Almelo. This was the city, after all. There was also much coming and going because the Schoutens' place served as a transit station in an underground railroad for people who had to find permanent hideouts or were on their way to Belgium or France. Niek and Aag understood the gravity of what was happening around them and believed it was their duty to save lives regardless of possible negative repercussions to themselves.

But more important, Aag and Niek, who became our dearest friends, were both idealistic and totally down to earth. In fact, they went about their resistance work so calmly (the word "calm" was never used to describe me), as if it were the most normal thing to do. Aag and Niek were socialists and pacifists. He had been a conscientious objector and spent time in prison to avoid serving in the Dutch colonial army. Both were active in the Volkshuis, a Settlement House in Rotterdam-Zuid, which formed the center of their lives. Volkshuis members believed in mutual help and attempted to reduce the role of money in their lives and thinking.

Niek had three responsibilities. He was a youth leader, the principal of the School of Social Work in Rotterdam, and the head of the entire Volkshuis. The Volkshuis leaders were extraordinary human beings best compared to Jane Addams, founder of the Settlement House in Chicago called Hull House. Both houses were part of an international social movement to end poverty. Both were socialist, democratic and pacifist. Both attempted to make fine art and literature, the music of all nations, poetry, and philosophy accessible to others with minimum ostentation or bureaucracy.

I do not want to idealize [the Volkshuis], but nowhere, not even in the Israeli kibbutz, have I seen such comradeship, such willingness to share, as in the Volkshuis. Among the hundreds of member families, almost all sheltered a Jew or took part in resistance work. Throughout the entire occupation, the Germans never caught on to the actions of the Volkshuis. Whenever I contemplated an ideal future society, the image of the Volkshuis came to mind. In turn, the Schoutens admired our form of Zionism and our efforts at building a socialist society in the homeland-to-be. The closest the Schoutens came to our world was through the "I-Thou" philosophy of Martin Buber.[105]

A habit of the Schoutens that my parents valued was sitting in silence or walking in silence on hikes. Because Jehuda and I did not know about the Schoutens' preference for silence, we had to get used to this practice when we visited them in Holland. When they sat down to eat, they didn't speak at all. Sitting in silence was foreign to me. In my German Jewish family culture, people were always talking, quoting, or arguing about some point or another. Even the study of holy texts was based on arguing/debating with one's study partner (called *chavruta*).

Quite aside from sheltering us and sharing their last morsel of food with us, Aag and Niek shaped our character. The Schoutens – two modest, highly intelligent yet practical people – had a crucial role in saving Ilse and me physically and spiritually. From a Jewish perspective, this Dutch Gentile couple were two of the 36 Righteous People of their generation.

The Theater and the Piano

Niek had a keen eye for finding just the right way to help someone. For me, he arranged an evening of theater at the Volkshuis and a 24-hour uninterrupted period to practice the piano there. These were gifts from the gods, a chance to partake of culture. The clandestine Volkshuis theater group had planned a performance of Henriette Roland Holst's play, `Thomas More,' a masterpiece of magnificent language, but alas, never translated from the Dutch. What made the play even more significant was that it represented a protest against German brutalities. The amateur actors of the Volkshuis had worked on it for months, and at each rehearsal they had to post guards at the various entrances to the building.

I sat in one of the last rows and acted totally unconcerned, as if I was a Volkshuis member. The place was packed. Some people shook my hand, others paid no attention to me. I believe that everyone in the hall knew I was a Jew-in-hiding. There may well have been others present, in the same situation. I can't say enough about the moral encouragement I received from watching that performance, from crying with the audience when Thomas More said goodbye to his favorite daughter before he went to his execution. As I look back on my life, that performance of Thomas More *stands out. I think there were moments during the play, performed in secrecy and under great risk, when all of us in that Volkshuis hall felt as one, united in thought and feeling, as though a mystical bond tied performers and audience together. The small, printed program for this theatrical event, decorated with sketches of stars and planets, was nestled among the papers in my parents' basement.*

Throughout our stay with the Schoutens, we were extremely lucky to be ignored by the Germans. And so as the weeks went by, I was permitted an occasional visit at night with some of the Schoutens' friends, allowing me to make new friends myself. In addition, one night Niek took me to the Volkshuis and locked me in a room so I could practice piano all the next day until evening when he returned me to our hideout. The delight of playing the piano for a full day was indescribable.

The Schoutens' Library

There were many books in the Schoutens' home, although none of their friends, nor they themselves, had a college education. Simply put, their thirst for knowledge led them to read good books all the time. They were particularly drawn to the work of that saintly (she would certainly protest this label!) Dutch writer, much too little known abroad, Henriette Roland Holst.

During the occupation, Holst refused to join the Nazi-imposed Chamber of Culture. Moreover, her calls for support of the Jews led to the founding of the illegal newspaper *De Vonk* (Dutch, *The Spark*) to which she contributed from early 1941 on. Holst's work was a key component of Dutch clandestine literature during the Occupation and put her and her readers in great danger. Her magnificent, inspiring poem about the fate of Dutch Jewry was circulated in various underground groups leading her to become the greatest spiritual influence on this entire generation among a segment of the Dutch people.[106]

Jeroen Dewulf's 2010 book about Dutch clandestine literature includes a section on Holst that is reminiscent of the White Rose anti-Nazi student group in Munich. The White Rose group is famous, in part, because its members tossed anti-Nazi pamphlets into the atrium of the University of Munich's main building. The bronze reproductions embedded in the floor serve as a memorial to White Rose members.

Similarly, "the most famous action of the De Vonk group was scattering Stars of David from the Amsterdam department store De Bijenkorf, in the hopes that if everyone wore the star, *Jews* and non-

Jews would be indistinguishable."[107] Unfortunately the hoped for outcome did not materialize.

Ilse in Rotterdam

Ilse's lack of "pronounced Jewish features" and her documented false name [Tina Ressen], enabled her to move around relatively freely. She decided to help one of the Volkshuis' children's groups, and from then on, she worked professionally with children all her life. It did not take long for Ilse to become well-liked by the Volkshuis crowd. Nobody asked any questions. Tina was just one of the Schoutens' new friends who stayed in their house.

There was folk dancing and community singing, there were outings and poetry readings and camping trips. Of course, I had to be excluded from all of this, but Ilse's new life helped me regain a sense of proportion beyond my absurd, indoor existence. Yes, there was another life out there, not only executions, deportations, people going into hiding, and needing to find identity papers and food stamps. Nevertheless, it was hard for me to endure being alone in the hot apartment on a nice summer weekend when Ilse was out on some resistance errand, constantly alert for unusual noises, never permitted to open a window, and certainly not to answer the doorbell. Nor was there a telephone, for better or worse.

Helga

Aag had given birth shortly before Ilse and I began living with the Schoutens. Helga, their first child, was six weeks old when I arrived. Two or three days later, Aag had to go on some errand, and Aag's mother, who knew all about me, asked me to hold the baby for a few moments. "Do you see something?" she said to me, and I told her that I thought that little Helga was a Mongoloid child. "The doctor did not want to tell Aag," the grandma said, and "Aag did not want it to be true." Why God selected these good people for this misfortune (and more) has remained one of the many unanswered questions in my life. However, to see Helga grow up, especially after liberation, and to witness the way her parents treated her, was an inspiration. They made an accepted, valuable, cheerful human being out of her.

If I were to write about Helga today, I would express these thoughts in completely different terms. Writing in the 1980s, I see that my language is characteristic of an earlier era when people still used the phrase "a Mongoloid child" rather than "a child with Down syndrome," a time when doctors did not tell parents their child's diagnosis, and a time when parents were thought to make human beings out of their children, particularly special needs children. But my insensitive language should not diminish the point I was making, i.e., that I admired the way Niek and Aag raised and adored their daughter. Helga was a lovely person with interests and friendships. We met numerous times and I saw how she brought joy to her parents and everyone around her. She was not, as I mistakenly wrote, the Schoutens' misfortune, but rather their very good fortune. The Schoutens taught us to value life profoundly. When their second daughter was born, they named her Ilse in honor of my Ilse. Their third daughter was Wanda.

An Inside Hideout

Toward the end of summer 1944, Niek and Aag invited Ilse to accompany them on vacation. For safety reasons, I could not join them, nor did I want to stay by myself. So I decided to go to the home of a new friend, J.W., who had just returned from the Russian front as a forced laborer for the Germans. He told us how he had sabotaged much of the work behind the German lines. At J.W.'s request, his mother gave me a room in the attic of her house. Although this attic room was probably secure, I took no chances and asked him to set up a "hideout in my hideout."

And thus, a leader of a parallel underground group built me an ingenious "inside hideout" which is worth describing. It consisted of a large chest for old rags and clothes, called a "lappenkist" [Dutch, rag box), something Dutch families liked to have in their attics. My friend sawed out the bottom of that chest and made it into a trap door, leading into a closely fitted, sawed-out portion of the floor, with a compartment the size of a large coffin, which in turn, formed the upper part of a clothes closet on the floor below. All I had to do was climb into the rag chest, go through the trap door, lie down flat, and pull everything close on top of me, with the rags falling into place by themselves.

There were a few air holes for breathing and the rest would have to be a matter of luck, meaning above all, no search dogs in case we had a razzia or were betrayed. Fortunately, I never had to use the much-admired contraption. Nevertheless, the very existence of this special hideout made me feel safer.

D-Day and its Aftermath

On June 6, 1944 (D-Day), Allied forces stormed the Normandy beaches in France and began to take possession of the German fortifications atop the cliffs. The successful invasion allowed the Allies to gain a strategic position from which they planned to push back the Germans and liberate the Western European countries under their control. One of those countries was the Netherlands. In the summer weeks following D-Day, the Allied military forces advanced, liberating Paris on August 25 and entering Belgium on September 2. The Allies began their attack on the Netherlands that same week. Labelled "Operation Market Garden," the Allies' goal was to proceed from the south to the north of the Netherlands via the Dutch city of Arnhem. The Allies' next objective was to liberate the rest of the Netherlands, the last German stronghold in Europe.

While hiding in Rotterdam, I was able to witness the Allied preparations for the Arnhem battle. Endless rows of big warplanes trailing long chains of gliders come over from England on their way to Arnhem where British General Bernard Law Montgomery (aka Monty) launched his ill-fated assault against the Germans. It was a beautiful evening when these endless, serene, processions came quietly over a clear sky, unperturbed, radiating a message of hope and little interfered with by German planes. There was only an occasional flak salvo in our neighborhood. Our expectations were high as we looked heavenward – only to be dashed during the next few days when Monty became bogged down.

Part of the Allied military strategy was to drop airborne troops to secure key bridges and towns along the route of the Allied advance. At first the Allied troops made good progress. So much so that on September 4, Pieter Gerbrandy, the Dutch Prime-Minister-in-exile, broadcast from London that the city of Breda had fallen to the Dutch, a sign of "inevitable" Dutch victory. When they heard the news, the residents in southern Dutch towns began celebrating the end of the war. The next day, September 5, the frenzy reached Rotterdam where people danced in the streets. But their dancing was premature. Instead of an Allied victory, the warring sides were locked in battle from September 17 to September 26.

After nine days of fighting, the shattered remains of the British 1st Airborne Division were withdrawn. This Division had lost nearly three quarters of its strength and did not see combat again. The celebrations ceased and were renamed "Mad Tuesday." Two films on the ill-fated Battle of Arnhem vividly depict the bravery and errors of this attempted liberation.[108] Instead of an Allied victory, the Dutch people of the northern half of the country had to endure an eight-month stalemate.

There was, however, an upside to the premature announcement of victory: anticipating an Allied victory, 60 percent of the Dutch Nazi Party (60,000 out of 100,000) fled to Germany. Similarly, fearing defeat, some German soldiers in the north abandoned their posts, destroyed documents, and ran for shelter.

Dad wrote, *"I realize that when I describe the liberation of the north on May 5, 1945, my writing seems somewhat subdued. Perhaps this reflects the false promise and dashed hopes of the 'first liberation.'"*

Strikes and Hunger

The long military pause that kept the northern part of the Netherlands (where Dad was hiding) under German occupation produced a series of events collectively known as the "Hunger Winter," which could just as well be called "The Hunger and Cold Winter." This period of misery began when the Dutch government-in-exile decided to retaliate against the German offensive in the south by ordering a universal railway strike. All railway personnel obeyed, but the Germans turned the deed to their own advantage when Seyss-Inquart imposed an embargo on all provisions. The western district (where the big cities of Amsterdam, Rotterdam, Utrecht, and the Hague were located) was doomed to hunger.

The Dutch railway strike to punish the Germans backfired. In retrospect, the Dutch leaders should have realized that the Germans would implement some sort of reprisal, as they always did. Dad's memoir contains his interpretation of the railroad strike and its consequences.

A grandiose operation, faithfully carried out with great bravery, it paralyzed much of Holland that was still under the German heel. This strike hurt the oppressor while binding the native population together in one gigantic resistance group. Without wanting to idealize, this, at least, was our feeling at the time.

I think it was the 20th [of November] when the tension that had been building up finally exploded. The Germans seemed to be uncertain as to where to shift their troops. The Allies had liberated the entire south of Holland, but the North was still in enemy hands. Allied air bombardments had become so routine that we paid little attention to the humming in the sky day and night. Through the dark streets you could also hear the rumbling of German troop movements.

Occasionally soldiers would confiscate bicycles and food from women who had made their way like strings of insects to the farms on the island south of our city. Some of the German soldiers were even friendly.

Moving to a New Home

Ilse and I hid in Niek and Aag's Rotterdam home together with their infant daughter, Helga. In late September, right after the unsuccessful "Market Garden Operation," Niek and Aag told us that Aag was pregnant again and thus they had decided to move to a different house to accommodate their expanding family. We either had to go with them, which would make the new house very crowded, or find another place to hide, which we did not want to do. The situation was resolved in a positive way. Niek's parents had been vacationing in Brabant over the summer and were barred from returning to Rotterdam. Their little house in Rotterdam stood empty. Niek suggested to Ilse and me that we move in there. This idea had many advantages – space above all, and with it a chance, finally, to take a more active part in underground work. But it had its drawbacks, too: we were separated from our friends by at least a ten-minute walk, not a small problem at the time.

And so Ilse and I moved into Niek's parents' house and, for the first time, lived together on our own. My War Diary entry for October 1944 conveyed an upbeat tone: *Despite many disappointments, the day of liberation is slowly coming into sight.* (It would take another six and a half months!) *A little more patience and we may enjoy daylight again. Although we have much more freedom of movement, the German police and their traitorous Dutch helpers are more active than ever. Europe resembles an empty fireplace because of the cold. Possessions are destroyed to get temporary warmth. Nowhere can we find the reverence for human life that has been crushed for so many years.*

True, the railway strike harmed the German armies, which could no longer transport its troops, but it also paralyzed the Dutch civilian population. The punishment the Germans inflicted was systematic starvation of occupied Holland... There were no longer any differences – Jews, resistance fighters, collaborators, everybody hungered except the Nazi higher-ups. The Germans wanted to bring the entire Dutch people to its knees, a people who had acted very kindly towards Germany in the past. To name only one example, Holland took in thousands of German children after World War I and nursed them into good health on Dutch butter, eggs, and cheese.

Had the Arnhem operation succeeded, the war would have been over before the winter, and 25,000 people who died of hunger might have been saved, including those left in the Dutch concentration and transit camps.

When we learned that things did not go well in Arnhem, we knew that the war would continue much longer, and that the Germans, although they knew they would lose, would turn more and more irrational, repeating their Gotterdämmerung of 1918 that brought World War I to an end.

Dad's apprehensions were justified. The last winter of the occupation was the worst. The only Dutch people who did not suffer were members of the Dutch government-in-exile who lived in England and who had ordered the strike. German revenge took the form of enforced starvation and murder. German authorities rededicated themselves to the goal of killing all the Jews in hiding as well as others defined as enemies. Thus, in November 1944, and in full understanding that they would soon be defeated, the Nazi forces in Rotterdam alone ferreted out and deported thousands of Jews in hiding and sent them "to the east" to be murdered.

In case a rescuer was betrayed, the Germans would shoot the rescuer and the Jew on the spot. The German rulers of the Netherlands did not limp to defeat when they realized they would lose. They increased their ferocious behavior.

I wrote my final entry of the War Diary *just before the start of the Hunger [and Cold] Winter. I urged all of us to face the future with a plan to rehumanize young Germans. "Our task is not to produce an endless enumeration of our sufferings…; we should not get involved in a repetition of all the atrocities, so extensive that the mass of German youth won't believe it anyway. Our task is something completely different, and that is what we owe the survivors of those atrocities. We must help educate young Germans into socialism, into pacifism, into becoming human!" When General Eisenhower considered how long it would take to reeducate Germans to uphold democratic principles, he estimated at least 50 years.*[109]

Before embarking on the gargantuan task of re-educating the German youth, everyone had to make sure that they themselves survived. That was not an easy task, given that the Germans interfered with basic human needs for food and warmth. As Ilse and Dad moved into the elder Schoutens' home, the "Hunger Winter" moved in with them. Nevertheless, they did not devote every waking minute to scrounging for food or coping with cold and fear. *I fill the long empty hours with contemplation. What is evil? What is justice? Is socialism the answer? Is Zionism the Jews' salvation? My writings are filled with these philosophical and existential inquiries. I plan to produce articles on these questions for resistance newspapers.*

Before the war, German leaders looked upon the Dutch people as spiritual and physical relatives who were rooted in the same "Aryan" stock. But the Germans had come to hate the Dutch for engaging in resistance. At the same time, some German military personnel began switching sides and deserted their posts as they anticipated defeat.

After the fiasco of Montgomery's September attack on Arnhem, we faced a much more difficult life. The Germans were nervous. Many of them realized that the war was lost for them, and some tried to "hedge their bets" by contacting some of the underground people and helping us. We had none of this in Rotterdam yet. But it was soon to come. We had to protect ourselves from the vengeful Germans and Dutch Nazis who pursued us until the war's last day.

There is a debate about how many Jews became "*onderduikers*" – probably 28,000 – and how many survived – approximately 8,000. After November 1944, the Nazis conducted mop-up *razzias* to kill Jews and non-Jewish members of the resistance. Their goal was to root out the 28,000 and finally make the Netherlands Judenrein. The main fury of the Germans at this stage was reserved for the Hollanders who increased their resistance as the war continued, knowing that Hitler's end was inevitable. It was a question of time, of nerves, and of the stomach.

Dr. Banning's Report

To describe more precisely the Hunger Winter and its impact, consider material published in *The British Medical Journal* of April 19, 1947, two years after liberation. Written by C. Banning, M.D., the Chief Medical Officer of Public Health in the Netherlands, the article, "Occupied Holland: Public Health," states:

> Before the war, Holland ranked among the highest [i.e. best] of nations regarding health. The death rate of babies was extraordinarily low. During the war, the infant mortality rate increased... Immediately after the liberation, in the summer of 1945, despite the restored good food supply, the death rate of babies was very high. Many babies died within a few days of being born with toxic appearances lacking a definite cause.
>
> Malnutrition did not occur in the entire population of Holland,

only in the western district where 4-5 million people or half the Dutch population had not yet been liberated. Malnutrition affected *in utero* development and led to the quick post-partum demise of newborns. Malnutrition was not the consequence of a poor crop season or bad weather – it was the product of a deliberate German policy...enemy starvation.[110]

This policy was used as a tool of genocide throughout the Holocaust. Dutch women, especially Jewish women, had to locate "food" that had escaped the Nazis' dragnet. They ate this "food" themselves and fed others. Banning explained this phenomenon very clearly:

> Officially, no provisions were allowed to be transported, but it was often possible for people to break through the German line towards the north and east. In that cold winter, thousands of girls and women, on bicycles without tires, badly dressed, with poor footwear and starving, went in search of food. Journeys of 100 to 200 miles were no exception. They came home laden with 30-50 kg. of potatoes and some wheat and could live for a few more weeks on that. Men between 16 and 50 years of age did not dare show themselves in the street as they would be rounded up and deported to Germany. Consequently, our women and girls had to carry out this almost superhuman task alone.

Fifty-six years later, in an interview on November 25, 2000, Ilse described the Hunger Winter, saying, "People's metabolism changed because they couldn't get any fat content." She tried to adapt to the situation by eating less on a regular basis rather than "stuffing herself" if she found something and then not having enough for several days. What seems to have saved them was the sugar beets that Ilse boiled and then mashed. Under normal conditions, this mush is used as cattle fodder. People scrounged in farms to find leftovers from the cattle and from the factories that processed these beets. Ilse found one farmer who gave her a shovel when she asked for potatoes. All he said was "dig!" Which she did.

Courageous, persistent, and strong, Ilse found a farmer who gave her Brussel sprouts and let her sleep in the hay of his barn.

Ilse's feet swelled, a sign of Hunger Oedema. "But then, a non-Jewish friend visited and brought a cooked potato," she explained. "We also got some food from the organization that helped us hide and sometimes came simply to visit, talk to us, and give us ration cards and coupons. The most we could get for these coupons was two loaves of bread, for which we had to line up at a soup kitchen." Never one to exaggerate, Ilse explained that while she stood in line, people were collapsing onto the street and even licking the pavement if they suspected the presence of some food droppings.

In our little house Ilse and I suffered just like everybody else. Had we been in the country, things would have been easier. We ate everything we could lay our hands on – raw vegetables, flour, actual waste. I saw people poking through garbage heaps for some edible vegetable leftovers. Black market operations helped a little, if one had the money to pay the prices, but even those sources dried up after a while.

In February 1945, three months after the German retaliation and three months before liberation, most Dutch people were living on 340 calories per day, less than what was provided to Jews in Auschwitz.[111] The only ray of hope was the Allies' progress. In March 1945, the neutral countries of Europe reached out to feed the people of the Netherlands. The Swedish Red Cross provided the entire occupied Dutch population with a loaf of white bread per person. Then they organized another distribution of bread including margarine.

During the week before liberation there was barely anything to eat at all in Rotterdam; only a distribution of 230 calories per day that would last a few days. As the calories decreased, the death rate increased. Children living on their own were particularly vulnerable. People in hiding had to rely on the willingness of their helpers to share the continuously shrinking supply of food.[112] The one factor of "luck" in all of this was that the war came to an end soon after the lowest point was reached. If the Canadians had not liberated the north on May 5, there might have been mass deaths by starvation for the people who lived in the most affected areas.

An Especially Cold Winter

Food was not the only item to disappear. As Banning wrote: "The population [of the northern part of the Netherlands] lived without light, gas, heat, soap or adequate clothing and blankets." And one should remember that Banning was writing about the Dutch in general, not specifically the Jews in hiding whose situation was always worse. People began to chop down trees for firewood. "The beautiful trees in the parks, in backyards, along the highways, were victims of the Occupation, too!"[113] In the face of the destruction or theft of their resources, the Dutch became very creative. People burned whatever was expendable in their houses: doors, walls, banisters, floor beams, etc.

Dad wrote in his memoir that "*a friend came over to show us which cross beams could be removed safely without the house losing its essential support. When there was no more electricity, somebody came up with the idea of a small dynamo in the shape of a waterwheel strapped to the water faucet. If you kept the water running, it would give a little light for half an hour or so from a bicycle lamp activated by the waterwheel. We read underground news in this fashion. But when enough households resorted to that arrangement, the Germans ordered the water pressure to be lowered. It was a rough fall and winter, that last year of the war, worse than anything we had lived through before, brightened only by the ever-growing hope of Germany's collapse. And by now the spirit was one of total resistance. Everybody was against the Germans, and you could trust people as never before.*"

Ilse Saved My Life

In November 1944, during the `Hunger and Cold Winter,' the Nazis conducted razzias in Rotterdam to root out all the Jews and others in hiding. On November 20, during one of these razzias, the Germans came to the little house in which we were staying. Under very difficult circumstances, Ilse saved the day and prevented both of us from being murdered. I told my children this story countless times, usually concluding by saying that I could never repay Mom for what she had done for me. This is the story.

Early in the morning on November 20, things began to get quite dangerous in Rotterdam. We heard shooting in the streets. People were screaming and running. I went down into the basement hideout several times including when Ilse stepped out for half an hour to bring home our daily ration of soup from the community kitchen nearby. When she returned, she said that a German razzia was in full swing to press 40 or 50,000 Rotterdammers into forced labor in Germany.

Since morning they searched one neighborhood after another, scaring people with their wild shooting. One woman simply looking out her window was shot and killed. The Germans picked up any man in the street they thought was fit for work. When Ilse finished her report, I descended into my special hiding place, the crawl space underneath the house. Heaps of dirt and ashes had fallen through the grate of the hearth on the ground floor. I pressed against the thick outer foundation wall as hard as I could, all the while burying myself deeper and deeper into the debris, covering myself completely.

Suddenly, the noise in our little street increased, and then came the inevitable doorbell ring. Ilse was my guardian angel. She acted cool and composed. In fact, she behaved as though she was a bit annoyed at the inconvenience imposed by the German Nazis. She was a "German nurse," all alone in the house since the owners were away temporarily, and she took care of things for them. The German gangsters entered through the front door, looked in all the rooms, went out the back door to search through the little patio and the garden patch, and then came back in. I was quaking in the basement.

It was pure luck that the Germans had no dogs with them. Those beasts would have sniffed me out in no time. I heard the soldiers' boots over my head, every word, every noise they made with their banging gear. I prayed that I would not have to cough or sneeze. When they were directly above me, I pushed myself even further into the wall because sometimes the Germans liked to shoot through the floor randomly. If so I hoped their bullets would somehow ricochet away from me, off the hard rocks of the foundation wall. Once again, I was lucky. I made absolutely no noise and even stopped breathing.

Then there was a moment of additional tension. We had a photo of Shushu on the chest in the living room. He certainly did not look like an Aryan specimen. One of the men pointed at it and asked Ilse whether that was her boyfriend. She gave an evasive answer and added: "You gentlemen haven't searched upstairs yet, and here are some more closets you have overlooked." That was a stroke of sheer genius: they forgot the photo, looked around a bit, and got ready to leave in no hurry.

As they retreated through the front door, they turned to shake hands with Ilse, their "fellow German." And it was at that moment that I think we faced the greatest danger in our underground existence. Ilse instinctively recoiled from shaking their hands. They hesitated, obviously stunned, and then... O miracle, one of them laughed and said, "Ach, we are not like those guys who molest our own girls...!"

Was it God's intervention that made that bum follow this line of thought, or was it his stupidity? I did not know, and fortunately, never needed to know. All of Ilse's sangfroid would have been for naught had those idiots said to themselves: "Why doesn't she shake our hands?" Later, when we had a chance to talk calmly, we realized how little it would have taken to turn matters the other way... Those bandits must have thought that Ilse was frigid, a prude or what have you, some spinster nurse that had never shaken a man's hand. She saved my life, and in all probability, her own along with mine. We cried with relief.

Years later when Mom and Dad were in their 90s and spent their time holding hands on a couch in their Fort Lee, New Jersey, apartment, Dad would ask me, "Do you know that Mom saved my life?" He loved her for that. And he never altered the story by saying that he also saved his own life by hiding effectively in the ash pit under the hearth.

This incident affected me so deeply that on that day, I resolved to change. I wanted to repay my debt for having been saved so far. I made a commitment to help others rather than just continue to hide. We both resolved to take a more active part in the resistance movement. Neither Ilse nor I could sit back any longer and let others risk their lives for us.

Joining Resistance Organizations

It would have made sense for me not to press my luck now that the war was creeping to an end. But Ilse and I did the opposite – we joined the organized Resistance. And we did so under the challenging conditions of intense cold, crushing hunger, and being hunted relentlessly. We both had evaded danger for so long. Why did we volunteer to endanger ourselves now when the end was so near? The answer lies in the pain of idleness associated with hiding. Ilse felt the same way.

But what effective action could we undertake? Jewish men couldn't venture outdoors. How could I aid the Resistance while staying indoors? Ilse's situation was different. She could go outside as "Tina Ressen." As a native German speaker, she could pass as a German Gentile woman who had been in the Netherlands long enough to learn Dutch. So using her wide network of Volkshuis friends, Ilse contacted members of the Resistance to see what kind of help was needed.

The Dutch formed resistance organizations relatively late in the occupation, but by this point various groups had emerged, each with its own goals. A few made saving Jews a priority, some were male-only, some were armed, some were church-based. The two main contenders for Ilse and Dad were the Socialist Group that repudiated arms and was not tied to a political party, and the underground communist organization, the first resistance group to organize in the Netherlands.

Our communist friends were tightly organized, totally pragmatic, and daring to the point of recklessness. No questions were asked when a mission was ordered. And there was the Communist Party – all-powerful, palpable, and yet invisible. People carried out the organization's work with limited information about the organization itself or about the higher-ups in the party hierarchy. This way anyone captured by the Germans would be unable to betray leaders. A strict command structure was in place. Impressed by the organization's structure, I joined the Dutch Communist Resistance.

But the communist group had a major problem. They tried to remain loyal to the Soviet Union even though, on January 23, 1939, Russia had signed a non-aggression agreement with Germany. This pact meant that the Soviet Union, now allied with Germany, had become the communists' enemy! After Germany turned on Russia, Europeans looked to the Soviet Union as a symbol of hope.

Our gratitude to the Soviet Union increased even further on January 27, 1945, when the Russians liberated Auschwitz as well as Belzec, Sobibor, and the Treblinka killing centers. But I had my doubts and after working for/with them for a while, my admiration diminished further. My main problem was that the communists ignored the very people that their ideology was supposed to aid. They were not very involved in "passive" resistance, such as hiding Jews and refugees or taking in abandoned children.

We youngsters were intrigued by some of the communists' ideological lures in the fall and winter of 1944. When the entire might of Soviet Russia was organized against the Germans in the name of the international proletariat, we hoped and prayed every single day that Stalin would win. It is not surprising that I began teaching myself Russian.

In the various resumés I wrote in the early 1950s when pursuing jobs in the US, I omitted my connection to communism. Americans would have been suspicious and perhaps even reported me to the government, which was hell-bent on capturing communist spies. After all, the Rosenbergs were executed at that time, on June 19, 1953. Nor did I mention working for the communists in my application for a visa to the US. By the time I arrived in America, I had outgrown my admiration for the communists altogether. I had become disenchanted with the ideology and the people who represented it, especially the ruthless antisemite, Josef Stalin.

At the same time, the US disappointed me by staying out of World War II until December 1941, a year and a half after Germany had invaded the Netherlands. I recognize that America entered the war only after Japan attacked the American naval base in Pearl Harbor. The US certainly was not on a mission to save or admit European Jews.

The Dutch Chamber of Culture and Illegal Newspapers

From the start of the Occupation, the Germans tried to elevate Nazi ideals by banning "subversive cultural content." As mentioned earlier, they did this by creating the Dutch Chamber of Culture and compelling all writers and artists to become members. Dutch people who defied mandatory membership in the Chamber – and there were many – were barred from showing their work. Illegal newspapers were a popular means of defying the Chamber (approximately 1,300 such newspapers appeared in the Netherlands!).

When the German secret police discovered illegal newspapers, the editors, writers, and distributors were shot. For example, Anton de Kom, from Suriname, was found circulating the illegal newspaper *De Vonk* and was executed 11 days before liberation. De Kom was one of 700 cultural workers killed during the occupation. The staff of these newspapers was undeterred. And when no more ink could be found, they devised a way of making ink from precious potatoes.

In no other country under German occupation during World War II was more clandestine literature published than in the Netherlands.[114] Historians attribute this phenomenon to the Dutch history of free-thinking. Ignoring the danger to their lives, Dutch librarians, bookstore owners, publishers and intellectuals wrote, organized, published, and distributed material that challenged the Nazis.

The underground press published opinion pieces about political and religious issues, as well as articles about post-liberation planning. *De Waarheid* was established in 1940, the day after General H.G. Winkelman, the head of the Dutch government on Dutch soil, shut down the earlier communist paper, *Volksdagblad* [People's Daily Paper]. When the Dutch military surrendered in 1940, members of the party defiantly and cleverly continued the *Volksdagblad* under a new name – *De Waarheid*.

The journalists and printers of the renamed paper set up a nationwide network of distribution handout points [*stencil posten*].

Major articles were written centrally, complemented by localized news that people in the *stencil posten* wrote. These local versions sometimes had their own names, including *Het Noorderlicht* [Northern Light], and even their own philosophy.

When I worked on De Vonk, it had become affiliated with socialism rather than communism. The paper continued publication for decades, but De Waarheid circulation dropped after the fall of the Berlin Wall on November 9, 1989. On April 28, 1990, it ceased publication altogether.

By working on the communist newspaper, I became acquainted with the higher echelons of the Communist Organization in Rotterdam, all of them a certain type: courageous, disciplined, self-sacrificing, non-sentimental and matter of fact, with no interest in the special problems of Jews or the values of the Volkshuis crowd. I had not met people like that before. In fact, the closer the end of the war came, the more pronounced my opposition became and turned into contempt. Stalin had no use for dreamers, for social idealists who created outings and folk dances for working-class families. He had no use for people who spoke of peace and friendship and adult education. Stalin was interested only in class warfare and Soviet Union dominance. The party was their church. Practically overnight I changed from a young Jew in enforced passivity to a journalist willing to jeopardize my life for the sake of producing a communist newspaper.

True, I was always interested in writing as well as in new social arrangements that might prevent future fascist movements. Ilse and I knew the risks we were taking. But we were determined. It's as if the Germans' one last push for murder was matched by our one last push for resistance. Even though there was no longer any doubt about the outcome of the war, the Germans made life unbearable for everyone. Ilse offered her services as a courier to the Communist Resistance Group in Rotterdam. And I, who had to stay indoors, offered my services on a clandestine mimeograph machine in the cellar of our house.

Ilse, the Courier

As a courier, Ilse was told she would be distributing documents for both the socialist and communist movements, a highly dangerous activity. In this role, she would go to a certain address, pick up a parcel and receive instructions about where to deliver it. Ilse drudged, half-starved, for miles through Rotterdam, all on foot, past guards and Gestapo patrols. After she delivered her parcel, she returned with another bundle. These parcels contained news items, instructions I had to mimeograph, or slogans for the next underground issue of De Waarheid. *When I finished my job, Ilse would take some bundles of printed sheets, hide them in her underwear, and carry them through Maas tunnel to the other side of Rotterdam for distribution.*

We soon discovered that Ilse was not only risking her life, but risking it unnecessarily, because often, the parcels contained only personal items: liquor, tobacco, and underwear for some of the communist resistance bosses. Outwardly these "bosses" rejected luxury items as a symptom of the distorted values of capitalism. Privately, however, they treasured the material perks of their positions. The question of justifiable risk to a courier always had to be weighed. There is a profound difference between risking your own life for the "cause" and risking someone else's.

The communists' chain of command could also be called a chain of fear. One of its purposes was to quell dissent. It was not for us to ask questions. When Ilse quite apologetically and after a sticky passage through a Gestapo line expressed doubt about the need for a certain shipment, she was rudely ordered to do her duty to the party. On the way home that day, she was forced to witness the street execution of 20 young Dutchmen whom the Germans, in a fit of rage, had grabbed from a Dutch jail. Those boys had been put there overnight by the Dutch police because they were caught cutting down trees in one of the parks to provide firewood for their families.

The Underground Newspaper

And yet, we did not quit. We diversified! I ran off the Waarheid *on my underground machine, and I worked for a second group much more congenial to us, a socialist-pacifist group, close to our heart, that produced* De Vonk. *Besides news items, it featured an ideological article reflecting socialist philosophy. There were occasional poems by Henriette Roland Holst or a quote from a pacifist or humanist thinker. A small group sponsored this sheet and after the war it continued as a monthly under the title* De Vlam [Dutch: The Flame] *because by now a flame had grown out of the spark. But this paper, too, soon ceased publication for lack of funds. We had always found the most beautiful, stimulating people in the* Vlam *circle. The Marxists and Communist Party robots would say that the* Vlam *was not class-based, too intellectual, and undisciplined in its criticism of the Soviet Union.*

Our printing and distribution of underground sheets became a daily routine. Ilse brought me the rough copy, stencils, and paper, and I would sit in the hidden, airless cellar doing the layout and typing, and then hand-cranking the machine. We thought less and less of the risks because all possible precautions had been taken. The rest was a matter of luck. After the liberation, I received laudatory certificates attesting to my role in the Resistance, including my work with the underground press.

The Deserter

During those bitter months of the Hunger Winter, Ilse and Dad became friendly with the de Jong family, relatives of one of the leaders of the Volkshuis. Cor de Jong, the young father, was an active resistance fighter. He participated in raids on offices to obtain food ration coupons, and he helped procure weapons and uniforms for resistance fighters that he stole from the Dutch *marechaussee*, the equivalent of American highway troopers, perhaps the riskiest of all underground exploits. For a while, some of those uniforms and weapons were stored in Dad's house. Finding anything like that was sufficient cause to be executed by the Germans.

Cor's group had become interested in German deserters, whose numbers grew as the war turned against the Germans. One of these fellows had given us his uniform and sidearms. These items and more enabled Cor's group to carry out "requisitioning" actions for coal and foodstuffs.

At one point, Cor met a young German soldier who wanted to join the Dutch cause, a difficult and dangerous undertaking because the soldier had to separate from his own unit and hide. Who would take him in? As could be expected, the German military police treated deserters harshly.

During the war, at least 15,000 German soldiers were executed for desertion, and up to 50,000 were killed for insubordination.

Before Cor admitted the German soldier into our group, he put him through a cruel security test in an empty apartment where he could be observed by underground people day and night. We wanted to see if he would ever leave. Did anyone come to see him? There was no telephone, no way of communicating with the outside. The deserter was given neither food nor water for several days. It came to a point that he started eating the geraniums in the window flowerpot rather than leave the apartment, which had been his solemn promise.

Cor's group decided that the deserter had proven himself. He then entered the de Jong household, an important resistance center. The boys built an arms cache and hideout in the crawl space under the living room floor. This was essentially a contraption for quick disappearance in an emergency. Even under "normal" rules of war, the authorities would have the "right" to sentence to death anyone carrying or storing arms.

The de Jong household consisted of Cor and his wife, both in their late twenties, their little daughter, Sonya, who was perhaps one and a half years old, Cor's frail mother, and his beautiful sister, Manya, in her early twenties, who managed to look attractive even under the most difficult circumstances. It did not take long for a love affair to develop between the deserter and Manya.

At least one or two evenings a week, Ilse and I went to the de Jongs' house to plan underground actions with Cor's group and engage in long talks with the deserter as he rested on the sofa, his arms around his sweetheart. I knew that relationship could have only one result unless the war ended quickly: death for the two of them.

At the same time, I, myself, became fascinated with the mysterious German deserter, Ludwig. I was drawn to him as someone who spoke German well, although it was foolhardy to risk my life just for that. Throughout the war and the period before it, I went out of my way to meet people with whom I could have an intelligent conversation. I had many long talks with Ludwig. Our dialogues were so exhaustive that I put them on paper when I returned home after each visit. That collection grew into something I titled "Letters to a German Deserter."

Gradually, I began to see Ludwig, approximately my own age, as representing the German future, and Ludwig began to see me as a kind of guide to improve that future. Consequently, the two of us began corresponding. I kept a copy of my letters to Ludwig but for some reason was unable to keep more than a few scraps of Ludwig's letters to me. Our semi-weekly meetings continued until one tragic evening when, for no apparent reason, I left Cor's house earlier than usual. Another miracle?

It was nothing but sheer luck that made Ilse and me leave an hour early. Later that night a courier awakened us with the news that Cor's home had been raided, the boys arrested, the weapons and uniforms confiscated. Cor's mother had been beaten so fiercely that she was never able to walk again. Ilse and I did not wait for one minute. We ran to Niek's apartment and the next day he found us a hiding place with an elderly couple [the Van Straalens].[115] *We feared that the criminals who had betrayed Cor may also have known about us.*

We tried hard to have Cor released through some contacts with friendly Germans, but to no avail. Cor was executed in public in downtown Rotterdam together with a handful of our comrades from the Resistance. They were among the last victims before the German surrender. After our liberation, the German commander of Rotterdam, Herr Vizeadmiral, told me that according to the law (!), Ludwig had been "umgelegt" [executed].

When we arrived at the Van Straalens' doorstep, we learned that a Jewish "onderduiker," whom we happened to know, was already hiding there! His brother was one of those young boys who followed the call-up for "Harvest Help" out of sheer idealism. I am still sad when I think of this good-looking, strong boy who had blond hair and blue eyes and could so easily have gone into hiding. Mr. Van Straalen was a retired railroad clerk, who spent his days and nights distributing union aid to the railroad workers on strike against the Germans. Having a few young Jewish people in his house during those last weeks of the war gave him added pride in resisting the oppressors. Later I mentioned the Van Straalens in a letter to my Father and requested help for this kind protector.

Dear Father,

Our host during the three last months of illegality, Mr. Van Straalen and his wife, of Rotterdam, wrote to me with a request. We had to flee to them twice: the first time for a week, the second time indefinitely. Mr. v. Straalen, a retired railroad man, has bronchitis chronica together with pleuritis chronica ("dry pleuritis"). He tried everything with all kinds of doctors and had whole periods of serious illness when he had to stay in bed. Now he is working again but does not feel well at all, and the doctor thinks he is deteriorating. He wanted me to ask you whether doctors in America have used penicillin successfully in such cases.

By return mail, my physician Father sent penicillin to Mr. v. Straalen's doctor in Amsterdam.

And so we faced another few weeks together hiding in the van Straalen home, our main problem being the lack of food. It got so bad that the Allies, with German consent (!), dropped flour, bread and canned milk from airplanes flying over the city. I doubt the Germans approved the request out of humanitarian concern. They probably were trying to win favor with the Dutch people as the war was coming to an end. Killings, food deprivation and cold were my parents' constant companions.

The Canadians

While I was talking to and corresponding with Ludwig, publishing a newspaper for a communist underground group, nearly starving to death, and moving in with new hosts who also hid Ilse, the Allied and German armies were battling each other ferociously in the Netherlands.

Freeing the northern half of Holland after the failure of the Arnhem assault required a vast international effort. Liberating forces came from the US, Britain, Canada, France, Poland, and other countries. Although the military might of numerous nations was involved in the final defeat of the Nazis in Europe, the Dutch people continue to give most credit to the Canadians. Perhaps this is because so many Canadians died in the process of liberating the Netherlands. Perhaps it was because on April 12, 1945, the Canadians liberated the notorious Westerbork transit camp where they found 876 "lucky" Jewish inmates who had not yet been shipped east. Perhaps it was because the Canadian soldiers stayed so long, leaving the country only on January 7, 1946, eight months after the end of the war. Or perhaps it was because a Canadian,

General Charles Foulkes, signed the papers with which the German commander-in-chief, Johannes Blaskowitz, acknowledged German defeat.

On May 5, 1945, victory finally came to all Dutch people. On that day, the *onderduikers*, including 8,000 Jews, came out of hiding. In Holland, May 5 is celebrated annually as Liberation Day with festivities throughout the country. The preceding day, May 4, is Remembrance Day with wreath-laying by the head of the government and two minutes of silence nationwide. Fifty-five years after the liberation, on May 2, 2000, the Dutch government erected a memorial sculpture opposite the Palace Het Loo, the royal palace in the town of Apeldoorn, where Dad hid briefly in the Jewish Insane Asylum. This memorial by Dutch artist Henk Visch is of a very tall *Man with Two Hats*. Nine days after the statue was in place, a twin statue was unveiled in Ottawa, the capital of Canada.

The identical sculptures evoke the solidarity of the two nations. The two hats, in turn, might signify war and peace, repression and freedom, life and death, sadness and joy.

Liberation

In all my writings I devoted only four brief sentences to the end of hostilities:

And then, at long last, freedom – Canadian troops moving through our city, the last enclave in Europe to be liberated. Ilse immediately helped in picking up half-dead children with swollen bellies from the hallways of houses all around. We danced and sang in the streets; we embraced strangers; we lit bonfires. A new life began with many questions.

What did I, Max Rothschild, do with my newly gained freedom? I was one of the three and a half million Jews who survived the Holocaust and had to start over again. How did they do it? How did I do it?

I am looking back to the time of my greatest happiness – May 1945. And I am trying to uncover some feelings beside those of utter elation, of a freedom that could be touched with one's bare hands, when even the still lingering physical hunger would not matter; a feeling of community, of unity with all the liberated people, when you just wanted to embrace everybody in the street. What went through my mind? Hoping to see the family again; being able to do things on my own, not being forced to remain passive all the time. All these hopes would be fulfilled.

After gaining freedom from the Nazis, feeding the Dutch became the nation's top priority. A massive program was put into place to provide food and electricity. Food had to be consumed in small amounts until people could digest normal quantities. Hunger persisted for three more months. Dr. Banning reported how the feeding operation functioned:

> By dint of extraordinary and well-organized efforts to bring thousands of tons of food into the affected area that began when the Germans surrendered, and the creation of 50 Special Feeding Teams, each headed by a physician, there was a considerable decrease in the number of deaths from malnutrition by May 15, ten days after the war's end, a decrease which continued until the beginning of August, when it disappeared altogether. [116]

Ilse and I were among those who were fed. I thought of all the years I had wasted fending off Nazi violence and oppression. Obviously, I was relieved that Ilse and I had survived, but I was also thinking about our friends who had not. These unfortunate souls had been betrayed, caught in hiding, sent to Auschwitz from Westerbork, or were active in the resistance. People like my beloved friends Shushu and Hannemann. One of the profound impacts their deaths had on me was the disappearance of my fear of death. If they could "do it," i.e., die, so could I. This, for me, is one of the great legacies they left behind. It is their silent testimony to their humanness and their Jewishness. Today's armchair heroes, Jewish and non-Jewish, would of course, have nothing but contempt for such an attitude. Over the years I have tried to prove worthy of my friends' suffering and death.

When the war finally ended, I realized it meant something different to Dutch non-Jews and Dutch Jews. Dutch non-Jews had seen much of their country destroyed and many of their fellow Nederlanders killed. For

Jews, their entire community had been nearly exterminated, and their future aborted by the loss of so many children.

Disillusionment

The immediate euphoria after the end of World War II and of "the war against the Jews" did not last long. Quickly it gave way to disillusionment and a return to old ways. As one author put it, "After a few days of celebration, the mood in the Netherlands was at best one of grim resignation about the work of rebuilding that lay ahead."[117]

This is yet another topic I wrote about. My disillusionment was directed against nearly everyone, starting with the Zionist personnel who delayed rescuing members of the youth groups. It applied to the Allied governments' gentle treatment of the Nazis after the war; to the scholars (or "so-called" scholars) who thought they understood the Holocaust better than those who endured it; to Russia, of course, which was transforming idealistic socialism into totalitarian communism; to the United States, which claimed it could not afford to bomb the death camps or bring Jewish refugees to its shores. And more.

Dad's description of the public response to the end of the war in Holland makes it sound briefer and calmer than the familiar American scenes of rowdy crowds celebrating with abandon. In Holland there was less to rejoice about. After all, Holland had been occupied by a hostile army for five years, whereas the US had not suffered German armies within its borders. Dutch cities had been the site of battles and bombing. Not so the US (other than Pearl Harbor). The Dutch celebrated the fact that both the home front and the military had been freed; the Americans celebrated that their soldiers would be coming home.

Perhaps it is not surprising that right after the word "liberated," I mention half-dead children. Although there was dancing and singing, I was immediately reminded of all the life that had been, or was about to be, lost. 19,000 Dutch people had died in combat, 8,000 non-Jews died in Dutch prison camps, and 25,000 non-Jews died because of starvation during the Hunger Winter of 1944. Over 100,000 Jews – non-combatants and guilty of no crime – were killed by Germans and Dutch forces, either in the Netherlands or in distant extermination camps. Ilse and I were two of the very few Jews in Holland who lived to see the end of the "Hitler period" in that country.

By virtue of a network of Jewish and Christian friends and helpers, organizations, resourcefulness, miracles and luck, Ilse and I had survived in the Western European country with the highest rate of Jewish extermination, the country that was the last to be liberated in Europe, the country whose operations to kill Jews SS officer Reinhard Heydrich considered to be "a model for other nations to follow." This model was almost "perfect" in exterminating the Jews in the Netherlands, except for those who went into hiding and the few that returned from the concentration camps. Finally, it was over.

It was difficult for me to grasp what had just happened. The Nazis had finally lost. They had retreated and fled. Hitler had committed suicide. The Germans were no longer in charge. I had been forced to deal with them since I had been a child. Most of the freedom-denying conditions preventing Jews and other people in the Netherlands from working, listening to the radio, riding a bike, protesting, or simply living were no longer in place. The Jewish Council ceased to exist, its leadership having been deported and killed when the Nazis no longer needed them. Some Dutch people had been active collaborators; many had betrayed Jews; and some had saved Jews.

How could I make sense of all that had occurred since January 1939 when I arrived in the country? What could I go back to? I had never been a Dutch citizen. I had no home of my own in Holland and very few people waiting for me when I came out of hiding. There certainly was nothing to return to in Gunzenhausen or Munich or Ellguth. The signing of the armistice was not like a light switch ending all the suffering. It rather was the beginning of new difficulties.

Resolutions

I remember distinctly that when the war ended, I made two resolutions of gratitude for the fact that Ilse and I were saved. I resolved to let nobody step on me and I resolved to live Jewishly, to help my people, to fight for my people. When I am depressed, it is because I have allowed somebody to take advantage of me – a boss, a colleague, an official or a store clerk. I tried not to feel sorry for myself, or sorry for being a Jew, which was beaten into me in Buchenwald, where we were made to feel guilty simply for being a Jew. Those are attitudes I am trying to correct for the rest of what's left of my life.

I believe I was successful in communicating the value of Jewishness to my children and grandchildren. My oldest grandchild showed me an essay she wrote about me. It started,

> The person who epitomizes 'Jewishness' for me is my grandfather... When I think of his values and his life, that is what gives me inspiration and confidence. A man of books with a deep love of learning, sharing stories and telling bad, repeated, and very non-PC jokes, he was a Holocaust survivor turned nomadic rabbi from New Jersey who traveled to disparate congregations around the country. I turn to him for Jewish wisdom and ridiculous humor when I face challenges. I have absorbed many important values from him: respect for others, respect for debate, gratitude for how lucky we are to do what is meaningful to us, let alone to be alive, and resistance...

In late November 1944, about 6 months before the end of the war, the British Army formed the Jewish Brigade in response to requests by such prominent Jews as Dr. Chaim Weizmann, head of the World Zionist Organization. Some members of the Brigade were British Jews; others came from Palestine. The Brigade served in the Allied campaign in Italy and was disbanded in summer 1946, a year after liberation. In the postwar period, members of the Brigade helped Holocaust survivors immigrate to Palestine illegally, a project called Aliyah Bet.

They also assassinated Nazis in Europe and smuggled weapons into Palestine, along with lifting our spirits.[118] After the war, I received a Jewish Brigade uniform and planned to kill a Nazi in my hometown of Gunzenhausen. I didn't care who the target was. But when the time and opportunity came, I couldn't bring myself to do it. For Ilse and me, the Jewish Brigade became our primary social organization until we left for the US at the end of January 1947.

Dockworker sculpture in Amsterdam, created by Dutch sculptor, Mari Andriessen

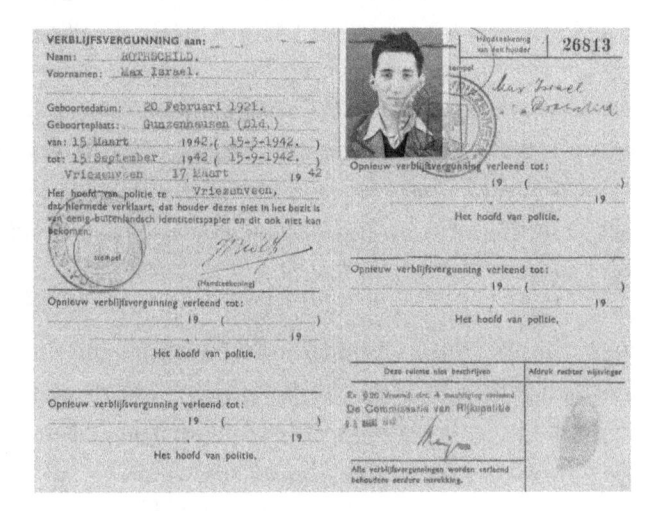

Residence permit for Max Israel Rothschild.

Women raking hay on Habonim Hachsharah in Poland as Ilse Strauss did alone in Almelo, Netherlands

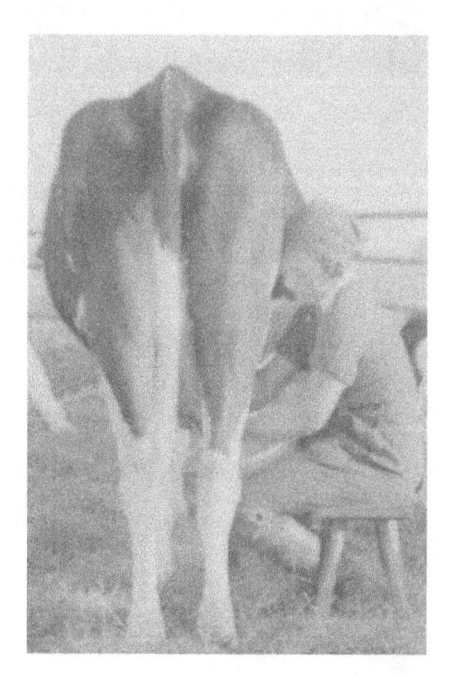

Mom milking cow.

Dad wearing wooden shoes and milking a cow.

Bernard Natt exemption from forced labor, document has Dad's photo.

Shushu when he advised Dad to hide.

Shushu's Headstone in Breda, Netherlands Jewish cemetery.

Dad's Photo before going into hiding, 1940.

Mom's Photo before going into hiding in 1940.

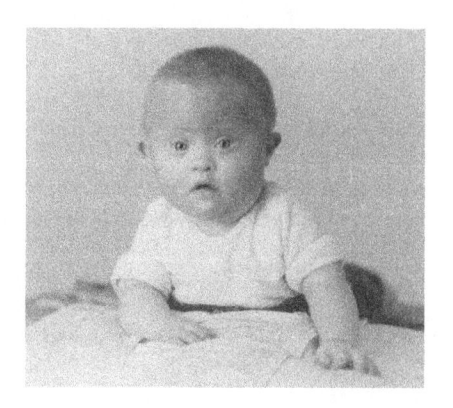

Helga Schouten as an Infant.

---

1. Chana Benninga Arnon, "Jewish Resistance in Holland: Group Westerweel and Hachshara," *Judaism: A Quarterly Journal of Jewish Life and Thought* (49: 4), pp. 449-453.
2. http:/www.nationalarchives.gov.uk/education/resources/holocaust/dutch-jewry
3. See encyclopedia.ushmm.org/content/en/article/escape-from-german-occupied-europe for a list of countries that let in Jews and how many Jews were accepted.
4. See *An Unknown Country*, a film by Eva Zelig. https://anunknowncountry-movie.com/film_team.php
5. See Vivian Jeanette Kaplan, *Ten Green Bottles: The True Story of One Family's Journey from War-Torn Austria to the Ghettos of Shanghai* (New York: St. Martin's Press, 2002) and David Brailovsky, *A Covenant in Shanghai* (New York: Universe.com, Inc., 2000).
6. Ben Braber, *This Cannot Happen Here: Integration and Jewish Resistance in the Netherlands, 1940-1945,* Studies of the NIO Institute for War, Holocaust and Genocide Studies (Amsterdam: Amsterdam University Press, 2013), p. 159.
7. Paul R. Bartrop, *The Evian Conference of 1938 and the Jewish Refugee Crisis* (Cham, Switzerland: Palgrave Macmillan, 2018), p. 58.
8. United States Holocaust Memorial Museum's Inventory of papers on Max Rothschild, focusing on "his whereabouts after Kristallnacht – based on Munich police reports and Dutch residence permits, 1938-1941." Author's Archive.
9. Dienke Hondius, *Return: Holocaust Survivors and Dutch Antisemitism* (Westport, CT: Praeger, 2003), p. 134.
10. J.C.H. Blom and J. J. Cahen, "Jewish Netherlanders, 1870-1940," in J.C.H. Blom, R.G. Fuks-Manfield, and I. Schoffer (eds.), *The History of the Jews in the Netherlands* (Oxford: The Littman Library of Jewish Civilization, 2007), p. 272.
11. David Koker, *At the Edge of the Abyss: A Concentration Camp Diary, 1943-1944* (Chicago: Northwestern University Press, 2012).
12. See Shoah Resource Center, the Netherlands, https://www.yadvashem.org/righteous/stories/netherlands-historical-background.html

13. Chaya Brasz, "Expectations and Realities of Dutch Immigration to Palestine/Israel after the Shoah," *Jewish History*, Vol. 8, No. 1/2 (1994), pp. 323-338.
14. See an essay Dad wrote: "Bialik 1956: Reflections on his Yahrzeit," p. 8. Unpublished essay, author's archive.
15. Bernard Natt, *Growing Up in Nazi Germany: Experiences and Memories of Bernard Natt* (Scotts Valley, CA, CreateSpace Independent Publishing Platform; 1st edition, 2013).
16. E. H. Kossman, *The Low Countries, 1780-1940* (Oxford: Oxford University Press, 1978), p. 621.
17. See David Sassoon, *One Hundred Years of Socialism: The West European Left in the Twentieth Century* (New York and London: Tauris, 2014). Bloomsbury Publishing as of 2018.
18. United States Holocaust Museum, 230/381 18267.
19. Werner Warmbrunn, *The Dutch Under German Occupation, 1940-1945* (Stanford, CA: Stanford University Press, 1963), p. 144.
20. Eric Kohler, "Relicensing Central European Refugee Physicians in the United States, 1933-1945," Revised version of a lecture delivered at the Simon Wiesenthal Center, Los Angeles, 2 April 1987.
21. The newly required additional documents had to be presented with the previously required papers. "These declarations are to be produced supplementary to the necessary police behavior testimonies stretching over an uninterrupted period of the last 5 years." Labeled Form VI/14, this regulation written in Dutch, and labelled Amsterdam, November 1940, was signed by the Foundation for Special Jewish Interests, Subcommittee: Committee for Jewish Refugees, Dept. of Emigration, in other words, the Jewish group established by the Nazis to handle Jewish affairs for Nazi benefit.
22. Germany reiterated its peace-abiding commitment to Her Majesty Queen Wilhelmina of the Netherlands on April 29, 1939, three months after Dad's arrival in Holland. But documents procured after the war show that Germany spent the entire year from May 1939 to May 1940 planning for offensive action on the northern flank of the Western Front including the area of Luxembourg, Belgium, and Holland. The objective of this attack was to acquire as great an area of Holland, Belgium, and Northern France as possible.
23. Leni Yahil, *The Holocaust: The Fate of European Jewry* (Oxford: Oxford University Press, 1991), p. 172.
24. Ibid.
25. Bernard Natt, Yad Vashem Documents Archive. Record Group 0.33, File number 8241
26. Seyss-Inquart was a particularly cruel individual. The purpose of his office was to control the pre-existing Dutch governing bodies, which, from then on, were "supposed to act only in accordance with German interests." Dutch government leaders set an example of collaboration and encouraged all officials and the entire Dutch society to follow their lead. Seyss-Inquart's administration was free to rule and rob Holland at will, killing nearly all its 140,000 Jews. In addition, during the five-year Occupation (May 10, 1940–May 5, 1945) the Germans plundered the assets of Dutch Jews, including bank accounts, insurance policies, stocks and bonds, real estate, valuable art, jewelry, furniture, and more.

27. Gideon Hausner, *Justice in Jerusalem* (New York, Schocken: 1968), p. 111.
28. Warmbrunn, *Ibid.*, p. 11.
29. *Documents of the persecution of the Dutch Jewry 1940-1945* (Amsterdam, Netherlands: Amsterdam Joods Historisch Museum), Translation document 138, p. 36.
30. *Ibid.*
31. Leon Poliakov, *Harvest of Hate: The Nazi Program for the Destruction of the Jews of Europe* (Philadelphia: The Jewish Publication Society of America, 1954), pp. 55-56.
32. Poliakov, *Ibid.*, p. 279.
33. Hayes, *Ibid.*, p. 196.
34. Warmbrunn, *Ibid.*, pp. 166-167.
35. Bernard Natt, *Ibid.*
36. Benjamin Aaron Sijes, "The Jews in Occupied Holland," in *Rescue Attempts during the Holocaust: Proceedings of the Second Yad Vashem International Historical Conference – April 1974* (Yad Vashem, Jerusalem, 1977). *Persecution of the Jews*, p. 535.
37. Edith Velmans, *Edith's Story, The True Story of How One Young Girl Survived World War II* (United States: van Horton Books, 2014), p. 45.
38. *Documents of the persecution of the Dutch Jewry 1940-1945, Ibid.*, p. 40, #365.
39. *The Jews of Holland during the Shoah: a catalogue accompanying the exhibition in Beit Lohamei Hagetaot* (Beit Lohamei Hagetaot, Israel, 1996), pp. 58-59.
40. Dad did not explain or describe how and why he was fired.
41. See http://www.holocaustresearchproject.org/nazioccupation/holland/netherdeports.html
42. Raul Hilberg, *The Destruction of the European Jews* (Eastford, Connecticut: Martino Fine Books, 1961).
43. Jozeph Michman, "Historical Introduction," *The Encyclopedia of the Righteous Among the Nations: Rescuers of Jews during the Holocaust, The Netherlands*, vol. 1 (Jerusalem: Yad Vashem, 2004), p. xviii.
44. Bart van der Boom, "'The Auschwitz Reservation': Dutch Victims and Bystanders and their Knowledge of the Holocaust,'" *Holocaust and Genocide Studies, (*31:3, 2017), pp. 385-407.
45. Yad Vashem. The word *"Judenrein"* can be translated as cleansed of Jews, free of Jews or emptied of Jews. See the play by Robert Skloot, *If the Whole Body Dies: Raphael Lemkin and the Treaty against Genocide* (Madison, Wisconsin: University of Wisconsin, 2006), p. xix.
46. See Hannah Arendt, *Eichmann in Jerusalem: A Report on the Banality of Evil* (New York: Viking, 1963), p. 45. Although Arendt uses quotation marks, she does not cite a source.
47. For a fictionalized, sometimes terrifying, other times hilarious, account of a Jewish Council, see Leslie Epstein, *King of the Jews: A Novel* (New York: Other Press, 1979).
48. Emuna Elon, *House on Endless Waters* (New York: Washington Square Press, 2016) p. 115.
49. Https://andocs.anglo-netherlands.org.uk/freedocs/ansAward2022Crumpton.pdf
50. My husband and I visited the hospital campus in summer 2008 and were able to imaginatively reconstruct where Dad and his friends hid.

51. Apeldoornse Bos: Deportation of Psychiatric Patients to Auschwitz-Birkenau. Holocaustresearchproject.org/nazioccupation/apeldooornssebos.html
52. Hans Schippers, *Westerweel Group: Non-conformist Resistance against Nazi Germany: A Joint Rescue Effort of Dutch Idealists and Dutch-German Zionists* (Berlin: De Gruyter Oldenbourg, 2020), p. 28.
53. In summer 1942, 40,000 Jews began to seek hiding places, but only 28,000 found them. Perhaps more would have lived had they learned earlier of the need to find places to hide.
54. And yet, he is not listed among Yad Vashem's group of Dutch Righteous Gentiles.
55. Etty Hillesum, *An Interrupted Life: The Diaries, 1941-1943, and Letters from Westerbork* (New York: Random House, 1980). In a study of 53 Jewish diarists in the Netherlands during the occupation, 19 did not go into hiding and 34 did. Of the 19, at least seven could have hidden, but decided not to. Another eight did not even consider the option. Of the 34 who did go into hiding, 14 did so without hesitation while the others hid only after prolonged weighing of alternatives, and sometimes at the very last moment. The author of the study concluded that Jews could not decide what was safer: hiding from or obeying the Germans. Similar people with access to the same information decided differently. Memoirs and interviews yield dozens of examples of Jews who could have gone into hiding but decided against it.
56. See for example, Bart Van Es, *The Cut-Out Girl: A Story of War and Family, Lost and Found* (New York: Penguin, 2018).
57. Chana Benninga Arnon, "Jewish Resistance in Holland: Group Westerweel and Hachsharah," *Judaism: A Quarterly Journal of Jewish Life and Thought,* Fall 2000 (49: 4, 450).
58. Yigael Benjamin, *They were Our Friends* (Jerusalem: Association of Former Members of the Hachsharot and the Hehalutz Underground in Holland-Westerweel Group included, 1990), p. 21.
59. Oral history interview with Mirjam Pinkhof. Oral History | Accession Number: 1997.A.0441.67 | RG Number: RG-50.462.0067
60. Chana Benninga Arnon, *Ibid.,* p. 451.
61. See https://dirkdeklein.net/2016/09/09/johan-westerweel-hero/nations.
62. As mentioned, the Westerweel group was unusual in being comprised of German Jewish Zionists and Dutch non-Jews. Shushu, Kurt Reilinger (nicknamed Nano, a friend of Dad's), Ernst "Willy" Hirsch, and "Cor" Windmuller also tried to help the pioneers escape from Holland to a destination abroad, including Palestine. Joop's wife, Willie, was arrested on one such mission. Another team member, Franz Gerritsen, falsified identity documents. In the book, *They Were Our Friends, A Memorial for the Members of the Hachsharot and the Hehalutz Underground in Holland Murdered in the Holocaust* (1990), there is special mention of Reilinger, who participated both in the Werkdorp and individual *Hachsharah*. Born in Stuttgart, he was caught by the Germans in Paris in 1944 and deported to Buchenwald. "The Jewish Black Book Committee, *"The Black Book: The Nazi Crime against the Jewish People* (NY: Duell Sloan and Pearce, 1946), pp. 271-276.
63. See Stephen Ward, "Why the BBC ignored the Holocaust: Antisemitism in the top ranks of broadcasting and Foreign Office staff led to the news being suppressed," August 1993, http: www.independent.co.uk/news/uk.

64. Edith Velmans, *Ibid.*, pp. 93-97.
65. See Cnaan Liphshiz, "Dutch-Jewish fighter whose factory was used to make yellow stars dies at 98," *The Times of Israel,* August 1, 2020. See also Vered Weiss, "Dutch mayor [Roelof Bleker] refuses to sit next to Israeli ambassador at Chanukah event," *World Israel News*, December 14, 2023.
66. Peter Hayes, *Ibid.*, p. 197.
67. See Michael A. Grodin, Johnathan I. Kelly, Erin K. Miller, Robert Kirschner, and Joseph Polak, "Rabbinic Responsa and Spiritual Resistance during the Holocaust: The Life-for-Life Problem," *Modern Judaism, 39* (3): October 2019, pp. 296-325.
68. Corrie Ten Boom, *The Hiding Place* (New York: Bantam, 1971), p. 69.
69. Yad Vashem, Shoah Resource Center, "Order to wear the Jewish Star, the Netherlands 29 April, 1942."
70. Dad never wrote out E.V.'s name.
71. Reinhard Rurup, *Ibid.*
72. *https://www.haaretz.com/jewish/.premium-1943-bbc-chief-soft-pedals-holocaust-reports-1.5422838*
73. Rabbis who were asked specific questions did provide answers. For example, Jewish parents asked if they should circumcise their sons, given that this "mark" was likely to endanger them. See H.J. Zimmels, *The Echo of the Nazi Holocaust in Rabbinic Literature* (New York: Ktav, 1977).
74. It is a mystery to me how Dad was able to put on and take off his star. After all, the star had to be sewn securely onto outerwear.
75. Jack Mayer, *Life in a Jar: The Irena Sendler Project* (Middlebury, Vermont: Long Trail Press, 2011), p. 79.
76. Ad van Liempt, *Hitler's Bounty Hunters: The Betrayal of the Jews* (Oxford, England: Berg Publishing House, 2005).
77. See Raul Hilberg, ed. *Documents of Destruction: Germany and Jewry, 1933-1945* (Chicago: Quadrangle Books, 1971), p. 140.
78. See Hilberg, *Ibid.*, p. 93.
79. The Holocaust in the Netherlands and the Rate of Jewish Survival, Marnix Croes Research and Documentation Center of the Netherlands Ministry of Justice, doi:10.1093/hgs/dcl022 474 *Holocaust and Genocide Studies* (V20 N3, Winter 2006, pp. 474–499).
80. See Ad van Liempt, *A Price on their Head* (Oxford: Berg, 2002).
81. Anthony Deutsch, "Nazis Paid Bounty Hunters to Turn in Jews, Book Says," *Los Angeles Times*, December 1, 2002.
82. See Hilberg, *Ibid.*, p. 148.
83. See also Bert Jan Flim, *Saving the Children: History of the Organized Effort to Rescue Jewish Children in the Netherlands, 1942-1945* (Bethesda, MD: CDL Press, 2004).
84. See Roxane Van Iperen, *The Sisters of Auschwitz: The True Story of Two Jewish Sisters' Resistance in the Heart of Nazi Territory* (New York: Harper, 2019).
85. Sijes, Ibid, p. 542.
86. Vera Laska, *Women in the Resistance and in the Holocaust: The Voices of Eyewitnesses* (Westport, Connecticut: Praeger, 1983), p. 84.
87. Max Rothschild, *From the Hidden: A War Diary, 1942-44,* German, unpublished manuscript, translated by Abby Huber, pp. 10-11. Author's archive.
88. Rothschild, *Ibid.*, p. 27.

89. P. Romijn, "The War, 1940-1945," in J.C.H. Blom, R.G. Fuks-Mansfeld and I. Schöffer (eds.) *The History of the Jews in the Netherlands* (Oxford, The Littman Library of Jewish Civilization, 2007), pp. 296-335, p. 316.
90. See Lucy Dawidowicz, *From that Place and Time: A Memoir*, 1938-1947 (New York: W.W. Norton, 1989), esp. ch. 1.
91. For a description of life inside Vught, see David Koker, *At the Edge of the Abyss: A Concentration Camp Diary, 1943-1944* (Chicago, IL: Northwestern University Press, 2012), edited by Robert Jan van Pelt.
92. See Jacob Presser, *Ashes in the Wind: The Destruction of Dutch Jewry* (Detroit: Wayne State University Press, English translation, 1988).
93. See https://www.bakschrijft.no/vrind.html
94. "During the Holocaust, Friesland's vibrant Jewish community was forever obliterated, including its endemic customs and distinct Yiddish dialect. It is one of the starkest examples of how the Holocaust decimated and irreparably changed Dutch Jewry." For the story of a Dutch Jewish wedding film from this community, see Cnaan Liphshiz, "Discovery of a Lost World," February 5, 2017, *The Jerusalem Post*, p. 24.
95. Erna Berg's memoirs contain a description of a similar hideout within a hiding place. See Erna Berg, *Memoirs of Life Underground: A Jewish Woman from the Village of Berne in Hiding in Amsterdam, 1943-1945* (Oldenburg: Isensee Verlag, 2010), pp. 44-45.
96. Gideon Hausner, *Ibid.*, p. 113.
97. Gideon Hausner, *Ibid.*, p. 115.
98. The Greens were Nazi officers whose task was to carry out arrests, mass raids, deportations, actions against strikers, and executions, in other words agents of police terror. See Werner Warmbrunn, *Ibid.*, p. 41.
99. Lenore J. Weitzman, "Kashariyot (Couriers) in the Jewish Resistance during the Holocaust" in *Jewish Women: A Comprehensive Historical Encyclopedia*, March 1, 2009. Jewish Women's Archive. http://jwa.org/encyclopedia/article/kashariyot-couriers-in-jewish-resistance-during-holocaust
100. See https://www.joodsmonumentzaanstreek.nl/durlacher-lore/
101. Jaap Polak and Ina Soep, *Steal a Pencil for Me: Love Letters from Camp Bergen-Belsen, Westerbork* (Scarsdale, NY: Lion Books: 2000).
102. See "The Jews of Holland during the Holocaust," https://www.gfh.org.il/eng/Exhibitions/82/The_Jews_of_Holland_During_the_Holocaust, p. 59.
103. Letter from Mr. te Riet to Max and Ilse, Almelo, February 4, 1997. Author's Archive.
104. "Jan Smit," in Joseph Michman and Bert Jan Flim (eds.) *The Encyclopedia of the Righteous Among the Nations: Rescuers of Jews during the Holocaust: The Netherlands* (Jerusalem: Yad Vashem, 2004, vol. 2), pp. 696-697.
105. Martin Buber, *I and Thou* (New York: Charles Scribner's Sons, 1923, 1970).
106. *https://jacobinmag.com/2022/03/henriette-roland-holst-hrh-netherlands-poetry-socialism*
107. Zijlma, Amber, "Between Humiliation and Pride: Describing Resistance and other Responses to the Yellow Star Badge in the Netherlands through Images, 1942," https://www.niodimagelab.nl/between-humiliation-and-pride
108. *Theirs Is the Glory* (also known as *Men of Arnhem*) is a 1946 British-focused film about the Battle of Arnhem during Operation Market Garden. Another film, *A Bridge too Far* (1977), includes British, Polish, Canadian and American forces.

109. Geraldine Schwarz, *Those Who Forget* (New York: Scribner, 2020), p. 4.
110. Banning, *Ibid.*
111. http://www.holocaustresearchproject.org/othercamps/auschwitzbasics.html
112. Banning, *Ibid.*
113. Scientists are now concerned about the impact of war on the environment. See Karl Mathiesen, "What's the environmental impact of modern war?" *https://www.theguardian.com/environment/2014/nov/06/*
114. Dewulf, *Ibid.*
115. The Van Straalen couple is not included in the Yad Vashem compendium of Righteous Gentiles in the Netherlands.
116. Banning, *Ibid.*
117. van Esp, *Ibid*, p. 190.
118. Robert Rockaway, "Jewish Vengeance: After World War II, some Jews searched for Nazis and Germans and killed them," *Tablet,* June 19, 2020.

3

COMING OUT OF HIDING

When the war ended, I asked myself: "How should I deal with the effects of being cooped up indoors for close to three years, always on the alert, not knowing if hiding would ever end?" Dad asked how he could begin a meaningful life in the postwar environment when the challenges he faced were far greater than those of Dutch gentiles.

The website of the US Consulate in Amsterdam describes the city's devastating conditions immediately after liberation, which are even more remarkable given that the Germans had dropped "only" a single bomb on the city. "There were no streetlights, no street cars or other public transport, no operating stores, except a few food shops with very limited supplies...no gas and no electricity except a very limited amount for official buildings."[1] Jewish Amsterdammer, Sem Goudsmit, wrote in his diary, "The neighbors are celebrating... Music is playing, everyone's singing loudly... But we remember the 95,000 Dutch people in Auschwitz. Families have been destroyed, burned, their heaped ashes in foreign places."[2]

In addition, although evidence was all around them, the Dutch government refused to acknowledge that the Holocaust had occurred on Dutch soil. No special measures were taken to come to the aid of the Jews during or after the war.

The [Dutch] State provided no help whatsoever to the repatriated Jews, arguing that such help should come from the Jewish communities of the Netherlands or elsewhere in the world. The Germans had departed, and the food supply had improved, but only 10,000 of the 70,000 Jews of Amsterdam survived the war – a number hardly sufficient to re-establish a community that had existed in the Netherlands for almost four centuries.[3]

Moreover, the Dutch Police required stateless Jews to report weekly until June 30, 1945, as if we were criminals. For me, the 17-month post-hiding period – until we left Holland – was almost nothing but challenges.

When Ilse and I came out of hiding, we found Rotterdam, like Amsterdam, disfigured by war. An entire culture was wiped out. The Jews were gone – women, men and children who had been betrayed or captured. Some killed by their neighbors, others by the invaders. Vanished. Not even buried. When the war was over, the remaining Jews in Holland took on a new identity – survivors. Surviving Jews sought immediate assistance.

Everyone wanted to find relatives. Everyone who had given up a child wanted that child back. The late Manfred Gerstenfeld, a vocal and persistent critic of Dutch policies and behavior toward Jews, wrote that "The remnants...had to fight an uphill battle to return Jewish war orphans to family members or Jewish institutions. The government commission appointed to decide on these cases was stacked with Christians who had their own agenda, and with baptized and assimilated Jews."[4]

Some survivors wanted psychological care. Later they would seek reparations and restitution for their persecution, slave labor and property losses. Later still, they would provide survivor testimonies, arrange for the memorialization of murdered family members and destroyed communities, and create organizations and institutions to care for disabled and aging survivors.

Survivors had to process the news of people's deaths and find ways to accept the fact that they, themselves, had survived. As was true in many countries, some Jews faced acts of antisemitism by

[Dutch] non-Jews who feared the survivors would demand the return of their stolen property. "The doors of the United States, Canada and the rest of the countries of the West remained closed to the refugees for quite some time, despite humanitarian and political efforts to the contrary (only 12,000 Jewish refugees succeeded in immigrating to the United States before 1948)."[5]

Because survivors, including Ilse and me, typically had no or few remaining family members in Holland or Germany, we were forced to seek help from and live with the people who had hidden us during the war! These people continued to help my parents and other survivors.

Rarely could Dutch Jews rebuild their lives in their former homes. Gerstenfeld wrote about Joop Voet who worked at the Beheersinstituut, the government body which acted as custodian of Jewish property. He was often told that "legal restitution to the Jews would be in conflict with the postwar economic reconstruction of The Netherlands!" Gerstenfeld also wrote about postwar Dutch Prime Minister Schermerhorn...who told his Zionist visitors "that they could not expect him as a socialist to help restore money to Jewish capitalists."[6] For several months after the war, stateless Jews were incarcerated in the same camps as Nazis because both were German.

Getting in Touch

At war's end in May 1945, I began an extensive correspondence with my family in the US that lasted until late January 1947 when I left Holland for America. In my letters, I tried to convey how I re-entered the world of the living, which I experienced as the "after-war disaster."

After leaving my hiding place, my first goal was to let my parents know that Ilse and I were alive. This turned out to be a drawn-out process that became successful only when a parallel effort was made by Daniel Roth, a London-based Jew whose family sheltered Hannah after she arrived in London on a Kindertransport in 1939. Because Hannah and Mr. Roth had stayed in touch, he knew that I had been trapped in Holland. After the war, Roth reached out to Irma de Miranda, a British woman who worked for the Red Cross in the Netherlands, asking her to locate me. She responded to Mr. Roth: "This is just to let you know that our Jewish Committee has seen that Max Rothschild and his fiancée, Ilse, are both safe and well. I suggest that if you would care to write to him, you send me a message, which I will then convey with the greatest pleasure."

The terse follow-up telegram to Malden where Dad's parents lived read: "Red Cross state Max Rothschild and fiancée well, writing Daniel Roth."

The Question of Justice

Even with the telegram, it was difficult for Dad's parents to believe that Ilse and I were alive. When Ms. De Miranda finally was authorized to send me Father's address, I wrote my first letter which was enroute to Malden for a month. "We have such a lot to tell! Yet the main thing is that we are safe. You need not worry about us. I cannot tell you how happy we are to be free at last. I was literally not free: I have been living indoors for nearly three years... [After liberation], I found nothing but anarchy here. It is very difficult to get regular work, so we are financially supported by our relief committee. We have enough to live on, but not to buy furniture, household goods, or clothes (ours are all ruined). Ilse is helping children at a Toynbee Hall (Volkshuis), and I work at a socialist newspaper. Writing will be my true calling because it is the only thing I really like to do.

But the great question is this: will I be able to support myself through writing? We both don't want to live in Holland. We would like to start a family but want to wait until we don't have to live with other people. The important thing is that we have safely come through the terrible war and will come through the after-war disaster too. Right now, we live in the home of the last couple to hide us, the van Straalens. We are so grateful to them for opening their doors to us once again."

Postwar Dutch non-Jews showed little sympathy or responsibility for the plight of the Jews during the occupation.

They did not admit to having been Nazis, betraying Jews, or stealing their property. "We saw nothing and did nothing," they claimed. A Dutch

Nazi lived across the street from one of my hiding places in Almelo. I am sure that at his arrest after the liberation, he would claim that he knew nothing... It seems to me that much of what happened after the war is but tacit consent to what was done to the Jews during the war, and sometimes it isn't even so tacit.

Only the big shots were punished.[7]

No legal punishment was adequate in view of the enormity of the crimes. The guilty went free and were now rich. I dwelled on the question of what people's behavior during the Holocaust and post-Holocaust teaches us about being human. Not a pretty picture. What is more, the entire denazification program to which we had looked forward so eagerly right after coming out of hiding turned out to be a farce. Besides Nuremberg, nothing – or so ridiculously little – was done, that my pain now is often greater than during the war years themselves. I suffer more from the failure to carry out a modicum of justice than I suffered from the brutalities themselves, and most of all I suffer from the total lack of understanding of what happened to us.

Finding People and Not Finding People

Survivors felt relief, despair, and uncertainty – relief when they learned that someone had survived, despair when they learned the opposite, and uncertainty when there was no definitive information. At war's end, Mom knew that her parents had been killed. But she soon received more terrible news: on May 13, 1943, her sister Shulamit (or Liselotte) had died of typhus in Palestine at age 26. She left a three-year-old boy (Iddo) and her husband (Alvan Treidel). For Ilse, the death of her sister spurred even further her desire to go to Palestine to be with Alvan and Iddo. "That idea helps me get through the most difficult hours," she wrote.

Ilse's immediate family had numbered five in 1940 and now was down to two. True, she was safe, but her heart was heavy and perhaps diseased. She continuously reached out to Dad's parents and began to consider them her parents as well. That feeling was reciprocated, as my grandfather wrote to her on June 20, 1945:

Mazal Tov to both of you... I embrace and kiss you, dear Ilse, as our daughter, as a hope and consolation for everything you went through. Lovingly, Yours, Father

The Desire to Help

Soon after liberation, I became Ilse's caretaker and she ceased taking care of me: reversing the roles we had while in hiding. I wrote to Father, Ilse's energy never used to flag. What should she do, dear Father? She is awfully nervous, tired, and among other things, she has lots of heart palpitations that scare me. Can you give us some advice or send medication? We do not have any energy for making [plans]. First, we must process some of the pain.

After the war, I assisted many Jews in finding their lost relatives, some of whom were languishing in former concentration camps. This led me to present a wild proposal to Father:

June 7, 1945

98 percent of all the Jews currently in the camps will not return. And the rest are in such a bad condition that only a few can survive. In one camp, 2,000 Jews cannot move about, 60 percent of them with T.B.!!! Two Jewish lieutenants went there. I read their report. It's a disaster. One is trying to get teams of doctors and nurses to help, and there are negotiations with the Red Cross about civilians being allowed to join those teams. Ilse and I are trying to join.

I would like to ask you dear Father, as a physician, to go with some nurses to those camps as soon as possible, i.e., above all to Bergen-Belsen-Celle. It's the only thing we can do for all the dear ones we have lost. And it's a shame if the people who have come through the war are not looked after. We will do everything to join a team. Now I hope you, too, will do what you can!

Despite my best efforts, my proposal to bring Father from the US to help survivors in German concentration camps did not come to fruition. Nor did Ilse's and my hope to join a team assisting camp survivors.

Survivor Guilt?

All my life, I struggled with the question of why Shushu and Hanneman died while I survived. I struggled with many unanswerable questions concerning my hiding experience, but the only guilt I experienced stemmed from two events in Buchenwald: when I held on to my sweater and when I stood by while a fellow inmate was whipped mercilessly.

There is a difference between asking these questions and suffering from "survivor guilt," which according to psychologists afflicts people who believe they have done something wrong by surviving a tragic event when others did not survive. Although Dad didn't suffer "survivor guilt," he probably suffered something that could be called "survivor anger" or even "survivor rage." These terms deserve examination as a description of how survivors felt after being liberated. From my perspective, "survivor guilt" is a phrase that seems to blame the victim.

I was angry that while I had to hide, my Dutch non-Jewish neighbors went about their business as usual, many of them carrying out the Germans' murderous plans, such as transporting Jews to the Westerbork camp.

Matthijs Kronemeijer and Darren Teshima, two fellows of an Amsterdam-based organization, Humanity in Action, explored the attitudes of Dutch non-Jews shortly after the war and found that Dutch gentiles expected gratitude from Jews for the assistance they received during the war. "Jews should thank God that they came out alive," they said. "Jews are certainly not the only ones...who suffered." Frequently, Dutch feelings about Jews were ambivalent... such as those reflected in a June 1943 diary entry by a Gentile inhabitant of Amsterdam: "What suffering [the deported Jews] had to go through... Granted they are not a pleasant kind of people. But after all, they are human beings."[8] In general, Dutch Gentiles believed they were victims, not perpetrators.

I did not have much time to dwell on these dilemmas. I had to deal with the endless practical problems Ilse and I faced, the most pressing of which was getting a roof over our heads. On July 1, 1945, almost two months after leaving our hiding place, I wrote to Father: For weeks we've been trying to find something without success...we are reduced to renting a room in the apartment of kind people. Two months later, in early September, I wrote: Our greatest difficulty is still the housing problem. I have lost hope and become a fatalist regarding housing. We long for it after years of always living with other people.

Endless Challenges and Choices

The day we came out of hiding, Ilse and I knew we had to create our lives anew. I visited a doctor early on to evaluate my health. I always tried to find food, and I tracked down survivors. Ilse volunteered in a hospital trying to help starving children. Everything was a challenge. Everything was a priority. Everything was bureaucratic. Four months after liberation, I was still writing to Father that Ilse and I wanted to stop living with our "hosts" but had nowhere to go. Thus, ironically, after the war, our housing situation seemed worse than when we were in hiding.

Young survivors in Holland, like Ilse and me, had to cope with our pasts and plan for our future. We had been forced to waste five years of our lives, years when under normal circumstances we might have gotten married, become gainfully employed, gotten a college or other education, and laid the groundwork for a career. Now that we had survived, we needed to find work. I wanted to be a writer and had already produced some manuscripts, but I needed help finding a publisher and had very few contacts in that field. Given the challenges of finding housing, getting enough food, finding work and more, I was very busy, almost frantic. But marrying Ilse was a priority among priorities. We wanted to marry as soon as possible and start a family.

As a young man with skills limited to writing, farming, playing the piano, mastering languages, Jewish Studies, and leading Jewish youth groups, I needed to broaden my education. To this end, I started taking courses at the University of Amsterdam, with Professor Kurt Baschwitz whose course "The Press and Public Opinion," was an excellent match for my interests. Professor Baschwitz hired me as a translator and research assistant and wrote me the following glowing reference:

MAX ROTHSCHILD...took my courses in social psychology and journalism. He has shown a peculiar zeal for the topics, works very carefully and displays...independent judgment far above the average students of his age. It is in the interest of science that such a promising power as Max Rothschild be able to complete his education.

Not only did Dad want to create an identity in society, but he also wanted to help rebuild the society itself, particularly the Jewish remnant. This meant re-establishing Jewish organizations that had been important before the war. *I summarized this experience in the resumé I later used to find work in the US: "After the liberation, I was active in Zionist and Jewish educational and communal affairs and took part in the rehabilitation of the Dutch Jewish community."* Not only did Dad's efforts strengthen all these projects, but, in return, his efforts bolstered him. As Werner Warmbrunn wrote, "The strength of their belief in a Jewish homeland enabled young Zionists to endure persecution...more successfully than their co-religionists.[9]

Where to Go?

German Jewish survivors in Holland had to decide where they *wanted* to go, where they *could* go, and *how to get there*. The three choices were to stay in the Netherlands; to return to their home country; or to try to go to the US, Palestine, or some other country that might let them in.

Returning to Germany was not even an option for Ilse and me. Nor did we want to remain in the Netherlands... I was disgusted with the Dutch denial of their collaboration in the murder of Jews.

Dad wrote to his Father: *You are all much too far away to be able to see what is happening here: how collaborators are walking free, traitors and Gestapo agents are being forgiven, war [criminals] are being put in office, rebuilding is being sabotaged, etc.*

Because Ilse and I were stateless, we needed Dutch permission to remain in the Netherlands, particularly since, when we entered the country, we were required to leave within two years. And to get to the unwelcoming US, we needed help from relatives or friends who lived there. Finally, there was the Palestine option. But to get to Palestine, one needed a British Certificate or risk entering the country illegally.

In 1945 the Jewish Agency issued no immigration certificates to Jews in the Netherlands. Instead, the Agency tried to use the few British Certificates it had to aid displaced persons in German camps. Triage rested on deciding who had the worst circumstances. Max's two sisters urged Max and Ilse to choose America, as they had done. Ilse's sister (Evi), on the other hand, and a few of her remaining relatives in Palestine urged Palestine. Else Scheuer, Ilse's aunt, for example, expressed her deep desire to have Max and Ilse move to Palestine. She wrote:

> Have you been able to make any progress toward your Aliyah? And if not, what can we do for you from here? We consider it a given that the two of you will be coming here as quickly as possible... You surely share our view that staying in Europe is not an option for Jews. You don't belong in any country other than this one.

Senta and Giora Yosefthal insisted that we come to Palestine and join them on a kibbutz. Senta wrote:

> For three years I have worked in the cowshed, and I like it very much. Our cowshed is one of the most economically developed branches in our kibbutz. We have 42 head of cattle, amongst them 20 dairy cows. I have raised most of them, and I'm very proud of that... I feel best amongst my good cows.

With enthusiasm, Senta described the kibbutz members' "feeling of creating something out of nothing":

> We do not have any influence on the distribution of certificates for *chalutzim* outside of Israel. We can only send a recommendation and it is worthless because there are thousands of requests. But we hope that you will come despite it all.

Ilse was sure she wanted to go east to Palestine and live on a collective farm; I was sure I wanted to go west to the US and live like my family. So we delayed our decision.

Ilse never abandoned the idea of moving to Israel, but she also never achieved it. When Ilse and Dad married and finally arrived in America in February 1947, 17 months after liberation, they assimilated into American life without shedding their Jewish, Zionist, or European identities. With effort they found a compromise. They became American Jews who went to Israel regularly and frequently invited our Israeli relatives and Dutch friends to visit us in the United States.

Writing Home

Thirteen days after my first post-liberation letter to my family, I found enough paper to write a second letter.[10] *Not only was the mail slow, but I needed the intervention of a friend to put the letter in the mail. "There is anarchy here in many matters..." I wrote in English, our new shared language. Underlying my description of the nearly futile attempt to find work was my desire to show Father that I was trying to be a useful member of the newly emerging social order in Europe. But the only work I found was writing an occasional newspaper article.*

I began my letter to my parents with an upbeat sentence: "I must say once more that Ilse and I, myself, are safe, well, and very happy to be free at last." And then Dad addressed the issue of work.

> Soon, the pace of finding work will pick up. For one set of investigative reports, I met with Jewish lieutenants who had come directly from three German concentration camps, including Celle, the camp where Fritz and Ruth had been imprisoned. When the British 11th Armored Division liberated Celle on April 15, 1945, the soldiers found 60,000 starving and seriously diseased survivors and 13,000 unburied corpses. Conditions there are still so terrible, that you don't even know if it is worth existing.
>
> It is a shame to hear of the treatment these people get after being "liberated" (some reports will be published and sent to the Allied Authorities, and we will publish them in the press, too). I still hope to be

allowed to go with the team as a pressman to report on concentration camp conditions, though it is nearly impossible for a civilian to cross the military zone frontiers. When the Jewish team goes to Celle, we hope to find out if Fritz and Ruth are alive.

Two survivors told me that except for the end of shooting, conditions have not improved since the SS left. The food and the hygienic conditions have worsened in the English and Canadian areas. The trouble is that we here in Holland may do nothing. We simply are not allowed to. There is a great need for relief teams. All these years, we have longed to do positive work, not only the nearly almost impossible negative work of sabotage. And now, when the moment finally has arrived, the old bureaucracy pops up again... And so once again, I must struggle with enforced idleness.

Employment is a real challenge for me because I have never been employed except as a "trainee" farmhand in Almelo or, for a very brief period, as an auto-mechanic "intern" and tutor in Amsterdam. I was more of a step-and-fetch-it than a trainee.

Ilse, on the other hand, has a job, Dad wrote to his Father. *She works at an emergency hospital started by the Jewish Relief unit for nearly starved children. She has a good practice in occupational therapy and keeps the poor creatures in the hospital busy. It is not easy work, but she does it gladly. Not only does she get enough to eat, but she may also take food home.*

On the other hand, I am selective about the employment I would accept. I will work only for the public welfare in a national Dutch context, or what would suit me a good deal more, in an international context. Perhaps you can imagine how much we long to leave this part of the world where every stone and every tree reminds us of a terrible thing. I am still so nervous, and I'm afraid that even you, who are so dear to us, won't understand our psychological condition after what we have gone through and are going through. We have worked hard to bring about the happy moment, but when it came at last, we were overwhelmed. Life is speeding along, but our minds linger in the past, in the well-known surroundings of danger, illegal work, hiding, and so on. Fortunately, I am not forced to earn now, because I am supported by a Jewish Relief Fund.

This week we moved again. We got a sleeping room and a sitting room with kitchen. Finally, we are our own masters. This is so much better than having to live with other people. Ilse feeds me splendidly, so I eat nearly all day long. And when I am not eating, I exercise my legs, which is critical. I haven't used them for nearly three years!!! I also play the piano. Sometimes I go to my newspaper office, but there is not much work to do there on account of the paper shortage. I've worked a few times for the Allied Staff as an interpreter. I have found the war criminals and murderers who killed our good friends.

During Dad's years in hiding, socialism was his preferred ideology, a topic about which he loved to write. But, *after hiding, my focus shifted to integrating socialism with Judaism and Zionism.*

Then, his letter of June 18, 1945, had good news.

I found the people who looked after the two younger Stein boys [Thomas and Michael]! They are both safe, one in Eindhoven and the other in Nijmegen. I found Wolfgang's name, the third son of the Steins, on an official list of persons from the mysterious [missing] train from Celle to Triebnitz [a village in Germany, with the Polish name Tröbitz].[11] However, *"poor Fritz, died in Celle."* [This was not true. Both Fritz and his wife, Ruth, survived].

The mail system was chaotic. Two of Dad's letters probably never got out of Europe, because Dad gave them to *"a Jewish chap of the Allied Forces to post and he told me that he may have forgotten about it."*

Finally, we have a nice home in Rotterdam but whether we will stay here is uncertain. I am "tramping" a little bit through the country to find hidden children, to see some old friends, to start some work, here and there, but it is really nothing to speak of... I am full of plans, but I cannot make up my mind and the whole situation here is still far too ambiguous. In any case, I shall try to continue my writing. As to my books, they cannot be published now because of the paper shortage. I'm going to Belgium and France for a few days to meet a publisher.

The Memorial Ceremony for Shushu

Four months after coming out of hiding, *Hachsharah* friends who had survived gathered to commemorate loved ones who had perished. In the southern Dutch city of Breda, they came together to mourn the death of Shushu.

Shushu always had a bit of a daredevil about him. I did not know too many details, since while we were in the underground, all of us had learned to keep information from each other. I knew, however, that he had taken care of many Jewish youngsters, finding hiding places for them and helping them avoid deportation. To do this, he had memorized dozens of addresses. I also knew that he had false papers and moved around freely whenever and wherever he wanted despite his Jewish features and the many curfews.

But then, tragedy struck. Shushu was caught attempting to cross the border between the area of Brabant in the south of Holland and Belgium. At the time he was on a reconnaissance mission to find ways for Jews to cross into Belgium and then travel south to Lisbon.

Shushu was put into the Koepelgevangenis prison in Breda to await questioning by the Gestapo. Because he feared that during torture he would reveal details of his underground organization, he asked the warden for a brush, comb, and razor so that he could "look proper" for his German interrogators. Shushu used the razor to cut his wrists. Even in death, Shushu saved Jews.

Now, in September 1945, we gathered around the tombstone we had erected in his memory. A contingent of the Jewish Brigade was there – Shushu's friends, like me, who had outlived the catastrophe, and a few representatives of the Dutch Jewish community. Although the ceremony was intended to be dignified and solemn, one person turned it into a highly emotional, furious event. The late Sam De Woolf, the aging Marxist theoretician who had lost his only son in Bergen-Belsen, screamed at the gravesite that all Dutch Jewry was guilty, because it had permitted this innocent blood to be shed, because it had not participated on a mass scale in the resistance movement led by such pioneers as Shushu.

"Today Shushu's grave is an unkempt, forgotten place," Dad wrote, "...hidden away in a small, walled cemetery (why is it so heavily walled? Are people afraid that somebody might run away with our dead?), guarded over by an old keeper and his wife who seemed disoriented."

Dad gave the primary eulogy in Dutch.

Chaverim [Hebrew: friends],

As we stand around this grave this morning, I am reminded once again, that for us here in the *Golah* [Hebrew: Jewish diaspora], *not much is left other than graves and memory.*

Shushu is one of those people you can never forget. Much has been written about him; he has been honored as one of the central figures in the Dutch Resistance. But I know that he...rejected hero worship. When I try to evoke the picture of Shushu today, I think first and foremost of the time we shared in Hachsharah in Germany. I think of our development as young people.

Shushu came from a highly assimilated milieu where he did not enjoy even the slightest Jewish education. Nevertheless, he chose the way of Judaism, of Zionism, and of chalutziut. We studied Hebrew together a lot. We celebrated life by reading Bialik and Shimonovitz, and it was always Shushu who...wanted to penetrate further into Hebrew literature and Jewish culture. It was a miracle that this chaver was able to conquer the Hebrew language given his background.

Shushu was the soul of our *chevra* [social group]. When you spoke about Shushu, it was always as though you were speaking about someone you adored – as a chalutz and chaver, but especially as a worker. Because he was not the strongest in our group, he went to work with the greatest enthusiasm. And his untamed drive to work made him so appreciated by our non-Jewish supervisors.

[Despite] the hostile world around us, we lived good lives in our group. Until deep into the night, we debated a portion of the Bible. In our youthful enthusiasm, we took a citation of [Chaim Nahum] Bialik or Berl [Katznelson] and enjoyed it for hours. This leads me to remember a *very special moment, a memory of a Shabbat evening, when as always, we sat in a large circle. Suddenly, Shushu jumped up from his chair and ran out of the building, into the woods, singing. We all ran out and followed him, singing and dancing, until late into the night. We stopped when we were exhausted. Such was Shushu, a flame that was always burning, a flame that lit up others.*

Later in the Buchenwald concentration camp, I was together with him for four weeks... He had been able to save a little copy of the Tanach [i.e. compilation of the Bible, the Prophets, and the Scrolls], *and so I see us to this day, sitting high above the ground in our 5a barrack, amid noise and rot, trying with difficulty to see the small letters of the tiny Tanach.*

Shushu was more passionate about the chalutzik idea than anyone else... He was so inspired that even in the most difficult hours, nothing was impossible for him. I remember how Shushu, along with the rest of us, was depressed when we got news of Holland's capitulation. But Shushu soon overcame the depression. He began acting with renewed courage, while others, apathetic and moping, sat bent over, unable to act.

He was the madrich [Hebrew: counselor] *for Youth Aliyah* [i.e. program to bring Jewish youngsters to Palestine]. *He visited chaverim who were working with farmers, and wherever he went, he knew how to inspire others through his personality, which was always upbeat and full of initiative. He knew how to strengthen people and give them courage.*

I had a long talk with Shushu that I shall never forget. We were on the way to the farmer where Shushu had been on Hachsharah, and where I came to visit him so often after a hard day's work, sitting until deep into the night, studying together. We spoke about the future but did not know the true circumstances that awaited us.

For him... impossibility did not exist. Eretz Yisrael, which was farther away than ever for us, seemed close by to him... With indestructible conviction, he had a solid belief in the future of the Jewish people. His deeply felt socialism and his fascinating personality allowed him to make good non-Jewish friends to whom he was bound in resistance. He worked illegally, sure of himself and his task, always courageous to the point of recklessness. He never rested and never thought of himself... We chalutzim honor his memory and his greatness... He could see the future of our people.

Shushu died in January 1943. Approximately ten years later, on February 6, 1953, economist and politician Sam de Woolf, the man who screamed at the first memorial service, published an essay, "Shushu," in the Dutch publication, *The Jewish Watchman*. It concluded with the following paragraphs:

> [When Shushu was] Seized by the Nazis in January 1943, he took his own life – so that his executioners... could not force him to betray his ideals. A few days ago, Dutch *chalutzim* [who live in Israel] commemorated Shushu's death in *Eretz* [Israel] exactly as they did in 1945... Shushu, you did what you had to do and literally gave up the last drop of your blood for others. As long as I live, I will commemorate you with the deepest respect. It is such a warm thought for me that I had the opportunity to know you, a heroic comrade. Such thoughts are bright spots in the usually tragic human condition!
>
> Did Shushu do the right thing by committing suicide? Was it certain that he would have been tortured? These questions have been laid to rest with his body. No one will ever know. And this is another consequence of the Holocaust for Jews. There are so many unanswered questions.

My experience brought nearly daily moral dilemmas with life-and-death consequences. Should I have intervened when a stranger, a fellow prisoner in Buchenwald, was tortured before my eyes? Should I have taken the risk of moving from Almelo to Rotterdam while in hiding? Should I have risked my life to visit Ludwig, the German deserter? Should I have done what Shushu did – i.e., try to rescue Jews rather than go into hiding? Hindsight raises questions; it doesn't offer answers.

Care Packages

In various letters I asked my parents to send me necessities I couldn't obtain or couldn't afford at black market prices. When Ilse and I received a "care package," we shared it with our friends as a gift or a swap. If someone needed penicillin, I asked Father to send some. I always reported on my visa problems and employment opportunities. I shared descriptions of my volunteer efforts to determine who was alive and who had been killed. I wanted to visit graves of loved ones, particularly Ilse's father's grave in the Gurs concentration camp at the foot of the Pyrenees... I put together a list of the names of all our dear ones who are missing and gave it to comrades from the Jewish Brigade who are going to be traveling to Germany soon. If I hear anything, I will update you, of course.

Dad was not only a survivor, he had an additional identity as "member of the resistance." After the war, he sought documentation of his role as a resistance member in order not to be suspected of spying for Germany. The resistor status was not something that one simply took on. Rather, it was conferred by documents that organizations issued. Getting that status was particularly important to Dad, because as a former German citizen, he could have been accused of being the enemy, an accusation that was quite common. If he wanted to cross borders or enter the United States, it was crucial to be able to prove who he had been and what he had done during the war.

My first such document was an "attestation" (or declaration) issued by the FFI, Organisation Juive de Combat [French: Jewish Fighting Forces] in Paris on June 28, 1945, six weeks after leaving hiding. The "attestation" did not mean that I had fought in a French group. Rather, this document, issued by Captain Jacquel-Lazarus, commander of the Organization Juive de Combat de Paris, certified that Monsieur Max ROTHSCHILD took part in the Dutch Section of Jewish Resistance. This Section, Jacques-Lazarus continued, was "mobilized during the oppressive period in which the Jewish Fighting Forces were engaged. Max Rothschild participated in the clandestine work of this Section. This certificate is issued for all legal intents and purposes."

Lazarus, a leader of the clandestine Armée Juive under the *nom de guerre* Jacquel, had a background that qualified him to confer the status of "resistance fighters" on applicants. On July 17, 1944, when he tried to travel from France to England on a secret mission, he was arrested and sent to Auschwitz with 50 other hostages on the last train to leave Paris for the notorious camp. Remarkably, he escaped four days later by jumping from the train, an experience he described in his book, *Juifs au Combat* (1947).[12]

Among Dad's papers were multiple affidavits concerning his resistance work. One was a card issued by the Forces Françaises de l'Interieur, Organisation Juive de Combat on September 18, 1944. On the front of the card, his very serious headshot was attached with two staples. The co-signators were Jacquel and Dad. On the back, embedded in a tricolor pattern, it states: "Je jure de lutter jusqu'à l'ecrasement total de l'Allemagne nazie" [French: I swear to fight until the total destruction of Nazi Germany.] This is followed by "Pour l'honneur, la libertée, et le droit a la vie du Judaisme" [For honor, liberty, and the right to live Jewishly].

On October 8, 1945, five months after the German defeat, Dad went to the offices of the Dutch Internal Armed Forces, Rotterdam branch, and received the following stamped statement that also documented Ilse's status:

DUPLICATE

Dutch Internal Opposition – Battalion X, Punishment

DECLARATION

undersigned declared to have contact with

Max Rothschild

And his fiancée

Ilse Strauss

During the occupation, both were pursuing illegal activities.

Undersigned thereby confirms that both people were actively engaged in the opposition.

Rotterdam, October 8, 1945

Signed, A.A. van Meenen

. . .

With these stamped documents, Dad's past was clarified, and he was able to participate in "postwar resistance". On the same day, he went to an additional office and received another confirmation of his status.

October 8, 1945: Solidarity Fund

DECLARATION

Undersigned, W. Goossenaarts, living in Rotterdam, Blokweg 49,

President of the Solidarity Fund in Rotterdam, hereby declares

Max Rothschild (hiding name: A. Van de Wetering)

And his fiancée

Ilse Strauss (hiding name: Tina Ressen)

Worked illegally for the Solidarity Fund.

Working illegally was a badge of honor, evidence of being in the resistance.

Authorization to Find Child Survivors

"Tracing children," a post-hiding task Dad undertook, was urgent and emotionally complex. The Montreal Holocaust Memorial Center estimates that thousands of Jewish children were sent to live with non-Jewish families in the Netherlands. In 1946, 3,458 children were still living in foster homes; of those 2,041 were orphaned. These children were at the center of a controversy: the Dutch government wished to leave the children with the Christian foster families and the Jewish community wanted to retrieve the children and educate them Jewishly, thus improving the chances that the Jewish community would have a future. In 1949, 1,500 of the 2,041 children were returned to the Jewish community, while about 500 others remained with their foster families.

"After the war, Jewish organizations sent investigators to locate child survivors and reunite families. In home after home, they faced the devastation wrought by the Holocaust." The Montreal Holocaust Memorial Museum continues: "In hundreds of cases, rescuers refused to release hidden children to their families or Jewish organizations. Some demanded that the child be 'redeemed' [i.e., bought] and their caretakers financially remunerated. Others had grown attached to their charges and did not want to give them up. In the more difficult cases, courts had to decide to whom to award custody of the child. Some rescuers defied court decisions and hid the children for a second time," this time shielding them from their Jewish parents or Jewish organizations.

In the Netherlands, more than half the surviving Jewish children were declared *Oorlogspleegkinderen* [war foster children] and most were placed under a state committee's guardianship. Dad volunteered to locate both types of children in the Netherlands.

My first step was to receive authorization to carry out searches so that I could try to unite them with their biological parents or other family members or make other plans for them if they were orphans. On June 22, 1945, I received the appropriate document from the Jewish Coordination Commission for the Netherlands. Under the title, Jewish Youth Aid Foundation Employee IEMX2, the Commission representative stated as follows:

We hereby testify that Max Rothschild, born on February 20, 1921, is employed by us to trace down Jewish children and uses a motorcycle, number 812 TWN, which was made available by the Southern administration of the NBS.

That same day, the Netherlands Israelite Community of Rotterdam wrote to the National Traffic Licensing Authority requesting a permit for the motorcycle TWN number 812 that I would use to track down children in hiding.

"Tracking down children in hiding" had to be done as quickly as possible because very young children saw their "foster parents" as their only parents. If one or more of their biological parents was alive, all means were used to reunite the child and parent(s). If the parents were not alive, the Jewish community wanted the children to be adopted by Jews.[13]

Those who had been infants when placed in hiding had no recollection of their biological parents or knowledge of their Jewish origins. The only family they knew was their rescuers. Consequently, when relatives or Jewish organizations discovered them, the children were typically apprehensive and sometimes resistant to yet another change. As one child wrote later, "I had been separated from my mother for so long that she didn't mean anything to me."

Jewish parents spent months or even years searching for children they had entrusted to others. In the best-case scenarios, they found their offspring living with the original rescuer, that rescuer was willing to return the child, and the child did not fight being extracted from the foster family. But time and again, the search for a child ended in tragedy, including discovering that the child had been killed or had disappeared.

Those trying to reunite families often encountered antagonism or outright refusal from the foster parents or the child itself. Jewishness for some hidden Jewish children had come to symbolize persecution, while being a Christian meant security. Some children even repeated antisemitic phrases learned from classmates and adults. Many surviving children truly loved their foster families and refused to be given to a "stranger." Some youngsters had to be pulled physically out of their foster families' arms.

Creating a Resumé

The task of creating a postwar identity based on wartime activity occupied Dad for a long time, an ordeal shared by many "onderduikers." In brief employment-seeking resumés he wrote when he arrived in the US, he eliminated aspects of his life that would not be understood in the American context. He also emphasized aspects he wanted people to know, such as his involvement in Jewish education and Jewish life.

In one resumé from 1951, used when looking for work in the US, he wrote:

I was born in Gunzenhausen, a small town in Bavaria/Germany. After completing my elementary, junior high and high school education, I finished Junior College, the Hebrew Language Institute, and the Seminar for Jewish Studies in Munich in 1938. After the invasion of Holland in 1940, I became engaged in Jewish education, youth, and community work. I was a member of the board of the Federation of Zionist

Organizations in Holland, served in its youth and education departments and was a member of the Hebrew language examinations commission. I led several Zionist youth groups and published translations from Hebrew literature as aids in education and programming.

Resumés such as this one erased my father's formative experiences in Germany and Holland. He didn't even mention that he was imprisoned in Buchenwald! Nor that he hid for three years. His life in the Netherlands sounds almost normal. In another résumé, he wrote:

Mr. M. Rothschild, a former correspondent in Europe, was the editor of an underground newspaper during the war in conjunction with Allied Forces Headquarters. He is a graduate of Amsterdam University and then Boston University, where he obtained his master's degree.

A third resumé (after 1958) offers more information:

A native of Germany, Dr. Max M. Rothschild spent the war years in Holland as a member of the underground forces and editor of an underground newspaper in liaison with Allied Headquarters. Dr. Rothschild visited the occupied zones of Western Germany in 1946 under an assignment of several Dutch newspapers and published first-hand reports of the [DP, i.e. Displaced Persons] camps. In 1946, he attended the World Zionist Congress in Basel as a delegate of the Dutch Zionist Organization.

Most interesting is a fourth resumé, also composed in the US:

After the liberation in 1945, I was elected a permanent member of the Jewish Coordination Commission of the Netherlands, formed with the aid of the representatives of the American Joint Distribution Committee. I served on the first combined Jewish-governmental committee for the saving of Jewish children in non-Jewish homes and was active in their rehabilitation and the organization of the exodus to Israel in conjunction with the Jewish Brigade.

These variations illustrate that there is no single account of a person's life. Autobiographies are unstable. Each version is designed to meet the needs of the reader and writer in the moment, and each version reflects the time in which it was written.

In the US in the late 1940s, I did some journalistic work for The New Jewish Weekly Paper [Nieuw Israëlitisch Weekblad], *a publication in*

Dutch, produced in Amsterdam. Every three weeks I sent the publisher a "Letter from America." To increase my opportunities to earn money, the editors and management of the Dutch publication sent me a letter of recommendation:

"We are pleased to introduce to you Mr. M. Rothschild, a prominent Jewish journalist. During his stay in the Netherlands, he contributed regularly to our weekly, the only general Jewish weekly in this country, and to "De Joodse Wachter," the Zionist bi-monthly, and was chief editor of *Dwar He-Halutz*. Besides that, he published studies and essays about arts and literature... During the German occupation, Mr. Rothschild played an important role in the successful attempt to smuggle *chalutzim* out of this country in close cooperation with the Dutch illegal movement..."

Despite these glowing endorsements, the truth is that my efforts to publish items about Socialism and Communism met with rejection. But I could also share good news. For example [in a letter on November 6, 1945] *I wrote to Father, I have begun publishing in the local Jewish papers, and I hope to get into the others, the more important ones, too.*

These resumés removed the horror from my teenage years and wartime experience. They offer an image that everything was under control. But nothing was further from the truth. While it is accurate that "In 1942 I went into hiding to escape deportation" *I wrote that* "later on, I joined the underground fighting forces." *I never claimed that I fought. I had a very low caloric intake throughout my time in hiding. I didn't have the strength or training to fight, let alone the willingness to do so.*

Perhaps after having to endure years of language distortion under Nazi rule, it was difficult to speak clearly and truthfully about anything. For example, "Harvest Help" was a ruse to convince Jews to report for deportation. "Final Solution" was the umbrella term for the genocide of European Jews. Survivor and philologist, Nachman Blumenthal, created a gargantuan collection of words and phrases that Nazis distorted to disguise the fact that they were exterminating the Jews.[14] This vocabulary constituted a whole new language.

Most of the Nazi regime's restrictions for Jews were delivered in Doublespeak, a strategy for using one word to mean its opposite or something unrelated. For example, "Law for the Restoration of the Civil Service," passed on April 7, 1933, about 10 weeks after Hitler came to power in Germany, meant "the law to fire all Jews from the Civil Service." When coming out of hiding, I had to reclaim both my identity and my language. Gabriella Saab wrote: "What is life after war? Returning to the lives we left is impossible: creating a life anew feels nearly as insurmountable.[15] "Life after hiding" fell somewhere in between "the impossibility of returning" and "the impossibility of moving forward."

A Search for Normalcy

Survivors yearned to do something that seemed normal. They also hoped to make up for the time they "wasted" in concentration camps, hiding, or passing as a Christian. When the few thousand Jewish survivors came out of hiding or returned to Holland from concentration camps, they typically wanted to marry as soon as possible. The Dutch government, however, adhered strictly to a multi-step process. As a start, if the couple was under 30 years of age, they had to obtain written permission to marry from their parents as well as from the government itself.

In my August 8, 1945, letter to my family, *I summarized all the issues I was dealing with: First, our legal marriage. This is a very nasty affair, because we lost all our papers, i.e., birth certificates, permits for foreigners, etc., etc. The papers burned during a* [German] *bombardment at Almelo this spring* (we had left our papers there). *People we asked to take care of these papers decided to burn them just before the Gestapo held a razzia in order not to be compromised. So we have no legal papers. Unfortunately, the official registration of foreigners in The Hague, at which we had copies of our papers, was also bombed. Added to that, there is no postal contact with Germany, so we cannot apply to the town mayors in Gunzenhausen where I was born or Ludwigshafen where Mom was born for a copy of our birth certificates if those lovely institutions are still intact. So the Dutch authorities refuse to marry us.*

It will take months, dear Father, with boring lawyers and will cost time and money. You can help me, please, by sending me this statement:

That I, Max Michael R., am your son, born on the 20th of February 1921, at G.; that you know that I have always been in possession of legal papers such as birth certificates, that you, Father, consent to my marrying Ilse Hertha Strauss. That you know the latter from 1938 onwards; that you know she was born on the 9th of April 1920, at Ludwigshafen/Rhein and has always been in possession of legal papers. That you knew her parents and know that they have died in a concentration camp.

Father, please swear to this statement before a notary public and get his seal so that the sworn statement reaches us as soon as possible... I am very sorry to trouble you with this, but I see no other way. My only hope is that it won't cost you much time, dear Father. You will, perhaps, be a little amazed at this kind of "difficulty" and will ask why, in the name of God, are we not helped, etc., etc. You then will have caught a glimpse of the situation here.

Ilse and Max were perfect candidates for marriage. They both came from Jewish homes. They had met in Munich as young teens. Both had signed up for the same Zionist youth organization – *Habonim*. Essentially, they became and remained a couple from that moment on. Even before they met, their lives had overlapped: as teenagers, they had moved to Munich from their hometowns. After Dad graduated high school (which Mom did not do), they both went to the *Hachsharah* training farm in Ellguth; they both escaped Germany for the Netherlands in early 1939; they both worked on farms there; they both went into hiding in August 1942; they both worked for the resistance albeit in different roles; and they both were liberated on May 5, 1945.

There are, however, a few highly significant differences. Dad passed the Abitur exam and was studying part-time at a university. Ilse did not do this. Ilse was also not imprisoned in a concentration camp; Dad was. Dad did not lose a sister and both parents as Ilse did. Dad had an intact family in the US, Ilse had one sister in Palestine. Dad hid after August 1942, and although Ilse hid at the same time, she had more freedom of movement because she did not "look Jewish."

Max, the Groom

Ilse and I had wanted to marry just when we decided to hide, but once we became "onderduikers," we couldn't do anything above ground, let alone interact with the state bureaucracy for a marriage license. Now our opportunity to marry rested on Father writing an affidavit granting us formal permission.

When the affidavit finally arrived, Dad went to the Dutch Jewish Community in Rotterdam and obtained the following document with two strange errors, making it sound like Max and Ilse are already married and about to sanctify their marriage in a church (!):

...We confirm that Max ROTHSCHILD, born on

February 20th, 1921, in Gunzenhausen (Mittelfranken), Bavaria

and his wife ILSE STRAUSS, born April 9th, 1920, in Ludwigshafen, will sanctify their marriage in a church this month and accordingly will be taken into the community register.

Rotterdam, May 27, 1945

DUTCH JEWISH COMMUNITY

Mathenlaan 223

Secretary [illegible signature]

A month later, on June 26, a document titled "Alien Record Testimony for Marriage," stated that a marriage between Ilse and me could take place even though we were stateless. On July 8, I wrote to Father about the obscure technical impediments to our marriage. Two months later, Father's notarized document arrived...

I wrote to Father that Ilse is doing most of the "marriage work," sometimes having to stand on line half a day. But what can we do?

My financial position is not too bad, dear Father, but we also have many expenses. Were it not for all the fees and papers for our marriage, we could easily be self-supporting. My salary is nearly sufficient, and Ilse always can find work if she wants to, but I prefer that she relax a little.

There was one more obstacle – this one from the Jewish community in Amsterdam! Although Ilse and I wanted very much to marry in a Jewish ceremony, we insisted that the ceremony be meaningful to us *rather than done according to Jewish traditions with which we do not identify.*

Dad wrote, *I also hate the idea of this ceremony being held with nobody of the family present. I propose to hold the chuppah* [Hebrew word for marriage canopy or marriage ceremony] *in America once we are with you. But, on this question, I submit fully to your opinion, dear Father, and I await your reply.*

Five days later, on September 1, 1945, Ilse and I had to swear in Rotterdam that "our intention to marry has remained unhindered." Next, we had to travel to Vriezenveen and Almelo to swear the same thing. On September 5, four months after coming out of hiding, I wrote to the family about more obstacles. But one month later, with all the appropriate documents in hand, Ilse and I went to the Office of the Mayor of Rotterdam and received an elaborate, but error-riddled, marriage certificate, which is framed and hangs in my home.

Today, on October 10th, 1945:

> Two people are standing in public before me, the Civil Service Officer of Rotterdam, in the headquarters of the Municipality in order to enter into marriage: Rothschild, Max Israel [sic, my middle name was Michael; Israel was a name assigned by Nazis to indicate I was Jewish], 24 years old, clerk [sic, I was a journalist, not a clerk], born in Gunzenhausen, Germany, currently residing here, last place of residence Vriezenveen, the adult son of Rothschild Karl, doctor, whose current place of residence is unknown [not true] and of Katzenstein, Thekla, deceased, and Strauss, Ilse Sarah Strauss [sic, her middle name was Hertha; Sarah was the middle name imposed by Nazis on Jewish girls and women], 25 years old, unemployed [not true], born in Ludwigshafen, Germany, residing here, last place of residence Almelo, adult daughter of Strauss Heinrich, lawyer, and Gern, Therese, unemployed, new residence address unknown [they were deceased].
>
> The intent to marry has been received here on September 1st of this year and on September 8th in Vriezenveen and Almelo and has remained unhindered. Attached to this certificate are public records regarding the birth of the groom and bride and the

certificate of death of the groom's mother. I have asked the groom and bride if they agree to take each other as husband and wife in marriage and agree to fulfill all the duties that are required by law to enter marriage. After these questions were answered by those present, I, in the name of the law, pronounced them husband and wife.

Witnessed by:
Mulder Jacobus, 43 years old, deputy secretary and Scheepers Lambertus, 38 years old, courier; both residing here.

All told, it had taken Ilse and me seven months of affidavits, standing in lines, applying for documents, and paying fees before we were able to be married by a Civil Service Officer who composed a faulty document.

Ilse and Max received no special assistance. When the general topic arose of how Jews should be treated when they "return to Holland," the Dutch ministers insisted that Jews should be treated the same as others. But they weren't treated the same as others; they were treated worse. "The vast majority of Jewish survivors who made it back to the Netherlands [including those coming out of hiding] found arrival traumatic."[16]

A Wedding at Last

Ultimately, Ilse and I had two weddings. The first was authorized by the Registrar of Civil Status and the second was a Jewish affair presided over by a rabbi three months later, on January 5, 1946. The second wedding, the one that had many features of the centuries-old Jewish marriage rite, was scheduled to take place in the home of the Stein family in Amsterdam. Fritz's presence was remarkable since he had been presumed dead in the Celle camp and had been forced to participate in a Death March. Ilse's attitude was unenthusiastic because my parents could not attend and hers had been murdered.

Ilse wrote in a letter: "So the day after tomorrow our Chuppah will be happening. I think it's dreadful that Fritz and Ruth [Stein] are doing so much for our sakes and holding the festivities at their home. I hope it won't be too celebratory. It all means so little to us."

A couple of days later, our Jewish wedding finally took place. The marriage of two "onderduikers" represented a near miracle. We had found a rabbi in Amsterdam whose views about Jewish law and ritual were acceptable to us. I'm not sure how much it mattered to the rabbi that Ilse was approximately four months pregnant, although he did delete the word betulah [Hebrew: virgin], *appearing four times on the printed marriage certificate. Ilse seems to have become pregnant right after our first wedding in September.*

After years of persecution, this was the first time we were able to be part of a Jewish celebration, where two Jewish people entered the covenant. The happiness at our wedding was tempered by the absence of family members except the Steins. Ilse lamented the fact that her parents had not been present at the weddings of any of their three daughters. On the other hand, a few friends came from our Hachsharah days. Thus, the wedding was an occasion of joy and hope, but also of absence and sadness – as is true for most Jewish weddings. On happy occasions, we Jews always remember those who have died.

On January 5, 1946, shortly after the wedding, I sent a telegram to my family in Malden, Massachusetts and Ilse wrote a letter as well. Now that we were married, most of the concerns Ilse had before the wedding vanished.

"That was not a day that we will forget any time soon," Ilse wrote to Dad's parents. "Our friends, and Ruth and Fritz especially, tried to make the day as grand and celebratory as possible. Because most of the people present were not religiously minded, the rituals that day were quite an experience for them. All the speeches came from the heart. It was so touching how Ruth took care of absolutely everything. Our thoughts were with you, dear parents, and with my dear ones in Palestine..."

Dad composed his own description of the wedding one week later.

Today I want to write to you about the chuppah and send you the 20 different photos that we have just now gotten back... The small celebration took place on Sunday at the Steins' apartment. Ruth went to enormous trouble. Everything looked just as beautiful and inviting as it used to look at home. Also present were Arthur Kellerman and his wife;

Frau Dr. Berg and Renate Freund; two families who lived in the Steins' building; other acquaintances of the Steins; my best friend, Gideon Drach; and two soldiers from the Brigade.

Just the right number of people. We didn't want any more. I had to wear a suit jacket and white gloves, and Ilse, a wedding dress with a veil. Someone played the grand piano; the cantor sang very beautifully, and the brief but dignified words from the young rabbi were fitting. Rice was thrown according to the Dutch custom. The Steins gave us a gorgeous ring. If Fritz hadn't been able to provide it, we could not have been able to get it because gold is not available here. After the chuppah itself, there was coffee with real cakes and tarts on a glorious, beautifully decorated table, just like we were used to when I was a kid.

Ruth spoke about culture and tradition and our will not to let the beauty of Jewish traditions be torn asunder, despite the difficulties that have put us on completely different paths than planned. A cousin of the Steins made a wonderful speech in Hebrew, and the rabbi also spoke in Hebrew. My friend Gideon Drach prepared fine words and gave us a beautiful gift. A tree is being planted in our name in Palestine. As you know, we didn't want to make a big deal of the wedding. For Ilse, it was a bitter reality to have to stand up there as good as alone. The wonderful affair ended in the late afternoon...

We thought of you very much throughout the day, but we thought even more of the many family members from both of our families who would have gathered around the chuppah if cruel fate had not struck them... You already know how far removed we are from religious things and certain social conventions, but now we find it comforting that we have fulfilled this traditional custom. There are a whole lot of chuppahs, and bar mitzvahs being held now that couldn't be held in the past few years. Chuppahs where little children are already crawling around are not a rare occurrence.

I had already told my parents that Ilse was pregnant and that soon a little child of our own would "crawl around."

Ilse Falls Ill

Having finally succeeded in getting married, I now had a new, unexpected role – Ilse's caretaker. Right after the celebration, Ilse became so ill that we accepted the Steins' invitation to stay in their home for a week. We had to get the doctor, who immediately prescribed strict bedrest and gave her "pulom opii." With the help of American cigarettes as a bribe and with great effort, I was able to get the prescription. Can you please send vitamin E soon, dear Father? Our very nice family doctor, Dr. Dasberg, specifically requested that I ask you about it..."

The week of being taken care of, plus the good doctor and medications, seem to have worked.

Ilse feels a lot better. The Steins are always so wonderful to us. We have a great relationship... Ilse will write to you herself today or tomorrow, but for now, many greetings on her behalf. My planned trip to Germany had to be postponed because I don't want to leave Ilse until she is well. That is more important to me than anything else. Next week I will start working energetically on getting a visitor's visa for the U.S.A. Start looking into this from your end, too, please. After all, a visa can be extended or turned into an immigration visa once we are already there. (This was not true.)

After Ilse had recuperated at the Steins' home, she sent my grandparents a critique of the Steins' values. In contrast to the Steins, she wanted to lead a socialist life. "I realized that we actually belong to different social classes, and I want our ideas to shape our lifestyles."

Max, the Caretaker

During the entire occupation, including the final three years in hiding, Ilse and I were never, or hardly ever, sick. Even during the "Hunger/Cold Winter," we somehow managed to stay healthy. But after we were liberated, Ilse fluctuated between debilitating sickness and normal health for one and a half years until we left the Netherlands in January 1947. Two months into her pregnancy, she wrote to my parents, informing them that she was taking a Hebrew language seminar, something she did her entire life, leading to her earning an M.A. in Hebrew Language and Literature in the US.

According to her letter, Ilse loved the course: "It has completely taken over my life so that I barely have any time for housekeeping, let alone for writing. Once I'm done with the seminar, I'll be starting a job with Jewish orphan children here. I will do that for three or four half-days a week, because then I will also have enough time to take care of my housekeeping and still earn a little something. I really like that work."

She continued: "You really do not have to worry about my health. I barely have the heart palpitations at all. The only thing is that I get tired more quickly than I used to. The pills for the heart palpitations work wonderfully. I just take them as needed whenever I feel I could use one. Thank you for all your care and attention!"

Ilse seems not to have been aware that the excessive fatigue she was experiencing could be a symptom of A Fib (arterial fibrillation), and that A Fib might have been a consequence of the stress of hiding and taking chances as a courier.[17] To deal with her overwhelming fatigue, Ilse went to a spa or rested at home. Her fatigue might also have been connected to her pregnancy. With concern, Dad wrote to his father about Ilse's health.

She was doing well except that in the last couple of days, she suddenly had those heart palpitations again in the evenings and at night, which are very depressing for both of us. And then, she is always completely exhausted, even though she certainly isn't doing any tiring work. Could there be an explanation for that?

Later that month, Ilse wrote to Max's parents: "I used to spend the whole day jumping around without getting tired. Now, if I spend two or three hours on housework, I need to rest, which is quite annoying to me."

I am frightened. I want to find a doctor who can free Ilse from this awful thing, which overwhelms me each time it happens. I think that what is really missing from her life right now is the opportunity to talk with older people.

As it turned out, Dad was right. Ilse had psychological and not exclusively physical needs. Aside from the possibility of A Fib, Ilse might have suffered from PTSD, a condition that can occur in people who have experienced or witnessed a traumatic event such as a natural disaster, a death, a serious accident, a terrorist act, war/combat, rape, a violent personal assault, or the loss of loved one/s. Ilse certainly had experienced deaths, war, and loss of loved ones. It is possible that she, like other Holocaust survivors who developed illnesses after liberation, was afflicted by PTSD as expressed in her frequent heart palpitations.

On March 10, 1946, ten months after the war had ended, Fritz Stein wrote a letter to my parents commenting on the mental health of the people around him. "My dears! We are doing fine, but we are not doing great. We have what people here call *"inzinking,"* a psychic effect caused by the peace following the very tense life we were leading. We have the trappings of peace, but we have not been able to achieve real peace or calm internally."

English translations of the Dutch word *"inzinking"* include breakdown, depression, meltdown, and downturn. Later that month, Ilse wrote to Dad's parents:

The doctor prescribed bed rest for me for the past week, and I have strictly adhered to that. We've decided that I won't be working with the children for the time being, and that [someone] will help with the laundry and other things now and then. Right now, I really want to do everything that is best for me and the baby so I can get rid of this nervousness.

Psychologically, I am completely calm and functional, not hysterical. For a few days we hired a woman we know from Rotterdam since I had to stay in bed and Max had to go to work. She is the mother of one of our friends who died a hero's death during the Occupation. She is an older woman, the same age that my dear mother would have been. It did me an amazing amount of good just to have her here with me. I'm still young, and sometimes I have questions that I would like to talk about with a mother. I think that after that unnerving war and having to hide, we need a nice home that will contribute to our mental and spiritual health.

In her next letter, Ilse told Dad's parents that she was worried about not having heard from her sister in Palestine since December 12. She then exuded happiness about the packages Dad's parents sent containing egg powder, a coat, gloves, knitting wool, as well as vitamins for their friend.

When I saw the coat, I jumped almost to the ceiling, I was so happy. My old coat was damaged in the attack on Ellguth! I am so happy to have the chance to wear a new one. The packages remind me of my dear mother. She also knew how to send wonderful packages...

As an expectant woman, Ilse was entitled to extra rations of essential foods: "Twenty liters of milk per month, and also more butter and meat, which means that we really have plenty to eat." She told Dad's parents that after nearly five years of not being permitted to go to the movies, they had just seen *The Youth of Maxim Gorki* (Moscow, 1938). "An excellent film. We loved it." She craved more. "We would like to take a class in the evenings, on literary or artistic subjects. Everything we read or hear here is so one-sided, and in Amsterdam we have much less stimulation than in Rotterdam. We miss it."

Because Ilse was pregnant with her first child, she had neither knowledge nor experience. She wrote:

Ruth (the mother of three sons) reminded me of what sorts of things I need. It is just so awfully hard to get everything here, from a wash basin to a baby carriage. We are trying to trade for things (everything revolves around bartering here) and not use the Black Market with its exorbitant prices. Now I feel a bit relieved, now that I've written down what I need. I am writing about it now because many packages take three months to get here. I have gotten Vitamin E from someone I know here, so I don't need that anymore. The other vitamins that you sent, dear Father, I'll have to show to my doctor first. He thinks it's good for me to take two a day. He said that I don't need the iron tablets since I am not anemic. But I should still take one a day, he said. Max is also taking the vitamins.

Ilse has developed a complex, Dad wrote, *thinking about the items Ruth says she will need. She wants only the best for her baby, just like any mother, and she has already had sleepless nights all because of a* little piece of embroidery thread! It would help her psychologically if you could write that some things are already on their way and are not too expensive. I also try to protect Ilse's mental health by shielding her from bad news. It does worry me that we aren't hearing anything from Israel and Ilse's sister is not doing well, in terms of her own health. I will certainly intercept any discouraging news because Ilse doesn't need that right now.

The American Consulate does its best to needle us, and in general complete chaos seems to reign there. I have become fatalistic and just take things as they come. "Preference quota" does not seem to be an option, as it applies only to minor children of Americans or parents of Americans.

[I joked frequently about people "needling" me. Years later in the US, I talked about an organization with the name A.M.R., or Aggravate Max Rothschild. When a car ahead of us on a single lane road proceeded very slowly without giving me an opportunity to pass, for example, I would invariably say, "Oh, there's another member of the A.M.R. society." This idea made the situation less annoying. The A.M.R. was always growing.]

My next letter to Malden dealt with anniversaries of horrible events and funerals I had attended, my interrupted studies, my need for money to move my visa process along, and many other topics. I was fortunate that I could write to my family in an open way and get their advice.

Ilse is doing well now but my own mood is weighed down by memories. It was exactly one year ago that we had to flee our borrowed Rotterdam house for good. Then, on my birthday, my friend Cor was shot, after we had spent 14 days frantically trying to free him. Sometimes these things come up again inside me, such as recently, when I attended the burial of two young friends who were laid to rest along with over 400 others who had been shot. The royal family was in attendance. My depressed feeling raises the question of the meaning of these deaths. That's when I ask, "Why us? Why were we saved? Why is it that we were so lucky?"

Back to the topic of my studies. We have insufficient funds to allow me to enroll normally. Maybe I will try to get a scholarship. There is only one professor who lectures about journalism and social psychology, Baschwitz. The faculty has not yet been fully restored and I know that opportunities are opening in America in that area. So I will listen to

Baschwitz's lectures now and then, and that will also allow me access to the university library, where I can work as much as I like. The professor will tutor me privately for the next six weeks until lectures start again. I will also be starting an interesting internship, which will be at a sociology department conference regarding last winter's "Hungerfahrten" ["Hunger Trips"], capturing them in statistics about people from West Holland who moved to the farming regions to avoid starving to death. In a couple of weeks, I will participate in a second conference on measuring the population's willingness to work.

Ilse wrote:

Our desire for a cozy home life grows stronger every day, and that means having a certain degree of order, including a way of separating the rest of the week from the workdays with their never-ending treadmill. Why not have that be Friday evenings? We also like to invite people over now and then. We rarely go out, ourselves; it's always nicest at home.

In February 1946, just after my 25th birthday, I wrote to my parents that Ilse and I had contracted the flu, one after the other. The flu is always an unpleasant experience, to say the least, but on the other hand, it was a not unwelcome opportunity to take a little rest and read a little. Ilse cared for me well, in the splendid traditional way; it was marvelous, with lemon juice, etc., etc. Today I got out of bed for the first time and now it is Ilse's turn to have a fever. But it's nothing to worry about. There is a widespread epidemic of influenza and what is most interesting is that far more people are sick now than during the war, although the conditions are so much better now. Ilse is doing well in every respect, owing to the splendid food she gets from your parcels... Everything is arranged concerning the [post-partum] confinement in the clinic.

The next month – March – Ilse wrote to Dad's parents:

Our whole life is light and carefree right now because we received good news from Palestine. Evi spent three months under observation in the hospital, and finally her illness was diagnosed as struma.[18] She underwent surgery and already feels much better. She will now need to spend three weeks at a sanatorium near Tel Aviv to regain her lost weight, and then she will be able to go home.

At last, I feel hopeful that once I do make it to Palestine, a healthy sister will be there to greet me.

I feel really good and the problems with my nerves are behind me now. It is still about three months until my due date, and to be honest, I am getting a bit impatient. It is a shame that you can't pop by, even for a minute, to see how nice and cozy it is in our apartment.

As had become his habit, when Ilse wrote to his parents, Dad added a post-script.

I am very satisfied with my work and with my study at Amsterdam University... Ilse feels splendid. Every day that brings us nearer to the birth of our little one brings us joy and happiness. For the first time, after the war, we really are happy.

On April 5, 1946, Ilse again wrote to Dad's parents, expressing concern that Dad was exhausting himself with so much rushing around: "As soon as he's back, he'll write you all about it. I will make sure Max takes a little time to relax in the next few days." To gain her own strength, Ilse went to Rotterdam for a vacation that she enjoyed immensely.

First, I spent a couple of days with the friends who hid us, and then I went to the Barendrecht spa and stayed with people who have a beautiful garden. The weather was glorious. I sat in the garden all day and now I am baked tan. I believe I wrote to you that I was sick. I have been in Barendrecht for about a week now, a small suburb of Rotterdam, and I have recovered well and rested up.

Ilse concluded by expressing gratitude for the packages Dad's parents had sent and reassuring them that she has everything she needs for the baby. Max was her devoted caretaker, but his duties were about to intensify.

Visiting the Past

Dad wrote, *In addition to what I needed to do for other people, I also had a project I was eager to do for myself – visit Gunzenhausen and Munich. Motivated by nostalgia and curiosity, I made two trips: the first, a ten-day journey while Ilse was seven months pregnant. The second, half a* year later in December 1946, after our baby was born and right before the three of us left for the US.

Regarding Gunzenhausen, *it makes me anxious to go back to a country that should really be my homeland, a country of a thousand memories from my childhood and youth. A country that betrayed me in the cruelest of ways.*

Wearing a uniform of the Jewish Brigade, Dad traveled by train to the Occupied Zone in what would become West Germany. This trip – with a few friends – was paid for by several Dutch newspapers for which he was reporting. While traveling, he wrote five long letters home.[19]

My comrades and I were disguised as soldiers and traveled with military papers. The sole disagreeable aspect was that we had to lie when old acquaintances asked questions. I told people in Gunzenhausen that I was in the armed forces and had fought in Italy. Having to be untruthful about my military experience irked me. This trip was taking place one year after liberation, and yet, I was still not free to be who I was and to say what I was doing. The fear of being caught in my lies haunted me. True freedom – in terms of honesty – would come later.

My group stayed in Brussels and Paris for one day each. Paris was filled with German prisoners of war, a blight on the cityscape... From Belgium, we traveled on American military trains, always in the company of Americans. The care, feeding and treatment we received was simply grand. It would have been worth making this trip for the meal stops alone in Karlsruhe, Strasbourg, Augsburg, etc. I got the impression that the American armed forces want to make life as pleasant as possible for each soldier, private or officer. It makes you want to say, "In the next war, I'm signing up for the US Army!" Even though the trip from Paris to Munich took 29 hours with wooden benches serving as beds, I was moved by the gorgeous German landscape...and depressed about the attitude of the population. The D.P.s were unimaginably demoralized, and the unspoiled beauty of the landscape contrasted with the destruction the Germans had inflicted on others. Overall, my depressed state was so severe that I returned home earlier than planned.

Landscapes and Memories

The Americans in our train compartment were strangely surprised at our hostility to the Germans. Right after the war, when what was done to the Jews was still evident, they could not comprehend what happened. Clearly, their narrative of rebuilding Europe superseded any interest in Jewish suffering. I noticed the well-dressed and well-nourished Germans, so different from the Dutch workers, a clear reflection of the fact that during the Hunger Winter, the Germans ate the food stolen from the Dutch and others.

After Kehl, a small city, the train passed through the Black Forest. It was a sparkling spring day. We stood at the windows for hours and gazed out at the lush scenery that harbors people who brought so much pain and death to the world. All the villages are still there, in all their beauty. Clearly, I was still attached to Germany, especially its language and landscape. In Karlsruhe we made our first meal stop on German soil. It was a strange feeling to be waited on by servile German girls and waiters who must play music for you while you eat, and as soon as your cup of top-quality Nescafé is half empty, they run over to fill it up.

The Germans will do anything for cigarettes and cigarette butts, so these play an important role in public life. For a certificate stating that they were not Nazis, they will do even more. Picture an American military train pulling into a German train station. All the Germans, from the street sweeper to the conductor, surround the train, everyone has their own beat. And then you see a butt lying somewhere that everyone missed – but here comes the station master with an air of importance, ready to give the signal for the train to depart. When he sees the butt, he reserves it for himself. Or you're standing near a policeman whom you've asked how to find a certain street, and you toss your cigarette butt on the ground without thinking. But this fellow, who just a short time ago may have murdered your relatives, hurriedly crouches and picks up the butt in the middle of the conversation.

Munich, Then and Now

The military trains going to Munich stopped at the special military station at the Oberwiesenfeld Gaskessel Airfield where the American transit camp nicknamed "Hotel America" was located.

The transit camp is wonderful. It has everything: a movie theater, a hotel, giant cafeterias where the groveling Germans must serve you, bathing facilities, etc. You can have your pants ironed, your shoes cleaned, and everything taken care of. The next morning – a Sunday – we traveled into Munich. The city's former beauty has completely gone to hell and the people don't show the slightest urgency about cleaning it up. In many places, the facades of entire rows of houses lack their outer frames. At first you think they are undamaged, but when you look closer, you see that they are completely burned out. Then you reach a square with a statue of a rearing horse, with the front half of the horse completely missing.

I was in a melancholy mood, a soldier coming back as a stranger, seeing his homeland again, caught up in images of the past. And then one sees unfamiliar people, acting as though nothing has happened, who are more antisemitic than ever before... As soon as I had the chance, I went back to the old neighborhood around grandmother's apartment. Her building is still standing, though slightly damaged. I did not have the courage to ring one of the residents' doorbells; I was very upset. Thierschstrasse 19 [Dad's parents' apartment] is still standing, as well.

A Greek doctor occupies our old apartment and has his practice there. I did not go up; I just stood outside for 15 minutes, looking at it. However, I could not resist the temptation to look for familiar names on the nameplates across the street. Miss Baumgart still lives there, and I went up to speak with her. She was extremely happy to see me. Miss B. managed to save some of your books, dear Father. You may not remember this, but you gave her some to keep for you.

In the late evening, I walked around the city to look for people I once knew. The empty, burned-out window frames yawn at you even more frighteningly than they do during the day. There are hardly any lights; only from a restaurant now being used as an Officers' Mess. I saw women who were manhandled — clearly, during war and postwar situations, women are the spoils that go to the victor.

It would have been easy to go to the Ettstrasse police station and inquire about everyone, but I did not because it disgusts me to witness the slimy groveling of the police, the same police officers who — in a somewhat different-colored uniform and with a swastika in the imperial eagle's claws — mistreated our loved ones.

Dad did not spend all his time in the city itself. Rather, he went to Displaced Persons camps — Föhrenwald at Wolfratshausen and Indersdorf at Dachau. Föhrenwald was a forced labor subcamp of the large Dachau complex. On these visits, he conducted intensive interviews and collected material that he could use "in proper journalistic fashion."

I will send you a couple of newspaper clippings of articles I wrote. I was particularly interested in political and "cultural" life, if there still are such things. A study I published on the new German writers offers clear examples that Nazi ideology manifests itself even in the people one considers "the best." I saw hypocrisy everywhere. The war hadn't diminished the antisemitism. The Jews were still to blame, even if Germans were now living in Jewish homes. At present, the people are phlegmatic. They couldn't care less about anything. There is only one question: How can I make life as comfortable as possible for my family and me? There is no "guilty conscience" to speak of, none whatsoever."

The Gruesome Deaths of My Relatives

I then sought information about my two grandmothers — Caroline [Mammiah's mother] and Betty [Father's mother]. Oma Caroline was not deported, as we previously believed. Rather, after suffering a third stroke and weakened by an ongoing intestinal problem, she died on Mathildenstrasse in Munich the day before deportation. Dr. Spanier was present and said the Kaddish and other prayers himself. She was buried in the old Thalkirchner Cemetery where several bombs fell. The cemetery has not yet been fully restored. In a certain sense, this news about Oma Caroline is a comfort, because she was spared a worse form of suffering.

Oma Betty passed away on 6-24-1942 in the Theresienstadt

concentration camp. She was already very weak from the time she had spent in the Milbertshofen concentration camp. Starting on March 17, 1941, Jewish slave laborers were forced to build a concentration camp in the Milbertshofen district of Munich. As a result of the forced relocation of Jews to Milbertshofen, around 1,500 apartments in Munich became vacant and were given to "deserving party members." The Jews in the camp were then deported to the Piaski, Theresienstadt and Auschwitz concentration and extermination camps. Dr. Spanier was present when Oma Betty passed away. Her body was burned, and the urns were reused without the ashes being laid to rest.

Uncles Bob and Paul, along with many other young Jews from Munich, were shot at Lublin after performing hard labor for four weeks until their strength gave out. Siegfried Lonnerstaedter was taken to Auschwitz in a transport on 3-13-43 and was gassed in the night of the 16th/17th. (It is awful for me to have to write this to you. I will leave it to you to share the precise details with our relatives if you so choose.) Most of the people from Munich, including Ilse's unforgettable aunt and uncle Dr. E. Gern and Ms. Lisl, as well as her Einstein relatives from Kyreinstr., and other acquaintances including Otto Wolf and his wife, Dr. Schaeler, etc., were taken to Riga in two transports. But these transports never reached Riga. The first, in which all the people mentioned above were deported, left Munich on 11-20-41, and the second left Munich in February 1942.

The second transport stopped in a forest before reaching Riga where all the passengers were immediately shot with machine guns. The fate of those in the first transport was even more atrocious: these people were forced off the train before reaching Riga, ordered to remove their clothes, and then, completely naked, chased into the woods. A few days later, a Jewish Kommando [work detail] from near Vilna had to chop through the ice and snow to retrieve the bodies.

On Wednesday, when I received this information, I could not stand being in Munich. It was a relief to sit in the American transit camp and brood in silence over my cup of coffee, which I did until 1:00 a.m., when the military train arrived. To ignore these stories is inhumane, to pay attention is to rip out one's heart. This conflict occupied me from Munich to Gunzenhausen, the last stop on my trip into the past.

Return to Gunzenhausen

I arrived in G'hausen, where my highest priority was to visit Mammiah's gravesite. When I saw the town towers, however, I was overcome with fear. Fear – not pride or relief for having survived. Fear – not safety that my uniform provided. Fear – not nostalgia for the scenes of my childhood. I experienced the fear of not knowing what to expect from the people whose violent antisemitism caused me to flee 12 years earlier. I didn't want to encounter residual Nazism or the blatant denial of what the "fine citizens" of G'hausen had done.

The whole area, including the city itself, looks unbelievably idyllic and peaceful. There are neither cars nor soldiers. In fact, when you walk across that medieval market square, you feel like you are in an earlier century. But when I saw some of my old classmates, limping around on their crutches, I didn't have the courage to speak to them. The chasm between us was unbridgeable and I was trying my hardest to go unrecognized. Of course, a gaggle of children began to follow me right away. And all the adults were watching me with open curiosity: the strange soldier sneaking through the sunlit streets who looked troubled.

I wish I could have observed without being observed. Everyone was watching me. Was I armed? I believe they knew this strange figure was a Jew. I went into our house where the Wagners now live. The cook opened the door and recognized me immediately. But then it became too much for me, and I stood there crying...overwhelmed by memories of my childhood, my lost joys, and the unfair hatred. Overcome by thoughts of all the people who had been killed. I could have been one of those people. My town was now Judenrein. The Wagner family was extremely nice to me, waiting on me hand and foot. They also called the Riedel family over, as well as Frau Barth and God knows who else. None of these people were Jews, of course. There is just no way to really communicate with them. I stayed because of the atmosphere of the house, which still reminded me of earlier days to such a maddening degree. You are all the objects of everyone's questions.

People say that no one ever did anything to the Jews, and no one understands why you won't come back. And since the Holocaust never happened, there was no reason not to move back. Why did the Jews leave in the first place? They told me that you, dear Father, would have a booming medical practice if you returned to G'hausen, although now there are nearly 12 doctors in the town.

People remember that after World War I, the people of G'hausen were embittered by the "unfair conditions" of the Versailles Treaty Conference. They choose not to remember that they blamed the Jews for stabbing-them-in-the-back. Furthermore, because the Allies humiliated the Germans, Germans were justified in fighting them in World War II. But to my surprise, the citizens of G'hausen also blamed their defeat on top-level Nazis – including Hitler – who had performed poorly! Those pigs at the top, the officers, failed us. Otherwise, everything would have gone fine. Everybody has the right to wage a war, don't they?

Wagner was enormously happy to see me and sends his loving greetings to you, dear Father. During my whole trip to Germany, he was the only person with whom I was able to have a real conversation because he had the moral courage to admit he had been a Nazi. Why could Germans not bring themselves to apologize to me for what the townspeople had done to my family and all the Jews of G'hausen? Perhaps they feared I would seek financial restitution.

The mayor is now Mr. Kraus, whose shop used to be next door to Lehmann's. Like all the others, the public officials groveled in the Rathaus [City Hall]. How to explain the groveling? Perhaps it was a bodily expression of guilt and fear. The single purpose of my trip to G'hausen was to find a Nazi and kill him. I do not know if I really planned to carry this out nor do I remember if I had a weapon. Nevertheless, I soon realized that I could not take another person's life. Also whom would I choose as my target? Anyone at random who lived in the town? The former mayor? A single teacher?

The Certificate

My visit to G'hausen included the Realschule [middle school], now located in a new building, the Hindenburgschule, because the old building houses D.P.s. "All those foreigners are in there now, and they have completely ruined my chemistry lab," Prof. Marzell said to me." Prof. Marzell expressed no sympathy for or understanding of WHY there were foreigners in his chemistry lab. He commented: "Since everyone in Europe was a Nazi or a hidden Nazi, why should the German Nazis be singled out for blame?" M. has now become the school principal. It isn't easy for him. "Wouldn't I like to come and teach English?" he asked me.

Just as every Jew had to do all the time, now every German official, teacher, doctor, or what have you, needs to show his certificate. It is the most highly coveted item – and God knows, many of the people who have one did not earn it. You can't imagine the role the certificate plays in daily life. These Germans need external validation of their integrity, plus an official stamp from a government authority!

M. and Hundsberger are the only ones still here from my early days. They've been certified by the Americans because they did not become Nazis until after '36! Old Dash, the school caretaker, a former patient of yours, Father, was moved to tears when he saw me. He was always a good man. We Jewish kids used to pester him during our free period.

M. told me that the people of G'hausen now display a "love of learning" that has never before been seen. The reason? The impending currency devaluation. People want to invest their stolen or dubiously obtained war money and so they are paying several years' tuition for their kids in advance!

And now, this you should share with the Rosenfelder family: my encounter with Hundsberger. "Oh yes, it's Rotschild." And then came an avalanche of words. "How I used to scold all of you Jews in the back of the classroom, do you remember?" etc. I was astounded at how that old man groveled in the dust and how he would not leave my side throughout my entire time in G'hausen. Only with quite a bit of effort was I able to get rid of him when I wanted to go to the cemetery and be alone.

He came with me when I walked through the castle ruins and employed his full repertoire of language skills to lambast the Nazis. He showed me his "certificate" several times – as well as a letter that the Rosenfelder children had written to him from the U.S.A. in 1938. I am sure he is not a bad person, but the problem is that the average German tolerated the Nazis and became like them.

Hundsberger cluttered my head with his nonstop talking. Everything was still there including the water reservoir full of secrets. The Bismarck monument, the Hensoltshöhe [the site of Protestant nuns' work for the welfare of the community], *even one tree with a funny growth like a – forgive me – behind. We always had a special relationship to that tree, as kids! I thought of the days when our dear mother would take us on a walk through the castle ruins, and I almost expected dear old Mrs. Rehfeld to appear around a bend. She was always up there in the woods.*

But They Were Such Nice People

We passed the spot where Hundsberger hit me when our class was taking a walk and I made fun of him. He had been trying to point out the beauty of a certain woodpile. Now he was going on about how awful he had felt upon seeing a couple of old Jews being sent to the train station. "But they were such nice people," he said, even though he didn't know old Dottenheimer and the other man. I'm sure they were not particularly nice compared to anyone else. As though being nice had anything to do with it.

They were probably the most decent, aside from Eder and Muehldorfter (no one has heard from either of them, but they are spoken of with reverence), those two early conscientious opponents of the Nazis who retired and started receiving their pensions shortly after '33.

"If only we had our King's Party [i.e., B.H.K.P., Bavarian Homeland and King's Party] again!" Hundsberger said, "then we could all sit at the Braunskeller and enjoy a beer together on a Saturday evening, with all the Jews, like we used to do. Sometimes your father and mother were there, too.[20]

The Hitler Monument

On the way back, we passed the "Hitler monument." I remember how it was put up right away in 1933 by some enthusiastic citizens because the city of my birth wanted to be the first in Germany to do so. Some sort of fight emerged with a small city in northern Germany that claimed that it was first. It is still there to this day and cleaned regularly, only, a wooden board has been hung over the bronze plate that bears the image of the Führer's head. The wooden board reads: "Peace memorial of the city of Gunzenhausen, in memory of the lives lost in the 1939-45 war."

No mention of Jews. The wooden board is rectangular, and the bronze plate is round, allowing the dead Führer to stick out a little bit on all sides. I had a good laugh when I saw the whole get-up. At first, Hundsberger had no idea what had happened, but then he remembered that a few weeks ago, the mayor asked the municipal clerk to affix the "cover-up" board. Very quietly, of course. "That's an outrage," I said. "We have to let the mayor know that you can still see the bronze plate." "You are completely right, Mr. Rothschild," he answered. Schmidt, from the hospital, is currently in "Moosach" where the American occupation people put dangerous Nazis.

I saw our old shul. Its walls were standing, the interior in shambles. But somebody had forgotten to destroy the quotation from Isaiah (56:7) whose Hebrew letters were chiseled deep into the heavy granite headstones above the main entrance, reading "...for My house shall be a house of prayer for all peoples..." And thus ends my report on my trip "home" in 1946.

Joy and Concern

When Dad returned to Holland from Gunzenhausen, he resumed the myriad activities he had interrupted: getting American visas; earning money by writing for the local press and for the *Review* he was co-editing; translating for and working with his professor; taking care of Ilse who was in the last trimester of her pregnancy and not in the best of health; receiving visitors constantly because people wanted to resume relationships suspended by the Occupation; helping to locate missing people; and carrying out an extensive correspondence with his father – among other things.

Dad's letters of spring 1946 describe birthdays and a *bar mitzvah* ceremony as well as concern for his father's car accident. Unfortunately, as a physician, Dad's father had to drive all day long because at that time, general practitioners made house calls. *Forbes* magazine reported that in the 1940s, house calls made up 40 percent of US doctor's visits, a figure that began to decline in the 1960s before dropping to less than 1 percent today.[21]

The next big event for my parents was the arrival of Passover and the celebration of a *seder* [festive meal and reading of the story of Exodus]. *At the Stein's seder, we thought a great deal about you and all our loved ones. We reminisced together about the Seders of long ago... I'm sure the words of the "Avadim Hayinu" song were not empty [Hebrew: Avadim Hayinu, sung at the Seder, means "once we were slaves, but now we are free"]. Ilse is doing quite well but she tires very quickly. What she needs more than anything is a mother... You can imagine how we think about our baby all the time now, and I have to say that we are happier than I would have believed possible. We had many visitors on Passover, which was far too much for Ilse. During the war and especially when I was hiding, I wrote about my profound loneliness; now I have the opposite problem. There are too many people around me!*

Now, a thought you might find meshugge [Yiddish: crazy]. Couldn't one of you come and visit us? I can easily get a visa for you to come here, and we could pay for the return trip in guilders. We could make some trades and you would need to bring cigarettes I could sell. And perhaps the Joint [American Joint Distribution Committee] could contribute some of the cost of the trip. How nice it would be if one of you could be here for the birth! Couldn't one of you accept some sort of temporary job on behalf of the Joint or the UNRRA [United Nations Relief and Rehabilitation Administration] or some Jewish organization for Western Europe?

The reason my work is so taxing right now is that I have become co-editor of the Zionist newspaper Joodse Wachter *– a small "Review" – and need to produce two pages every 14 days. So I have started a feuilleton to have a bit of routine.*

Ilse added a p.s. to Dad's letter: "A great many *chaverim* have already left Holland for Palestine, which means that our movement is getting smaller and smaller here. I hope we will be able to emigrate to Palestine soon! What do you think about Max's suggestion of visiting us here?"

Looking after Ilse

No matter how interesting my work was, my primary focus was on the thrilling fact that I would soon be a father. And for this to go well, Ilse had to be in the best condition possible.

Ilse, who typically minimized her health problems, wrote to Dad's parents that she was having "heart palpitations" again. This intermittent but frightening condition changed Ilse from a brave, strong, and energetic woman in hiding to a weak woman who stayed home and rested. She wanted her mother beside her and that was impossible.

A full year after coming out of hiding, nutritious food was still scarce.

Fruits and vegetables are nowhere to be found here, and even potatoes are unavailable. To make up for it, we take vitamins... Until now, we ate whatever was put in front of us. Now, since we are expecting a baby, the question of nutrition is significant. If you have time, dear Father, could you give me your opinion about the vegetarian lifestyle?

I found out that Dutch people whose children are in the States are being issued visas [under family reunification programs]. I will arrange things with the bureaucrats here, but I would just like some sort of assurance from you that we will be able to go to Eretz, be it forever or just for a visit. I wanted to make sure you knew that I planned to visit or move to Palestine, even though I have mixed feelings about Zionist ideology and about being separated from you.

A Jewish Child Is Born

Since no Jewish hospital was functioning in Amsterdam, Ilse gave birth at the Catholic lying-in hospital Onze Lieve Vrouwe Gasthuis. Every day at 5:00 a.m., the nuns woke Ilse for an early morning mass. Like all Dutch expectant fathers at the time, Dad was not allowed into the delivery room even if he was wearing the uniform of the Forces Françaises de l'Intérieur, Section Juive, with a special armband signifying the corps.

That a Jewish child could be born in Amsterdam a little more than a year after her parents were freed was a matter of great significance. This birth was the very phenomenon that Hitler had feared; it signified that a remnant of Jews had survived and started reproducing, leading to the rebirth of the Jewish people. To Ilse and Dad, this new life was a victory – a new beginning for Jewish survivors. With the birth of children, parents could imagine leading normal lives. Moreover, a healthy child meant that the parents had not been irrevocably damaged by years of trauma, hiding, cold and hunger. Amsterdam, which for five years had been a city of death, could slowly become a city of new life. One friend wrote to Ilse: "A midwife told me that 400 babies are born per week in this area, whereas in previous years, the number was about 70."

On June 17, 1946, the day of my birth, Ilse began a German-language, six-month journal about me. "Today at two minutes past 1:30 p.m., our little Shulamith [SR: one of many spellings of my name, although I prefer Shulamit because there is no "th" in Hebrew] was born. Eight days ago, the doctor told me it would be a boy – but it was a girl. Max had wanted a boy."

"Second day of Shulamit's life: Before nursing, she lay in my arms calmly for a couple of minutes. Today she had her eyes wide open..." Dad wrote:

I did nothing except send telegrams to Palestine and to our friends here. I wrote endless letters and was so overwhelmed that I developed cramps and could not concentrate. Simply put, I was an ecstatic, nervous wreck. In the evening, I visited Ilse for half an hour and then waited in my room at home for the telephone call. It came ten minutes later than what we had agreed on. As I was waiting, I wrote a whole list of English sentences. I wish I would never have done that, then I could have spoken more freely. I hope you could understand what I was saying, dear parents. Because I was very confused speaking in both German and English. I could not understand you, dear Mother, as well as I understood you, dear Father. In all the excitement, I forgot to tell you the name of our daughter. Or did I?

I have to say, my nerves are shattered; I feel as if I, myself, gave birth to the child. I also think that I hung up while I was still owed three minutes! I thought over and over, "Now you are talking to your parents for the first time after such a long time, and you are telling Father that he became a grandfather. After all, not an everyday occurrence."

I think she already looks like a typical Jewish baby with her black hair – how can it be different with two such parents? Our baby is stronger than many other newborns I have seen lately because of her legs. Ilse's salt-free diet probably contributed to the fact that Shulamit weighed 6 pounds 100 grams. Fortunately, Ilse and I had been able to arrange for help, someone in the house for a couple of weeks who will take over Ilse's chores. I will see to it that Ilse is well taken care of.

We are printing cards for the many people we know. And we will put an announcement in the Jewish newspaper. I am writing to all the family members by hand. I greet you especially from Ilse. She is so happy that she would like to scream with happiness. Why, I wouldn't change my little dear one for another baby, not even for a boy. She is so very dear. I must say you can already tell by her face that she is a Jewish baby, different from all the others in the room! We are very, very happy!

Naming the Baby

Had I been a boy, I would have had a *bris* (Yiddish) or *brit milah* (Hebrew), the ritual circumcision performed on the eighth day of a Jewish boy's life. For newborn Jewish girls, there are no set rituals. In our case, Dad placed an announcement in the Jewish newspaper with news of my birth and my name. Emy Bartfeld, a German Jewish, Zionist refugee in Holland wrote to my parents: "Since I have been back from Hilversum, I have checked the *NIW* (*Nieuw Israelisch Weekblad*) each week to see if your public notice was there. And today it finally was. Mazal tov!"

By naming me Shulamit Tirzah, my parents had chosen neither a German nor a Dutch name even though I was born in Holland to parents born in Germany. Instead, they chose two Jewish Hebrew names from the Bible, affirming that some Jews had survived and were beginning to create a new Jewish world.

Notes of Love and Urgency

Dad reported to his parents that *Friends from all over the Netherlands and other countries contacted us with warm messages when Shulamit was born. Letters expressed stereotypes about Jewish babies being small and black-haired. A friend wrote, "One of my most important wishes is that she will grow up in Eretz Yisrael to be a truly healthy, real*

Palestinian kid." Another wrote: "Congratulations on the birth of your daughter. I hope she will come with you to Israel soon."

Ilse's sister, Evi, wrote with the wish that the three of us would join her in Palestine, "our country," soon. In her next letter, she wrote about the excellent childcare facilities in Palestine, and told Ilse that her husband, Hannes, "got such a shock from our daughter's powerful lungs that he moved out of their little house and lived in a tent for the first three months!" A while later, the Union of Palestine Pioneers in Holland made a contribution to the Jewish National Fund to plant a tree in Palestine in Shulamit's name. Our Zionist friends in Holland and elsewhere laid the foundation for a strong emotional tie between our little girl and the Land of Israel.

But letters also came in from the US. "Ilse, you should live here in America, where they have 'Diaper Service,' and baby food comes in lovely little cans and bottles." Some of the congratulatory notes reveal that the suffering of the war years was still present: "First things first – I am happy that both of you made it through the war... Five years of war with all its misery, and now after a year of freedom, the world still seems to be a gloomy place. Today there is the nuclear bomb that can bring the biggest destruction in just a blink of an eye. You hear about Palestine and wonder why people can't just leave the Jews alone. Haven't people learned anything?"

Post-partum Practice and Problems

In the 1940s, accepted obstetric procedure in the Netherlands was to keep the mother in the hospital with her baby for two weeks and allow very little contact between father and baby.

I am sending you the first picture of Shulamit. I must say, I did not yet see her like this, she usually is covered up to her nose and I am strictly forbidden to touch her. You can imagine our feelings. Ilse lying alone in the hospital. I am not allowed to see her more than one hour a day. Not to speak of the lonely atmosphere at home, which I simply hate.

There was also a strange practice to help women like Ilse who had "too much milk." *She had to take a little "guest" into her bed, a Dutch baby boy who fights with our Shulamit for his existence. While I did not move into a tent for three months as Evi's husband had done, I did leave town for several long trips. On July 16, 1946, when Shulamit was one month old, I went to Friesland for eight days – alone. I desperately needed some time to relax and rest up. Usually, I put my all into my work (I think that is a Rothschild family trait), and then I fall into bed, dead tired.*

I make a good living, dear Father. And now that we have Shulamith, we receive additional money from the government. Our standard of living is higher than it has ever been. The only thing dampening my joy now is the current situation in Palestine. I often ask myself why so many people sacrificed their lives, why so many of our young people died. I need to close, now. My daughter has just gotten in touch with me again.

Immigration to the US

The Immigration Act (or Johnson-Reed Act) of 1924 defined US immigration policy. This Act of Congress, which could just as well have been called The Anti-Immigration Act, was designed to limit new immigrants to 2 percent of their existing representation in the US population. In the mid-1920s, there were approximately 1.8 million Jews in the United States. Two percent would allow only 36,000 Jews to be permitted entry. By the time World War II had ended, of the 3.5 million Jews who had survived in Europe, the vast majority wanted to live in the US. The American quota was based not on refugees' needs but rather on lawmakers' and the public's anti-immigrant reasoning and feelings. One of the tools bureaucrats used to keep potential immigrants out of America was exhaustive, contradictory, and largely incomprehensible paperwork. Dad wrote to his parents:

When Shulamit was only two weeks old, I focused my attention on getting us to America. As a first step, I wrote to the US Foreign Service seeking permission to immigrate. It turns out that I had approached the wrong office, an error that wasted a full month! When they sent me the necessary form, I found the language nearly incomprehensible, and, of course, the rules need to be followed to the letter. A typical example concerns affidavits:

INSTRUCTIONS regarding AFFIDAVITS OF GOOD CONDUCT

[as issued by]

FOUNDATION FOR SPECIAL JEWISH INTERESTS

Subcommittee: Committee for Jewish Refugees, Dept. EMIGRATION

...[A]ccording to a regulation of the State Department in Washington of September 14, 1940, in cases following hereafter now also "affidavits of good conduct," meaning sworn declarations which confirm the good behavior of the visa applicant – must be presented in addition to the previously required papers.

These declarations are to be produced as supplementary to the necessary police behavior testimonies stretching over an uninterrupted period of the last 5 years...

Amsterdam, November 1940 Form VI/a4

The consulate loses registrations and people waste an additional month filing again. Clearly, the consulate is not interested in receiving immigrants. They don't care in the slightest whether we fought in the war or were in the underground. They don't pay any attention whatsoever to whether someone had already filed before the war, let alone whether they previously received a visa. When you are called in, you must take all the certificates and documents with you, including political character references from the war years, either from your time in the camps or your time in the underground!!!

Try not to laugh. We must even provide them for our little Shulamit. But they did tell me at HIAS [Hebrew Immigrant Aid Society] that if we make a big effort, we may be able to dissuade the consulate from requiring Shulamit to have a political character reference for the war years (!) at which point she had not yet been born. In any case, we won't be able to leave for months because no transportation is available. Flights are fully booked all the way through October.

If a higher quota for people with a German background is approved, we may be called in more quickly. But this may represent a preference for Germans not for German Jews. For now, there is nothing we can do but wait. Regardless, I would like to ask you, dear Father, to prepare a new affidavit. It should be for all three of us, and it should mention your status as a US citizen.

"By This Point, We Know How to Wait"

My June inquiry to the Consul dragged on throughout the summer. In mid-September, Dad sent his Father another update: *Yesterday I went to the Joint [Distribution Committee] to ask about our emigration. It doesn't matter that you, dear parents, are citizens. It doesn't matter that I'm over 18. It doesn't matter that we worked in the Underground. I was told that preference currently is for Jews in Poland, Czechoslovakia, etc., who need to get out much more urgently than we do here in Holland. You know, of course, that we want to go to Palestine in the future. And you know that Ilse and her sister are so deeply longing to see each other, just as deeply as I'm longing to see you.*

On October 13, 1946, I received "visa form 2" from the American consulate. The next day I went to the American Express office and decided to book travel for the end of January, because usually a period of circa three to three and a half months elapses between visa form 2 and the visa itself. To be on the safe side, I added a fortnight. Our plan was to fly via Malmö to Gothenburg [in Sweden] and board the ship there.

I cannot tell you what a terrible time I am having now, running to all kinds of offices to get papers and certificates required by the consul. Everything costs lots of money, and it takes nearly one whole person working a few months to get those papers. Not to mention that there is something like regular work to be done, too. My overriding questions were not only which type of visa to apply for, but also to which country we should go, America or Palestine, and in which order and for how long.

Although Ilse wants to go to Palestine, I am afraid to take her there because of the unrest. One good piece of news: I might go to Switzerland for four weeks to attend the Zionist Congress. Next week I am going to enroll at the university, though I do not yet know how to manage everything. Good news! We found a lovely house in Haarlem. We may be able to move there together with friends.

On November 14, 1946, Ilse and I each received a Military Entry Permit to cross the border from Holland into Sweden, with Shulamit's right to travel included on my permit. A comical note in Ilse's pass was her stated "object of journey" – "to travel by rail to America via Sweden." The permits are good until January 31, 1947. The final official stamps state, "British Passport Officer, January 28, 1947" and "British Passport Officer, January 29, 1947" because the three of us would cross through the British zone to get to Sweden.

I received another request from the consulate for additional evidence regarding the affidavits, but since I was unable to imagine what that could possibly have meant, I went to Rotterdam to ask about it. That cost me nearly a full day. While I was there, I told the official that I have already booked our passage for January 31, 1947. And I can only say that it's a good thing, because we thus "compelled" the consul to give us the visa in a timely fashion.

I am facing demands from every part of my life: I have been working under a lot of pressure lately. This week I wrote four articles and if time allows, I will keep writing from the US for a couple of publications located here. The pay is one good reason to do so.

In the six months between Shulamit's birth in mid-June 1946 and my departure to Bern, Switzerland to report on the World Zionist Congress, my letters to my parents focused on Ilse's serious case of mastitis and the joy of being new parents. Ilse's condition was not under control and there was no penicillin to be had. Regardless, when our doctor told me that he had been offered penicillin that had gone slightly bad for 300.fl., I took it!

August 21, 1946. After two months of severe mastitis, the penicillin worked wonders. After two days of injections, the crisis took a turn for the better. The fever went away, and the infection went down. Long live penicillin! It really saved us. Now we can take joy in our little sunshine again. She laughs so sweetly when she recognizes us...

Biblical Job

Report from the consul: No visa [to the US] can be expected. Notice given to leave the apartment by October 1. Everything at once. I feel like Job who said: "How many sins have I committed? What wrongs have I done? Show me where I went wrong or how I sinned (Book of Job (13:23). Then, finally, some relief!

The Zionist Congress

In mid-November 1946, Dad felt ready to leave Amsterdam for an extended period to cover the Zionist Congress in Basel for Dutch newspapers.

Given that I had a five-month-old infant daughter and a wife whose health was precarious, this trip was perhaps reckless or selfish. But essential nevertheless!

On November 26, I took the train alone from Amsterdam to The Hague, with the purpose of obtaining a document that would allow me to travel in Europe for more than three weeks in December. My next stop was Paris, 240 miles due south. There I went to the Croix Rouge Nederlandaise: Le delegue pour la France [French: The Dutch Red Cross: French Delegation] where I obtained a document identifying me as a Repatriation Official. I had one more appointment in Paris where I received a travel order, valid for one month. This document allowed me to travel from the Netherlands through France and then into Switzerland. Multiple permissions were necessary because the map of Germany, redrawn by Roosevelt, Churchill, and Stalin at the Yalta Conference carved out four zones for the victorious Allied forces: Great Britain in the northwest, France in the southwest, the United States in the south and the Soviet Union in the east.

On December 5, I set out on the first leg of my journey beyond Paris. My destination was not Munich as per the French document, but rather Basel, Switzerland, the site of the 22nd World Zionist Congress that I would attend as a Dutch reporter.

Dutch Zionism

Zionist activity in the Netherlands increased right after the war when the few surviving Jews in Holland successfully reactivated the Dutch Zionist Federation. After one year of operation, the Zionist Youth Federation of the Netherlands counted 800 members. This 22nd World Zionist Congress occurred just before UN votes were lined up for the creation of a Jewish state. Later, the Dutch Zionist organizations were successful in persuading the Dutch government to support the Partition Plan of the United Nations that divided the contested area into two states, one Jewish and the other, Arab. On November 29, 1947, a majority of the United Nations' member states endorsed the partition plan, a major accomplishment for the two-year old organization.[22] The tiny State of Israel could have been founded on that date, but the Arab states rejected the plan even after the U.N. vote. Instead, Israel was founded when the British Mandate ended on May 14, 1948, half a year later.

In his autobiography, *Trial and Error*, Dr. Chaim Weizmann, the future first president of the State of Israel, wrote despondently about the reconvening of the World Zionist Congress because so many delegates had been killed.

> It was a dreadful experience to stand before that assembly and to run one's eye along row after row of delegates, finding among them hardly one of the friendly faces which had adorned past Congresses. Polish Jewry was missing; Central and Southeast European Jewry was missing; German Jewry was missing. The two main groups were the [Jewish] Palestinians and the Americans; between them sat the representatives of the fragments of European Jewry, together with some small delegations from England, the Dominions, and South America. The American group, led by Dr. Abba Hillel Silver, was from the outset the strongest, not so much because of enlarged numbers, or by virtue of the inherent strength of the delegates, but because of the weakness of the rest.[23]

Dad wrote about the Congress in a completely different way

from Chaim Weizmann in part because he had not attended previous Congresses.

I saw what was now before my eyes rather than what was missing, and I was proud to participate as a correspondent who would inform Dutch Jews about Zionist and Jewish issues. Basel itself was a highly symbolic venue because it was there in 1897 that the *first* World Zionist Congress had convened, presided over by Theodor Herzl, universally acknowledged as the father of modern, political Zionism. *The Congress I attended was special as well because it came after a seven-year interruption during World War II and the Shoah.*

The proceedings were filled with passion, as each speaker referred to the fate of the worldwide decimated Jewish community. Much of the debate expressed outrage at British actions that were impeding Jewish immigration and land purchases. This outrage became embedded in the Congress's resolutions: "This Congress reiterates the inflexible resolve of the Jewish people never to acquiesce in these violations of its inalienable historic rights, acknowledged in the Balfour Declaration and the Mandate."

300 to 400 people milled around in this incredible Yiddish and Palestinian atmosphere, showing up hours too late and talking to each other without really caring what the other person had to say. In the evening, old friends were reunited. People kissed and hugged. When the Congress concluded, I boarded a train from Bern to Amsterdam. In many ways, this Congress symbolized the end of what I needed to do in Europe. I had survived the war. I had helped find other survivors. I had married and become a father, returned to my hometowns of Munich and Gunzenhausen, established my work as a journalist, and participated in the politics of creating a refuge for Jews in a new Jewish State in Palestine. I could now leave Europe behind. In a few weeks, I would be in America.

When I returned to Amsterdam from Bern, I poured my energies into writing articles and preparing for our immigration. The fact that we had gone through hell for five, six, 12 or 14 years, depending on how one defines the span of the Holocaust, played no role in the way bureaucrats treated us, although the JDC [Joint Distribution Committee] was a bit more helpful than others. No one seemed interested that seven years earlier, we had entered Holland on condition that we leave within two years! Now that we were trying to leave, neither American nor Dutch bureaucrats helped.

Lost Assets

Although our family in Europe was not wealthy before the war, they did have some property that had been confiscated or sold under duress at shockingly low prices. I didn't want to leave these assets behind. Thus, in addition to everything else, I spent a few days of my final month in the Netherlands trying to reclaim Ilse's parents' life insurance policies that had been deposited in Swiss banks. I didn't get very far. Years later, I discovered that my parents-in-law's assets were irretrievable from the Swiss bank where they had been deposited for safe-keeping. Nor did I receive compensation for stolen real estate – Henny's family home in Erfurt had been sold at what was called "the war price," i.e., far less than its value. Receiving payment to which the family was legally entitled was immensely important to me because I could not condone the way in which the Nazis were being left in peace. Why should those people be free to enjoy what they never earned?

In a letter three months before our family's departure to America, I asked Father to send me complete information about what he had lost through seized bank accounts and how much he had paid in "Jew taxes." Taking on these projects usually meant going to court, which required a great deal of money, good lawyers, and lots of free time, none of which I had.

Ilse's Parents

Not only was I making all the arrangements to get the three of us to America and trying to retrieve family assets, I was also pursuing exact information about what had happened to Ilse's parents. A few days after the liberation, I had contacted the Fédération des Sociétés Juives de France to determine what had taken place in Gurs, the concentration camp in which Ilse's parents were incarcerated. Located in southern France, Gurs was a large camp that held 20,000 European Jews, many *from Germany. French personnel cooperated in its administration. After the war, the Fédération created Sérvice de Recherche et Régroupement des Families [Research and Family Reunification Service] to communicate with interested parties. At the end of May 1945, shortly after war's end, an official of the Fédération wrote on my behalf to the newly installed Gurs Camp Commander inquiring after Therese Strauss, Ilse's mother.*

In November, six months after my inquiry, I was advised to contact the Toulouse Region Chaplain, R. Sommer, who wrote me the following about Ilse's father:

> Mr. Heinrich Strauss died at the Gurs camp on February 8, 1942. The medical death certificate is number 875: the grave is number 1010. The gravestones are perfectly maintained by the Department of Public Works. A small tombstone on each grave bears the first and last name of the deceased and the date of death. Naturally, one is allowed to visit the cemetery without prior authorization. I would like to provide you with precise information concerning your mother-in-law, but you probably will never know. I recommend that you contact the European Research Services in Paris. They will be able, I hope, to indicate the date of Therese Strauss' deportation.

Although the chaplain predicted that we would never know what happened to Terèse Gern Strauss, I, Shulamit, was able to find out a lot. One document, now in the archives of the United States Holocaust Memorial Museum (USHMM) lists Terèse Gern Strauss, born February 19, 1890, as having resided – before deportation to France – in the German city of Ludwigshafen. After many pages listing the names of people on the same transport to Auschwitz as she, there is a photograph with the caption, "Sur la rampe d'arrivé á Auschwitz-Birkenau: la selection" [French: On the arrival ramp of Auschwitz-Birkenau: the selection] with unending rows of bedraggled Jews, unknowingly "slouching toward" the gas chambers.

The USHMM document "Convoy no 17, August 10, 1942" concerns SS officer Heinrichsohn, who sent a message to

Eichmann in Berlin as well as to the commander of Auschwitz. The message stated that on that very day, at 8:55 a.m. under the direction of Feldwebel Kruger, convoy D901/12 left the train station at Drancy headed for Auschwitz with 1,000 Jews on board – 525 women and 475 men. The train started from Gurs near the town of Pau and traveled to Drancy near Paris to pick up more deportees. In total, there were 290 women between the ages of 46–60, and 309 men between the ages of 41–61.

When they arrived in Auschwitz, 140 men and 100 women were "allowed to live." The younger or older Jews were gassed immediately. At the time of the liberation of Auschwitz on January 27, 1945, there was only one survivor from the 1,000-person transport: Herbert Fuchs. For Ilse, the important question was whether her mother died on the train or immediately after her arrival at Auschwitz. Ilse hoped her mother died on the train, thereby avoiding selection and gassing. Not knowing haunted her forever.

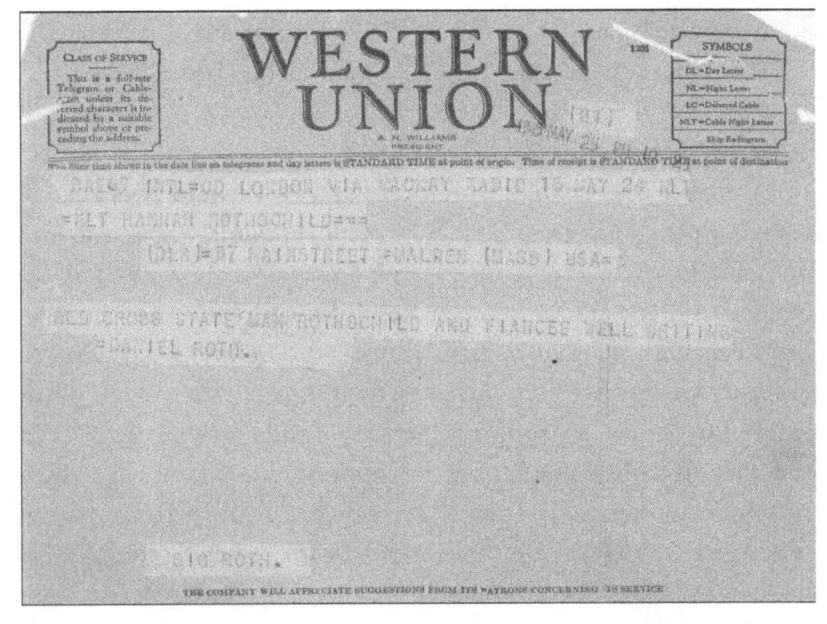

Telegram informing Dad's parents that he and Ilse were alive. The text reads "Red Cross state Max Rothschild and fiancée well, writing Daniel Roth." This was the first sign my grandparents received that my parents had survived.

22nd Zionist Congress ticket. 1946.

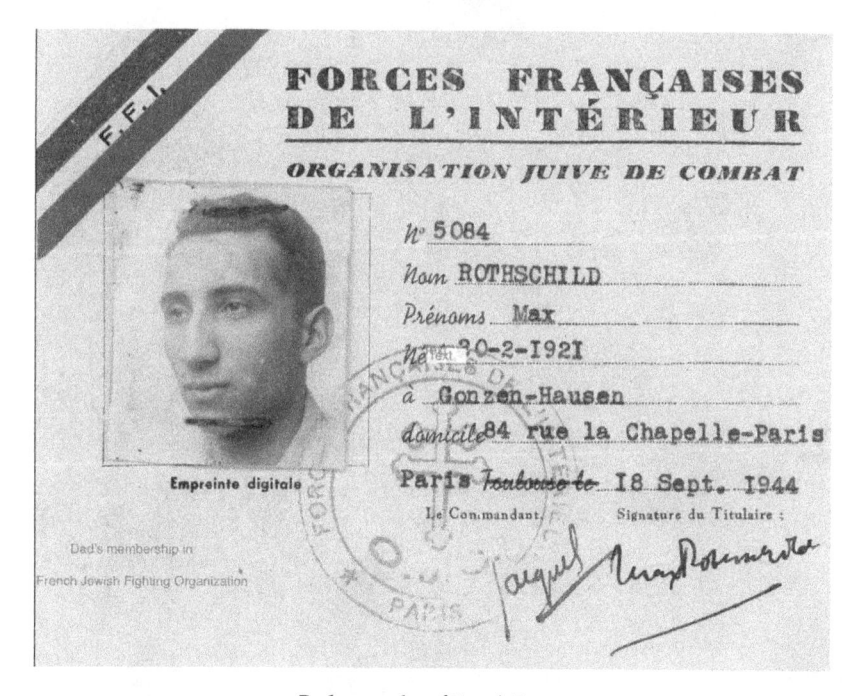

Dad as member of French Forces.

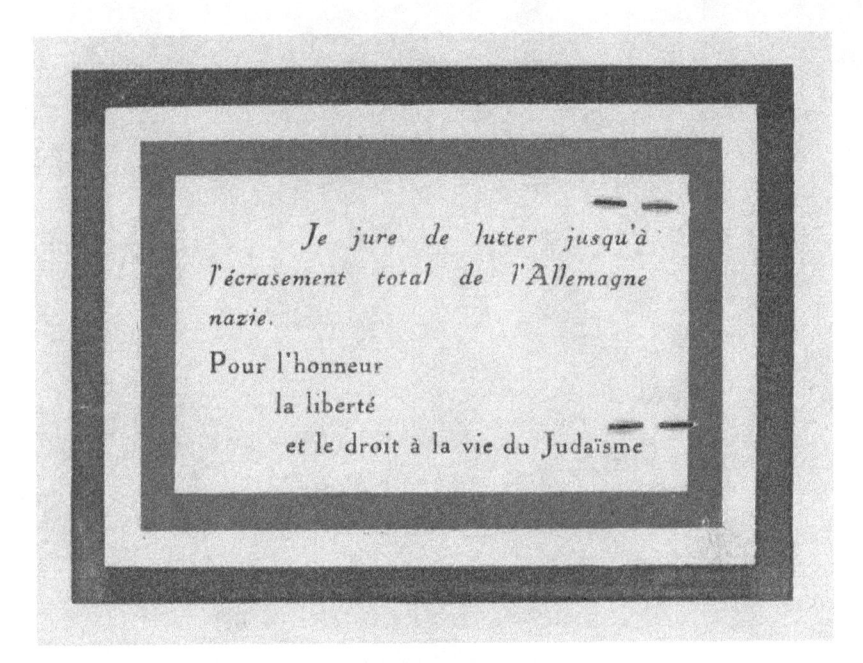

Je jure de lutter jusqu'à l'écrasement total de l'Allemagne nazie.

Pour l'honneur
 la liberté
  et le droit à la vie du Judaïsme

Verso of Forces Françaises identity card.

Mom and Dad's Wedding Photo, January 5, 1946.

Memorial for Shushu, Hannemann and others near Kibbutz Gal-ed. Kibbutz member Amir Rozental on left, author on right.

---

1. https://nl.usembassy.gov/embassy-consulate/amsterdam/history/
2. "10 Things you need to know about the end of World War II in the Netherlands," *DutchNews.nl*, March 3, 2015.
3. See "Brief History of the Holocaust in the Netherlands," Montreal Holocaust Memorial Center.
4. Manfred Gerstenfeld, "Wartime and Postwar Dutch Attitudes toward the Jews: Myth and Truth," *Jerusalem Letter/Viewpoints*, VP:412, 3 Elul 5759/15 August 1999.
5. https://www.yadvashem.org/articles/general/liberation-and-the-return-to-life.html
6. Manfred Gerstenfeld, see above and *Judging the Netherlands: The Renewed Holocaust Restitution Process, 1997-2000* (Jerusalem: Jerusalem Center for Public Affairs, 2011).
7. "Arthur Seyss-Inquart, the German administrator of the occupied Netherlands, was condemned to death at the Nuremberg trials and executed. The Dutch executed forty Nazi officials and collaborators, including Hanns Rauter, the SS chief in Amsterdam. The death sentences of Ferdinand aus der Funten, who directed the deportations from Holland, and of Willy Lages, the chief of the SS Security Service there, were commuted in 1951 to life in prison. Lages served 15 years, then died five years later. Aus der Funten served 39 years until the Dutch released him on grounds of ill health two months before he died. Albert Gemmeker, the commandant of the camp at Westerbork from which most Dutch Jews were sent to their deaths, got off more lightly with a ten-year prison term, of which he spent six behind bars before his release in 1955." https://www.tracesofwar.com/articles/2613/Gemmeker-Albert.htm
8. Warmbrunn, *Ibid.*, p. 265.
9. Warmbrunn, *Ibid.*, p. 279.
10. See also, Robert Rozett and Iael Nidam-Orvieto (eds.), *After So Much Pain and Anguish: First Letters after Liberation* (Jerusalem: Yad Vashem, 2016).

11. *The Lost Train: Bergen-Belsen to Tröbitz*, see film, https://www.yadvashem.org/exhibitions/last-deportees/bergen-belsen-trobitz.html
12. Translation: "The Fighting Jews." See Jessica Hammerman, "Lazarus, Jacques" in: *Encyclopedia of Jews in the Islamic World*, Executive Editor Norman A. Stillman, accessed March 3, 2021.
13. See film, Aviva Slesin, *Secret Lives: Hidden Children and their Rescuers during World War II* (2002).
14. See "This Man Cracked Nazi Doublespeak: A survivor's mission to decode euphemisms for murder," *The New York Times,* Tuesday, June 25, 2019, pp. C1 and C6.
15. Gabriella Saab, *The Last Checkmate* (New York: William Morrow, 2021), p. 369.
16. van Es, *Ibid.,* p. 191.
17. A Fib is an irregular, often rapid heartbeat that commonly causes poor blood flow. This condition may have no symptoms, but when symptoms do appear they include palpitations, shortness of breath, and fatigue. A Fib can lead to blood clots, stroke, heart failure and other heart-related complications.
18. Struma (medicine), a swelling in the neck due to an enlarged thyroid gland.
19. See David Nasaw, *The Last Million: Europe's Displaced Persons from World War to Cold War* (New York: Penguin Press, 2020).
20. I can't imagine that this is true. I doubt that Dad's parents were interested in sitting in a beerhall with their non-Jewish neighbors on a Saturday night after the end of Shabbat, a time when Dad's Father started his delayed house-calls.
21. https://www.forbes.com/sites/theapothecary/2015/12/09/explaining-the-decline-fall-and-possible-rebirth-of-doctors-house-calls/?sh=5fd74af8384d
22. The partition resolution was adopted on November 29, 1947 with 33 votes in favor, 13 votes against, and 10 abstentions. The Jews accepted the plan and the Arabs rejected it.
23. See Simon Erlanger, "A Dreadful experience." How the 1946 Zionist Congress in Basel Changed the Center of Gravity of Jewish Politics. Talk given to the "Jews in the Modern Europe Study Group," Harvard University, January 30, 2017.

4

POSTSCRIPT

My father's life did not begin from scratch when he passed the Statue of Liberty with my mother and me in 1947. He did not change his name to make it sound "less Jewish." He did not deny his past. He spoke German with my mother in our home, with his parents in theirs, and in a German-speaking synagogue in which he officiated as a rabbi for several years. For a long time, my parents had believed seriously and passionately that if they survived the war, they would move to *Eretz Yisrael* to fulfill their Zionist dream. But instead, like millions of Jews before them, the three of us moved to the United States where my parents lived for 66 years until they died in January 2013, one week apart.

Ilse and Max never considered returning to their birthplaces in Germany. Nor did they entertain the idea of staying in the Netherlands. "Europe was one large Jewish cemetery," my mother said, "a place for dead Jews, not a place where Jews could live." In truth, a cemetery would have been a vast improvement. Most murdered Jews were not buried at all.

When the time came to leave Europe after the war, my parents disagreed about what they would do next. Dad wanted to go to the US where his family had already relocated; Mom wanted *Eretz Yisrael* where she had one sister and a few other relatives, all that remained of her family. Each of them wanted family. Dad got his choice. Mom did not get hers.

When Dad finally succeeded in amassing all the visas and permits needed to enter America, the three of us flew from the Netherlands to Sweden and boarded the MS *Gripsholm*, a transatlantic ship operated by the Swedish American line.

Dad later described the trip to me as stormy with high waves and rough waters. He was seasick all the time. As a seven-month-old, I apparently rolled around on the shifting deck, enjoying the strange experience. Many refugees were on board in addition to the three of us, and Dad felt comfortable among them. In the US he always considered himself a refugee, not an immigrant. For him, this was an important distinction.

On Ellis Island, Dad encountered incompetent bureaucrats whom he deemed grossly under-qualified for their jobs. Few "seemed to understand any of the major languages the newcomers spoke": Italian, Yiddish, German, Dutch, Polish, Russian, Hungarian, Czech, and so on. "*One guy asked me if I was Mr. Gunzenhausen.*" Another asked "the nature of our professions" – Dad said "*teacher,*" Mom said "pediatric assistant." And then the worker pointed to me asleep in a basket. I had to "sign a document" stating that I was unemployed and not a prostitute.

When I was eight months old and living in Malden, Massachusetts, I received a stamped Alien Registration Receipt Card (no. 6564096) instructing me to "Keep this card. Keep a record of the number," neither of which I was old enough to do. The card said I was "Admitted Permanent at New York, New York," and informed me that "The Alien Registration Act of 1940 requires, under penalty, all resident aliens to report each change of address within five days of such change."

More than a year later, on September 3, 1948, I received a receipt for $3.00 (made out to the mistyped name of Shulanmit T. Rothschild), mailed to the wrong address. These three dollars were in repayment of for the payment of my permit to enter the US. No one knew what this meant. Five years later, Mom, Dad, Tova (born in 1949 in Israel) and I became naturalized American citizens.

Jonathan was born a few years later in the US. *The only one of us who could become president*, Dad said.

On May 14, 1948, the radio announced that David Ben-Gurion had declared the establishment of the State of Israel. Mom ran to Dad and told him we were now obligated to move there. So we did move to Israel in 1949 for what turned out to be a ten-month stay. Dad was employed by American newspapers to report on the new country. He also worked on building a road connecting the existing road with our cabin in Haifa's Carmel Forests.

After ten months of living in Israel, Dad became ill and wanted to return to his father's care in the US. So we returned, and Dad recovered quickly. I don't know if Dad ever understood how deeply the decision to return to the US disappointed Mom. Once again, Dad won, and she lost. She told me years later that those ten months in Israel were the happiest of her life.

In September 1949, upon my family's second arrival in the US, Dad worked as a necktie salesman before landing a position at a Zionist organization in Boston. For a while, Mom kept a packed suitcase near the front door of the apartment. "Ready to return to Israel at a moment's notice," she said. At the same time, Dad studied for an M.A. in journalism at Boston University, thanks to the department's defining his life experience and educational background as equivalent to "at least a B.A." In June 1950, when I was four years old, Dad earned his degree.

On the surface, life was good. Both times we arrived in the US, we were embraced by my grandparents and their wide circle of German-Jewish refugee friends. Mom took on part-time work with children and enrolled me in a Jewish pre-school program. I remember being afraid, however, that Nazis, in the form of uniformed policemen, would come to our house and "get me." How did I develop that frightening idea? Were my parents already telling me about the Holocaust?

When I entered kindergarten in the local public elementary school, I was afraid that corporal punishment was being meted out somewhere in the building. I imagined a "torture room" to which misbehaving children were sent. I wonder if my character was already being shaped by stories my parents were sharing with me or that I overheard. I was becoming a child of Holocaust survivors, a member of the "Second Generation."[1]

When I was about to enter second grade, my family moved to New Jersey from Massachusetts. Dad had just been hired as the Director of Regions for the United Synagogue of America, the organizing body of the movement for Conservative Judaism. The offices of what he jokingly called the U.S.A. were located in the same Manhattan building as the Jewish Theological Seminary, making it convenient for him to enroll in the seminary for evening classes while working full-time during the day. Dad chose to earn a doctorate rather than embark on rabbinic studies because he had not yet decided to become a rabbi.

Along with his daily commute, a full-time job, and three young children at home, Dad added the challenging task of writing his dissertation in Hebrew. My father received his Ph.D. in 1958. His thesis, *Rabbi Yosef ibn Caspi: His Life and Works (1280 Arles— 1345 Majorca)*, was a difficult subject given that Caspi, a medieval rabbi, traveled a great deal and was prolific – authoring at least 20 books of commentary on a wide range of Biblical topics. But Dad felt a kinship with Caspi, I believe, who, like him, loved studying Jewish texts with brilliant teachers. Most of his professors at the Seminary were Europeans, some of them Holocaust survivors, all of them knowledgeable – his kind of people.

Working at the United Synagogue of America provided Dad with material for an endless stream of jokes. For example, one of his responsibilities was to place rabbis in congregations that no one wanted to serve or that no other congregation would hire.[2] The stories of the mismatch between congregation and rabbi were so funny that Jehuda and I tell them to this day.

After a few years, Dad was ordained privately by his colleague, Rabbi Joseph Weisenberg, in Minnesota. Newly certified, Dad began to function as a part-time rabbi, a job which he enjoyed immensely and for which he received appreciative feedback. Occasionally, particularly on Holocaust Remembrance Day in the spring, he gave public talks about his Holocaust experiences. On one occasion he participated in a conference organized at the United States Holocaust Memorial Museum in Washington, D.C. Titled *The Courage to Care: Rescuers of Jews during the Holocaust*, Dad's essay in the conference book included ideas not found in his memoir. The most striking was the following: "I, myself, was not smart enough to make the decision to go into hiding and join the underground. If it hadn't been for my good wife, who didn't trust the Nazis, and others who convinced me... I would most likely not be alive today."[3]

Dad's first congregation, whose synagogue was squeezed in between a Chinese laundry and a Puerto Rican bodega on Manhattan's Upper West Side, was composed of German-speaking survivors who chose to name their synagogue "The American Congregation." Dad delivered his sermons in German and became the substitute son of his mostly childless old people's congregation. We three children listened with appreciation to his double sermons – one in German and the other in English – almost all of which managed to touch on the Holocaust.

At that time, Dad told us that should he not find a rabbi for a congregation, he would serve that congregation himself. And so he did, bringing Judaism to such communities as Nuevo Laredo, Texas; Ashtabula, Ohio; Oneonta, New York; and Ridgewood, New Jersey, all while we lived in River Edge, New Jersey. Usually, he would serve these congregations one or two weekends per month. The congregations were very grateful for his presence and commitment. For example, a brief history of Temple Beth El in Oneonta, New York states:

> The considerable scholarship Rabbi Rothschild brought with him and which he continues to develop has been a rich source of knowledge and inspiration to the congregation... One of the innovations he brought is the Jewish Study Group which has been meeting regularly on Sundays. Among the subjects dealt with were the Dead Sea Scrolls, various books of the Bible (Job, Ruth, Jonah, Ecclesiastes, the Prophets, Ethics of the Fathers, etc.), Judaism and Christianity, Jewish Life in the Enlightenment, and many others.

The sessions were marked by animated discussion. No study period ever reached its conclusion, however, without a generous sprinkling of Max's usually ironic, but always spicy, humor.[4]

Dad enjoyed lecturing around the country, as well. An article in the *American Jewish World* (2/1/74) announced a talk in St. Paul, Minnesota with the title "A Look Inside the Bible Today." In publicity for the talk, Dad described himself as an executive member of the World Jewish Bible Society and an author of articles on Hebrew, Midrash, and Jewish history. That was fine, but some aspects of his resumé were put in a strange way, e.g. "A native of Germany, Dr. Rothschild was educated in the Netherlands."

Years later, when Max and Ilse moved into a "retirement center," he told the family stories galore about the inanities of the place. One of our favorites concerned his asking a waiter what time it was. The man answered, "You're not my table." Dad did not want to spend his last years "as an inmate" in a Kafkaesque environment, so he and my mother left the facility and moved into a private apartment with their full-time helper, Angelies, whom they loved and who cared for them lovingly in return. Dad had a great time speaking Spanish with her, a language he basically didn't know.

When Dad obtained minor teaching jobs in local colleges, he would regale us with stories about the incredibly stupid students he was trying to teach. One cherished example concerned a European history class that ended with an essay exam about Karl Marx. Dad asked the students to list the most important of Marx's books and explain their contents. One student began, "One day, many years ago, Mr. and Mrs. Marx had a baby boy. They named him Karl..." After a few paragraphs, Marx died. Another wrote, "Karl Marx wrote too many books to mention." Dad laughed and laughed, but he also lamented the fact that he wasn't teaching "real students" at a "real university," and that he hadn't become a great teacher or a great writer. But when these thoughts threatened his self-esteem, he quickly shifted gears and told another story.

Dad accepted early retirement at age 59 and lived another 33 years. He spent his time studying Talmud, investing in the stock market, and showing my brother, Jonathan, how to do the same. Dad and Mom wintered in Florida (an environment that my mother didn't like) in a condo Jonathan bought for them. In their Florida beach town, they met many European survivors who became their friends. Mom and Dad loved traveling to Holland to be with the Schoutens, as well as visiting Israel and much of the US. Dad never left Mom's side as she slipped into dementia.

Dad wrote about the importance of preserving the names of those who did not survive; and of teaching one's children about what happened. Growing up in my family, it seems that almost everything about the Holocaust was divulged, discussed, debated, dissected – repeatedly. I even teased Dad and said, "You aren't having a good time unless you're talking about the Holocaust." My mother didn't like my comment at all.

So too, my sister didn't like hearing about the Holocaust "all the time" and was afraid that our father would incorporate a discussion of the Holocaust into her wedding ceremony at which he officiated. My brother liked to imitate Dad. My family was perhaps unusual, but certainly not unique. Recently, a Jewish friend sent me an email during a weekend-long Jewish wedding celebration: "There's a sit-down dinner at every meal – fun to be part of this family. Holocaust 24/7."[5]

Although Dad talked freely and frequently about the Holocaust, some of the horror stayed inaccessible to him, residing deep in his brain. On overnight visits to my parents' apartment during their final years, I would sometimes hear him scream in his sleep. To my astonishment, his screaming did not stop when he walked around the dark rooms, dazed. I tried to reassure him that he was only dreaming. "Everything is okay," I told him over and over. But clearly, everything was not okay. Writing and talking did not eradicate his traumatic experiences. Sometimes his memories came out as beautifully composed pages with precise information. Other times they came out as screams.

It is difficult to comprehend the concept of six million people, which at the time of this writing in 2023 was a bit smaller than the population of New York City (7,888,121) and quite a bit larger than the population of Los Angeles (3,769,485). In one project in Tennessee, children collected six million paper clips to help them grasp the number.[6] One researcher determined that if we held a moment of silence for each of the victims of the Holocaust, we would remain silent for 11.5 years.[7]

Dad didn't focus on the numbers. He was not looking for patterns in these sad statistics. He wanted something more. He wanted his children to remember specific people, friends and relatives who had been killed. Dutch Holocaust survivor, Haim Roet, felt the same way and created Unto Every Person There is a Name, "a memorial project that involves annually reading aloud the names of Nazi victims around the world."[8] "I Do Not Want Them To Be Forgotten," Dad wrote near the end of his memoir, each word capitalized. And then he wrote the names and explained what happened to each of these innocent victims.

A Charmed Childhood

The tragic deaths of his brother and mother when he was a child, along with the growing Nazi activity in his hometown, diminished Dad's otherwise charmed Jewish childhood that enabled him later to resist in multiple ways. His rich childhood and his Father's survival enabled Dad to lead a relatively normal life in America, fulfilling the stereotype of the immigrant/refugee arriving with nothing and gradually entering the middle class. On our cul-de-sac in New Jersey, we were the only refugees and the only Jews. All the families – Protestant, Catholic and Jewish – got along.

My father died in Fort Lee, New Jersey on January 18, 2013, one month shy of his 92nd birthday. Although I am grateful that Dad lived to a ripe old age, I wish he could have lived another seven years. He would thus have learned that the president of the Netherlands Red Cross visited Israel to apologize formally for the organization's conduct during the German occupation of the country.[9] If Dad had lived until November 9, 2020, he would have learned that the Dutch Protestant Church apologized formally on the anniversary of Kristallnacht for not helping Jews during the Holocaust.[10]

That same year he would have learned that then King Willem-Alexander of the Netherlands acknowledged the indifference of his great-grandmother, Wilhelmina, to the fate of Dutch Jews. "It's something that won't let go of me," he said.[11] Four months earlier, Prime Minister Mark Rutte "apologized for how his kingdom's wartime government failed its Jews."[12]

Dad had not been ill when he died, so I suppose he just didn't want to live without my mother who had passed away a week earlier. Perhaps he thought she needed him in the afterlife if there was one. My brother arranged for Dad's body to be placed in an El Al plane and sent to the vast cemetery Har Hamenuchot in the Givat Shaul neighborhood of Jerusalem. Dad was buried next to Mom who had arrived a week earlier. Their side-by-side graves are not far from the trees Niek and Aag Schouten had planted at Yad Vashem. My parents' graves lie close to those of Dad's Father and stepmother, on which the names of Dad's mother Thekla and grandmother Caroline are also listed because they have no graves. Dad's grave is also not far from that of his sister, Hannah, and her husband, Robby. The proximity in death of all these people is somehow comforting.

My parents survived the German occupation of the Netherlands because of luck, smart decisions, and people's help. It was the behavior of these exceptional people that led Dad to tell me what he considered the most important lesson he derived from the Holocaust: *There are some good people in this world.* My parents' lives were saved by modest people who contributed to the survival of a remnant of the Jewish people. Dad's belief is not to be confused with Anne Frank's naive idea that there is "some good in everyone." She wrote that sentence right before she was betrayed and shipped to the Bergen-Belsen concentration/extermination camp where she died. The subtle difference between the sentiments of my father and Anne Frank is important.

According to Jewish tradition, the world continues to exist because a few good individuals exist. The Schoutens, the van

Straalens, H. te Riet, Miss Veth, Jan Smit, Joop Westerweel, the Mondriaans and the anonymous people in Wieringen, among others, were a few examples, as was "the organization." Ilse and Max stayed in touch with the Schoutens, and with Miss Veth until her death on May 26, 1965. They vacationed with the te Riets in the US. They visited the Mondriaans who had moved to Nova Scotia, Canada. These relationships lasted forever. My parents invited their rescuers to visit them in New Jersey. They underwrote the Schoutens' children's higher education. Dad and Niek corresponded until their deaths. I found letters scattered throughout the house.

Dad emphasized that he survived by hiding and by the help of people who enabled him to hide. Hiding became a theme in his life even when he lived in the US and no longer had to hide. Dad survived, but when he emerged into broad daylight at the end of the war, he didn't leave hiding behind. For example, when I was growing up in the 1950s, a Catholic family lived across the street. The father in that family and my own father commuted in Dad's car to Manhattan every weekday. After about a year of this simple arrangement, my father "announced" to our family that if we ever had to hide, we should turn to Mr. Smith, the man across the street. He could be trusted. He wouldn't ask questions or seek rewards – he would just do what was right. We accepted what Dad said.

On Dad's 90th birthday in 2011, his younger sister, Eva, flew in from Seattle to celebrate with us in New Jersey. When asked to say a few words, she recounted an incident that occurred shortly after Dad had reached the US 64 years earlier: "We were overjoyed that Max and Ilse were alive," she said. "Our mom and dad had rented a modest apartment for them, and we all went to inspect it. When we came to the kitchen, Max looked it over, went to the sink, opened the cabinet underneath, and burst out, 'Two people could hide under there.' I shall never forget it as long as I live."

Hiding is a triangle with three roles: the pursuer, the hider, and the helper. Successful hiding cannot be done on one's own; it requires at least one helping person or, better yet, a whole network of helpers. Helpers, sometimes called "hosts," sheltered, harbored, fed, protected, and concealed. But during the Holocaust, these words all meant the same thing – hiding a Jew – a crime punishable by execution.

The Holocaust has become reduced in the public mind – if it is remembered at all – to concentration camps and extermination camps, particularly Auschwitz. The horror of Auschwitz is conveyed in images of Jews close to death or already dead, not of Jews surviving. Dad's story and the story of people like him present an alternate image – a person crouched silently in a basement or attic, a haystack or a cave – a person with a chance to live. We should remember that one third of the Jews of Europe did survive the Holocaust, a typically forgotten fact. Their survival has to be explained.

In a dramatically stunning area near the main entrance to Jerusalem, there is a special path on the grounds of Yad Vashem, along which a tree is planted for each Righteous Gentile whose acts of bravery and kindness during the Holocaust can be authenticated and documented. In 2004, Yad Vashem, Israel's national memorial to "the martyrs and heroes" of the Holocaust, and now a major museum and research center, published the informative and beautifully designed *Encyclopedia of the Righteous among the Nations: Rescuers of Jews during the Holocaust.* Two of the numerous volumes concern the Netherlands. This invaluable resource contains the names of the rescuers and their "guests," plus important essays by scholars.

The Schoutens are included in the book along with a description of their courageous activities during the Holocaust. Those rescuers who were not nominated or could not be documented, however, are not mentioned, suggesting that there were many more rescuers than those listed. Miss Veth and Ha.B. and Hennie te Riet, for example, are not included. Conversely, I found names of several Almelo people that I did not recognize. The essay about the Schoutens also opened my eyes to the assistance this magnificent couple gave to Jews other than my parents.

For years Niek and Aag refused Yad Vashem's request to honor them, saying, "What we did was not special. If we considered it special, then we would be saying that we don't expect everyone to do it." Many Dutch people who hid Jews similarly did not want to talk about their actions or be honored for what they did. After stubbornly resisting, the Schoutens finally conceded when my parents explained that they should allow the next generation to learn from their deeds. So on January 5, 1984, nearly 40 years after the liberation, the Schoutens made the trip from the Netherlands to Jerusalem where parts of our extended family met them at Yad Vashem to plant two trees in their honor.

After the tree planting, Niek gave a speech in Dutch to the crowd that assembled in an auditorium at Yad Vashem. His remarks addressed my parents directly and explained briefly and modestly how they had made the decision to rescue Jews.

> It was the end of 1942 when I saw how a group of Jews was assembled in South Rotterdam ready for deportation. As an individual, one was powerless to oppose such an act of violence. What the individual or family could do, however, was to help Jewish people go into hiding, so that they, at least, might be spared such a fate. This is purely and simply, the basis on which we, Aag, Bubi [Niek's mother], Helga and I lived with you at 36 Pioenstraat. We remember so clearly hearing the simple Dutch nursery rhyme *"rikke tikke teddybeer"* with Helga on Bubi's lap. We remember Max always studying and Ilse's boundless readiness to help.

Niek's phrase, "when we lived with you," rather than "when you lived with us" deserves comment. First, Niek used the word 'lived,' not "hid," probably because he did not relate to Max and Ilse only as Jews or as people in need of assistance; and second, "lived with you" creates a sense of equality even if the apartment belonged to the Schoutens. This little reversal of the expectable indicates sweetly that Niek and Aag never wanted my parents to feel indebted to them. On one of my visits with Jehuda to the Schoutens in Holland, they showed us to the "guest room," where we unpacked our bags and spent a few nights. It was only when we were ready to leave that we realized they had given us their own bedroom. There was no guest room. I have no idea where they slept.

The Schoutens frequently visited us in the United States. Together with my parents, they once drove cross-country in an RV. They spent a few summers together in Israel, a few winters in Florida, and took various hiking trips in Europe. In 2014, when Jehuda and I visited Niek and Aag in Holland once again, Niek showed us the very spot in Rotterdam where he watched Jews being marched off at gunpoint to the train station. This image clinched Niek's decision to save Jews rather than try to kill Nazis – to prevent harm rather than to murder perpetrators.

After Niek spoke at the Yad Vashem ceremony, my mother addressed the crowd on behalf of our family. With a glowing tan from the Jerusalem sun and a warm, modest demeanor, Ilse, who did not know she would be the only Rothschild family speaker, delivered her handwritten prepared remarks:

> Aag and Niek, honored guests, friends, and relatives,
>
> Max and I feel proud and privileged that we finally can honor you, dear Aag and Niek, here at Yad Vashem. We are thankful to you that you came to Israel and made it possible for us to have this ceremony and to celebrate this day together. It is not in my character to make long speeches. I normally leave this to Max. But I felt that today I had to say a few words.
>
> We just left the somber and impressive hall at Yad Vashem where Jews and non-Jews usually gather to remember the Holocaust and the suffering of our people, where we tell our children *Z'chor* – 'Thou shalt remember.' Remembering is the least we can do to keep the memory of our dear ones alive.
>
> But there is a different kind of remembering, a joyous one, and this is why we are here today. Max and I, and all of you in this hall, are here to honor Aag and Niek who opened their home to us when we were complete strangers. They saved our lives. At a time when our lives weren't worth a penny, when we were stateless, when we were hunted by the Nazis and we were supposed to be

extinguished in the concentration camps, Niek and Aag gave Max and me shelter. Not only us, but many others.

Niek and Aag, you endangered your own lives. You did it out of high moral values and because of your respect for the lives of your fellow man. You also gave us your friendship, and this is what made life in those days bearable and more normal. We shared fear and sorrow together, but also laughter and funny moments.

So I'm happy that today we can celebrate and remember together. I'm also glad that two of our children, Shula, and Jonny, could come. Our daughter, Tova, visited you last September and she is with us in her thoughts. I'm also thinking of your children who are precious to us. I am so glad that Wanda [the Schoutens' third and youngest daughter] is with us today in accepting your medal and certificate. Her presence brings us all closer together. [Ilse Schouten, their second daughter, named for my mother, could not attend, nor could Helga.] Aag and Niek, you are very dear to us, and I hope that our friendship will last forever.

Max did not have the chance to speak publicly at this event, but he saved a travel journal in which he wrote soon after the Yad Vashem ceremony.

The ceremony at Yad Vashem. Unexpectedly "successful," short, to the point. A bit too much Dutch language, but that perhaps contributed to the awed impression of our Israeli friends and relatives who wanted to see what those people looked and sounded like, people who helped Jews during the war. Ilse's short speech a masterpiece, putting aside my petty feelings of not being given a chance to say the words that I had prepared. The religious–liturgical element in the cantor's rendition was subdued. Among the highlights: the unimaginably beautiful spot where Aag and Niek's tree was planted. What a glorious view over those Southern Hills of Jerusalem. The party at the Roth's home afterwards. All in all, very favorable reactions, plus seeing old friends – as I expected, some of them we hadn't seen for over 40 years.

The meaning of my own life grips me with an irresistible force. Sentiments well up. The days of our youth – and our youth movement life are coming close to the surface again. It all goes deeper, for us at least, than a memorial ceremony. Its symbolism, and Niek's wonderful words about our family and the concept of Amor Fati. So full of danger, unhappiness, loss – and of happiness. All else sinks into insignificance. Look down on us with favor, dear God. Perhaps it was a divine spark (as somebody there remarked) that caused our saviors to act as they did, and that brought us together as friends for life. An unforgettable experience – and everything went smoothly, without a hitch.

During the various ceremonies, Niek and Aag seemed to be at peace with their decision to accept the gratitude and attention bestowed upon them.

A few years later, on a subsequent trip to Israel, Dad visited the region of the country in which his *Hachsharah* friends established several *kibbutzim*:

The sight of those kibbutzim evoked a stream of feelings in me. These feelings included pride in what my friends had created. But also shame or regret that I had not been part of the kibbutz story, that I had abandoned the goal of my Hachsharah. As I looked out at the gently sloping hills of the Menashe Plain[13] *of Israel with neat kibbutzim in verdant fields, I thought: Here is the world of our youth. To go to Kibbutz Gal-Ed, I couldn't bring myself even though that was the location of the memorial to my best friends, Shushu and Hanneman. The reason: Kibbutz Gal-Ed member Senta Josephsthal's strong and insulting letter, calling me "an unpleasant snob" for having written the invitation for the Yad Vashem ceremony in English rather than Hebrew.*

When Niek was 90 years old and Aag was recovering from an illness in a hospital near their home, Jehuda, Niek, one of Niek's and Aag's grandsons, and I went to visit her. Afterwards, we all went to Niek's farm in Hoogeloon, a small village in the "commune of Brabant" to which Niek and Aag had moved after Niek retired from his work at the Volkshuis. While we were sitting around the wooden kitchen table eating a simple meal in silence, Niek suddenly left his seat. He had a surprise for us.

Still tall (Dutch people are the tallest in the world) and erect, he walked over to a drawer and pulled out a large manila envelope. In the envelope he found his and Aag's "Righteous Gentile" certificates from Yad Vashem. He read us the citation as if we didn't know that he had been recognized for his great deeds. He had probably forgotten that I had been with him in Jerusalem on that precious occasion. Perhaps for the first time, he seemed to be saying that he was happy to have been a Righteous Gentile and that looking back on his life, "It was good." That was the last time we saw him. My parents died before Niek, and I did not receive a notice of Niek and Aag's deaths.

After the war, Dad wrote the following, with which I finish this book:

There is no longer any SS to be feared, thank God; but there are plenty of others who would gladly take away our dignity if you let them. I value and want to protect my freedom! – freedom from terror, freedom to make my own choices, including the choice of religion, and freedom from having to hide. For me, freedom's birthdate was May 5, 1945, the day the Allies finished the job they had started on the beaches of Normandy. I will be forever grateful.

Dad and me (age three) in Carmel Forests, Haifa, Israel, 1949.

Dad shares the stage with David Ben-Gurion, first Prime Minister of Israel. Dad is third to the right.

Dad earns Ph.D. from Jewish Theological Seminary, New York City, 1958.

Dad guiding a student in Beth El Synagogue, Oneonta, New York.

Niek Schouten, Mom, Dad, and Aag Schouten enjoying a vacation in Pompano Beach, Florida.

Gunzenhausen 2014, Author's first visit. Hostess of coffee hour is blonde woman, Emmi Hetzner, on my left. Emmi taught middle school and introduced the subject of the Nazi period in Gunzenhausen.

Tree-planting ceremony (July 2023) in memory of Jewish residents of Gunzenhausen who were murdered or driven out of town, making it ethnically cleansed of Jews. Author is in center with white jacket. Everyone else is a relative of the author, a member of the Gunzenhausen/Jewish descendants Dialogue Group, or part of the Rosenfelder family who were friends of my father's family when they lived in Gunzenhausen.

Last photo of Dad, taken in January 2013 at home of caretaker, Angelies.

ILSE H. ROTHSCHILD
APRIL NINE 1920 - JANUARY TEN 2013

MAX M. ROTHSCHILD
FEBRUARY TWENTY 1921 - JANUARY EIGHTEEN 2013

הנאהבים והנעימים בחייהם ובמותם
לא נפרדו

Death notice for Mom and Dad, January 10 and January 18, 2013.

---

1. See Helen Epstein, *Children of the Holocaust: Conversations with Sons and Daughters of Survivors* (New York: Putnam's, 1979).
2. See Stephen Fried, *The New Rabbi: A Congregation Searches for Its Leader* (New York: Bantam Books, 2002).
3. Max Rothschild, "Max Rothschild," in Carol Rittner and Sondra Myers (eds.), *The Courage to Care: Rescuers of Jews during the Holocaust* (New York: New York University Press, 1986), pp. 34-37.
4. http://www.templebetheloneonta.org/history/
5. Filmmaker Rachel Kastner labels a family such as this a "Holocaust home," defined as a household where the events were discussed all the time. See Rachel Kastner: "Living in the 'Third 'Generation," https://www.youtube.com/watch?v=-_XipotpWXU
6. https://oneclipatatime.org/paper-clips-project/
7. *snopes.com/fact-check/moment-of-silence-holocaust*
8. Daniel E. Slotnik, "Haim Roet, Who Kept Holocaust Victims' Names Alive, Dies at 90," *The New York Times*, June 21, 2023.

9. Ofer Aderet, "How the Dutch Red Cross Abetted the Nazis during World War II," *https://mosaicmagazine.com/picks/2018/03*.
10. Aaron Reich, "Dutch Protestant Church Apologizes for not Helping Jews in Holocaust," *The Jerusalem Post*, November 9, 2020.
11. *https://www.timesofisrael.com/dutch-king-admits-jews-felt-abandoned-by-great-grandmother-during-holocaust/*
12. *https://www.timesofisrael.com/dutch-pm-apologizes-for-his-country-failing-its-jews-during-the-holocaust/*
13. According to the *Book of Joshua*, the region is named for the tribe of Menashe.

ACKNOWLEDGMENTS

My first thanks go to my late parents, Max Michael Rothschild and Ilse Hertha Strauss Rothschild, for teaching me about their experiences and entrusting me with their papers. I especially thank my father for writing his memoir and for keeping the myriad documents I found in my parents' home. I thank my sister, Tova Rothschild Lovett, my brother, Jonathan Rothschild, along with their spouses, Barry Lovett and Stacey Halpern Rothschild for encouragement, answering my questions and overall kindness. At the same time, I acknowledge my late grandparents Dr. Karl (Opa) and Henrietta Rothschild (Oma) for teaching me what Judaism meant by example and showering me with love.

I thank the Schouten family in the Netherlands for saving my parents' lives during the war and for their friendship with my parents and our family after the war. In focusing on the Schoutens, I am very aware of all the other people who saved my parents. I am grateful to my cousins Sanne Kalter Dewitt (author of *I was Born in an Old Age home: A memoir*); Bea Schutz (who supplied me with Erna Berg's memoir of hiding in Holland during the Occupation); Tamar Yechieli (who translated my father's entire memoir into Hebrew) and my late beloved cousin, Netanel Yechieli, who helped me in countless ways.

I thank my dear friends, Ellen Golub, Loraine Obler, Phyllis Chesler, Viva Hammer and Lois Lindauer for talking through my writing process. My gratitude to Ellen Cassedy, author of the magnificent, *We Are Here: Memories of the Lithuanian Holocaust*, for steering me back on track when I strayed. I am grateful for illuminating discussions with many authors such as Bernice

Lerner, author of *All the Horrors of War: A Jewish Girl, a British Doctor, and the Liberation of Bergen-Belsen*. Thanks also to Ruth Gruschka and Reina Reiner in Jerusalem. These people commented on my book's topic or format, read and commented on individual chapters or the whole book, and applied their keen critical eye to individual words and overall tone.

I thank Anne Gottlieb, actor and playwright, for teaching me about Etty Hillesum. I thank Josette Goldish, an expert on the Jews of Curacao for teaching me about Dutch culture and translating my parents' ketuba from Dutch to English. I benefitted from Shirley and Kenneth Rendell, founders of The International Museum of World War II who shared original documents with me concerning children's literature in Germany. I enjoyed discussions of German Jewish culture in America with Gabrielle Rossmer Gropman and her daughter Sonya Gropman. I thank Chaya Brasz for inviting me to her Dutch home in Jerusalem and for her work at the Hebrew University's Institute for Research on Dutch Jewry. I thank Dr. Olivia Mattis for involving me in activities of the Sousa-Mendes Foundation that focuses on rescuers and survivors.

I thank my "Student-Scholar Partners" at the Brandeis University Women's Studies Research Center: Tova Perlman, Alona Weimer and Gabrielle Boloker, for their conscientious research assistance.

I thank my Israeli friends, Esther Carmel-Hakim who took me to Kibbutz Gal-Ed. I thank Professor Dan Michman, Head of the International Institute for Holocaust Research at Yad Vashem, for helpful conversations. Dr. Mordechai Paldiel, former Director of the Department of the Righteous at Yad Vashem, explained Yad Vashem procedures used to select individuals for status of Righteous Gentile.

I thank the members of the Brandeis University's Women's Studies Research Center and especially for members of the Holocaust Research Study Group for comments on my rough drafts. They are filmmaker Ornit Barkai; public artist, Karen Frostig; sociologist Debra Kaufman; professor of journalism, Laura Leff; public health specialist, Jutta Lindert of Germany; poet and architect, Rachel Munn; artistic photographer, Karin Rosenthal; and author, Sarah Silberstein Swartz.

I thank Sharon diFino for arranging for me to affiliate with the Summer School at the University of Utrecht. I thank the friends I made while living in Utrecht, especially Wanya Kruyer. I thank Tobe Levin Von Gleichen who supported my appointment as Research Fellow of Lady Margaret Hall at Oxford University, and who later drove me to Gunzenhausen to participate in the ceremony of 2023. I'd like to express gratitude to Lidia Sciama my landlady, fellow researcher, and guide to Oxford. I benefited greatly from conversations with Dr. Joanna Michlic, historian of the impact of the Holocaust on Polish-Jewish families. Judge Thomas Buergenthal, author of *A Lucky Child: A Memoir of Surviving Auschwitz as a Young Boy*, and his wife, Peggy, invited me to their home in The Hague for a weekend and taught me about legal issues in the Netherlands.

Translators were essential to this project: they include Simone Diender, Anna Simpson, Abby Huber, Rosalyn Leshin, Gabe Padawer, Eveline Weyl, and my husband, Jehuda Reinharz. Thanks to Josette Goldish who introduced me to fellow Curacaoan, Roz Leshin. I am grateful to Uri and Tamar Kupferschmidt of Haifa who helped with Dutch translations. And to Brandeis faculty member Ron Gomes Casseres who explored my mother's claim that Queen Wilhelmina of the Netherlands helped Jews in WW2.

I thank Emmi Hetzner who welcomed me to Gunzenhausen, Germany for my initial visit, and who worked with Stefan Mages and others to create our Residents and Descendants Dialogue group. I thank the late, Netanel Yechieli for becoming my friend and introducing me to Shirley Levi in Jerusalem whom I interviewed. Her family had been patients of my grandfather's in Gunzenhausen and then in Munich.

I thank the open, warm-hearted group of people who live in Gunzenhausen today. I also thank the town government of Gunzenhausen for all they are doing to create a living history of the Jews of Gunzenhausen. Similarly, I thank Peter Schnell for allowing me to reprint his speech about Gunzenhausen's behavior toward the Jews in the 1930s and beyond.

I thank Mustafa Ahdoudi, Utrecht City Archives in the Netherlands; Werner Mühlhaüßer, Municipal Archivist, Gunzenhausen; Anat Bratman-Elhalel, Director of Archives, Ghetto Fighters' House, Israel; and Sara Bloomfield, US Holocaust Memorial and Museum.

I thank my therapist, Dr. David Geltman, for helping me understand my family and myself. I also thank Dr. Anna Orenstein for illuminating psychological interviews about her Holocaust memories.

For travel and research support, I thank Brandeis University's Theodore and Jane Norman Fund for Faculty Research and Creative Projects in Arts and Sciences, 2007-2008 and 2008-2009.

I thank Sylvia Fried, producer of a wide range of books for the Tauber Institute at Brandeis, for suggesting that I speak with Sue Berger Ramin, Director of the Brandeis University Press, who in turn suggested I contact Liesbeth Heenk, Director of Amsterdam Publishers. Lois Lindauer, Joanna Gould and Lucia Coimbra helped me in countless ways. I thank EverPresent for producing usable photographs out of both old and new images; and I thank the Brandeis University Help Desk for years of technical support.

As the Hebrew saying goes, *Aharon, aharon, chaviv*, meaning "the last is best." My husband, Jehuda Reinharz, talked with me about this book the whole time I was writing it and did everything he could (a lot!) to get me the help I needed. I can't thank him enough. We are the proud parents of Yael Reinharz and Naomi Reinharz, and the adoring grandparents of Amalia Kit Reinharz and Jago Dylan Reinharz-Trainor. My parents would be delighted and relieved to know that their children had grandchildren.

Shulamit Reinharz, Brookline, Massachusetts, 2024

AMSTERDAM PUBLISHERS HOLOCAUST LIBRARY

The series **Holocaust Survivor Memoirs World War II** consists of the following autobiographies of survivors:

Outcry. Holocaust Memoirs, by Manny Steinberg

Hank Brodt Holocaust Memoirs. A Candle and a Promise, by Deborah Donnelly

The Dead Years. Holocaust Memoirs, by Joseph Schupack

Rescued from the Ashes. The Diary of Leokadia Schmidt, Survivor of the Warsaw Ghetto, by Leokadia Schmidt

My Lvov. Holocaust Memoir of a twelve-year-old Girl, by Janina Hescheles

Remembering Ravensbrück. From Holocaust to Healing, by Natalie Hess

Wolf. A Story of Hate, by Zeev Scheinwald with Ella Scheinwald

Save my Children. An Astonishing Tale of Survival and its Unlikely Hero, by Leon Kleiner with Edwin Stepp

Holocaust Memoirs of a Bergen-Belsen Survivor & Classmate of Anne Frank, by Nanette Blitz Konig

Defiant German - Defiant Jew. A Holocaust Memoir from inside the Third Reich, by Walter Leopold with Les Leopold

In a Land of Forest and Darkness. The Holocaust Story of two Jewish Partisans, by Sara Lustigman Omelinski

Holocaust Memories. Annihilation and Survival in Slovakia, by Paul Davidovits

From Auschwitz with Love. The Inspiring Memoir of Two Sisters' Survival, Devotion and Triumph Told by Manci Grunberger Beran & Ruth Grunberger Mermelstein, by Daniel Seymour

Remetz. Resistance Fighter and Survivor of the Warsaw Ghetto, by Jan Yohay Remetz

My March Through Hell. A Young Girl's Terrifying Journey to Survival, by Halina Kleiner with Edwin Stepp

Roman's Journey, by Roman Halter

Beyond Borders. Escaping the Holocaust and Fighting the Nazis. 1938-1948, by Rudi Haymann

The Engineers. A memoir of survival through World War II in Poland and Hungary, by Henry Reiss

A Spark of Hope. An Autobiography, by Luba Wrobel Goldberg

The series **Holocaust Survivor True Stories**
consists of the following biographies:

Among the Reeds. The true story of how a family survived the Holocaust, by Tammy Bottner

A Holocaust Memoir of Love & Resilience. Mama's Survival from Lithuania to America, by Ettie Zilber

Living among the Dead. My Grandmother's Holocaust Survival Story of Love and Strength, by Adena Bernstein Astrowsky

Heart Songs. A Holocaust Memoir, by Barbara Gilford

Shoes of the Shoah. The Tomorrow of Yesterday, by Dorothy Pierce

Hidden in Berlin. A Holocaust Memoir, by Evelyn Joseph Grossman

Separated Together. The Incredible True WWII Story of Soulmates Stranded an Ocean Apart, by Kenneth P. Price, Ph.D.

The Man Across the River. The incredible story of one man's will to survive the Holocaust, by Zvi Wiesenfeld

If Anyone Calls, Tell Them I Died. A Memoir, by Emanuel (Manu) Rosen

The House on Thrömerstrasse. A Story of Rebirth and Renewal in the Wake of the Holocaust, by Ron Vincent

Dancing with my Father. His hidden past. Her quest for truth. How Nazi Vienna shaped a family's identity, by Jo Sorochinsky

The Story Keeper. Weaving the Threads of Time and Memory - A Memoir, by Fred Feldman

Krisia's Silence. The Girl who was not on Schindler's List, by Ronny Hein

Defying Death on the Danube. A Holocaust Survival Story, by Debbie J. Callahan with Henry Stern

A Doorway to Heroism. A decorated German-Jewish Soldier who became an American Hero, by Rabbi W. Jack Romberg

The Shoemaker's Son. The Life of a Holocaust Resister, by Laura Beth Bakst

The Redhead of Auschwitz. A True Story, by Nechama Birnbaum

Land of Many Bridges. My Father's Story, by Bela Ruth Samuel Tenenholtz

Creating Beauty from the Abyss. The Amazing Story of Sam Herciger, Auschwitz Survivor and Artist, by Lesley Ann Richardson

On Sunny Days We Sang. A Holocaust Story of Survival and Resilience, by Jeannette Grunhaus de Gelman

Painful Joy. A Holocaust Family Memoir, by Max J. Friedman

I Give You My Heart. A True Story of Courage and Survival, by Wendy Holden

In the Time of Madmen, by Mark A. Prelas

Monsters and Miracles. Horror, Heroes and the Holocaust, by Ira Wesley Kitmacher

Flower of Vlora. Growing up Jewish in Communist Albania, by Anna Kohen

Aftermath: Coming of Age on Three Continents. A Memoir, by Annette Libeskind Berkovits

Not a real Enemy. The True Story of a Hungarian Jewish Man's Fight for Freedom, by Robert Wolf

Zaidy's War. Four Armies, Three Continents, Two Brothers. One Man's Impossible Story of Endurance, by Martin Bodek

The Glassmaker's Son. Looking for the World my Father left behind in Nazi Germany, by Peter Kupfer

The Apprentice of Buchenwald. The True Story of the Teenage Boy Who Sabotaged Hitler's War Machine, by Oren Schneider

Good for a Single Journey, by Helen Joyce

Burying the Ghosts. She escaped Nazi Germany only to have her life torn apart by the woman she saved from the camps: her mother, by Sonia Case

American Wolf. From Nazi Refugee to American Spy. A True Story, by Audrey Birnbaum

Bipolar Refugee. A Saga of Survival and Resilience, by Peter Wiesner

In the Wake of Madness. My Family's Escape from the Nazis, by Bettie Lennett Denny

Before the Beginning and After the End, by Hymie Anisman

I Will Give Them an Everlasting Name. Jacksonville's Stories of the Holocaust, by Samuel Cox

Hiding in Holland. A Resistance Memoir, by Shulamit Reinharz

The series **Jewish Children in the Holocaust** consists of the following
autobiographies of Jewish children
hidden during WWII in the Netherlands:

Searching for Home. The Impact of WWII on a Hidden Child,
by Joseph Gosler

Sounds from Silence. Reflections of a Child Holocaust Survivor,
Psychiatrist and Teacher, by Robert Krell

Sabine's Odyssey. A Hidden Child and her Dutch Rescuers,
by Agnes Schipper

The Journey of a Hidden Child, by Harry Pila and Robin Black

The series **New Jewish Fiction** consists of the following novels, written by Jewish authors. All novels are set in the time during or after the Holocaust.

The Corset Maker. A Novel, by Annette Libeskind Berkovits

Escaping the Whale. The Holocaust is over. But is it ever over for the next generation? by Ruth Rotkowitz

When the Music Stopped. Willy Rosen's Holocaust, by Casey Hayes

Hands of Gold. One Man's Quest to Find the Silver Lining in Misfortune, by Roni Robbins

The Girl Who Counted Numbers. A Novel, by Roslyn Bernstein

There was a garden in Nuremberg. A Novel, by Navina Michal Clemerson

The Butterfly and the Axe, by Omer Bartov

To Live Another Day. A Novel, by Elizabeth Rosenberg

A Worthy Life. Based on a True Story, by Dahlia Moore

The Right to Happiness. After all they went through. Stories, by Helen Schary Motro

The series **Holocaust Heritage** consists of the following memoirs by 2G:

The Cello Still Sings. A Generational Story of the Holocaust and of the Transformative Power of Music, by Janet Horvath

The Fire and the Bonfire. A Journey into Memory, by Ardyn Halter

The Silk Factory: Finding Threads of My Family's True Holocaust Story, by Michael Hickins

Winter Light. The Memoir of a Child of Holocaust Survivors, by Grace Feuerverger

Stumbling Stones, by Joanna Rosenthall

The Unspeakable. Breaking decades of family silence surrounding the Holocaust, by Nicola Hanefeld

Hidden in Plain Sight. A Journey into Memory and Place, by Julie Brill

The series **Holocaust Books for Young Adults** consists of the following novels, based on true stories:

The Boy behind the Door. How Salomon Kool Escaped the Nazis. Inspired by a True Story, by David Tabatsky

Running for Shelter. A True Story, by Suzette Sheft

The Precious Few. An Inspirational Saga of Courage based on True Stories, by David Twain with Art Twain

The Sun will Shine on You again one Day, by Cynthia Monsour

The series **WWII Historical Fiction** consists of the following novels, some of which are based on true stories:

Mendelevski's Box. A Heartwarming and Heartbreaking Jewish Survivor's Story, by Roger Swindells

A Quiet Genocide. The Untold Holocaust of Disabled Children in WWII Germany, by Glenn Bryant

The Knife-Edge Path, by Patrick T. Leahy

Brave Face. The Inspiring WWII Memoir of a Dutch/German Child, by I. Caroline Crocker and Meta A. Evenbly

When We Had Wings. The Gripping Story of an Orphan in Janusz Korczak's Orphanage. A Historical Novel, by Tami Shem-Tov

Jacob's Courage. Romance and Survival amidst the Horrors of War, by Charles S. Weinblatt

A Semblance of Justice. Based on true Holocaust experiences, by Wolf Holles

Dark Shadows Hover, by Jordan Steven Sher

Katie O'Connor, This Grey Place

Amsterdam Publishers Newsletter

Subscribe to our Newsletter by selecting the menu at the top (right) of **amsterdampublishers.com** or scan the QR-code below.

Receive a variety of content such as:

- A welcome message by the founder
- Free Holocaust memoirs
- Book recommendations
- News about upcoming releases
- Chance to become an AP Reviewer.